China's Enterprise Reform

China's basic work units, collectively known as the *danwei* system, have undergone significant reform, particularly since 1984. The heart of the *danwei* system are multi-functional units that constitute the bottom layer of the party/state machinery. They are engaged in planning, party ideology and providing social welfare for workers. The *danwei* system is now being progressively dismantled.

You Ji examines how the *danwei* system operates and how reform is generating change in the party at grassroots level. The book is particularly concerned with three major institutional reforms in China's state sector:

– political reform of the party leadership, the cadre appointments system, management mechanisms and the state/enterprise administrative chains;

– market reform with an emphasis on ownership;

– changes in the industrial social welfare system.

The author demonstrates how China's post-Mao reforms have produced a quiet revolution from below as the process of political and economic liberalization has accelerated. This book presents new research findings that will be invaluable to those wishing to understand the nature of change in China.

You Ji is a lecturer in the School of Political Science of the University of New South Wales, Sydney, Australia. He has published widely on China's political, economic and military affairs.

Routledge Studies in China in Transition
Series Editor: David S. G. Goodman

China's enterprise reform
Changing State/Society Relations after Mao

You Ji

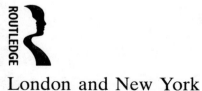

London and New York

First published 1998
by Routledge
11 New Fetter Lane, London EC4P 4EE

Simultaneously published in the USA and Canada
by Routledge
29 West 35th Street, New York, NY 10001

© 1998 You Ji

Phototypeset in Times by Intype London Ltd
Printed and bound in Great Britain by
Antony Rowe Ltd., Chippenham, Wiltshire

British Library Cataloguing in Publication Data
A catalogue record for this book is available from the British Library

Library of Congress Cataloging in Publication Data
A catalogue record for this book has been requested

ISBN 0–415–15726–9

To my mother Chen Shishu

Contents

Figures and tables

FIGURES

TABLES

Preface

In the late 1970s, as China's reform era opened, the Communist Party of China committed itself to first doubling and then redoubling the aggregate size of the economy of the People's Republic of China by the end of the millennium. At the time and into the early and mid-1980s it was a prospect greeted as a desirable aspiration by most academic observers of China, but as little more. Many economists in particular pointed out the difficulties in the project and the near-impossibility of its achievement. In the event the target was attained with almost five years to spare, sometime in 1995.

The rapid growth of China's economy is a useful starting point for this series, intellectually as well as chronologically. It is not only that China has developed so spectacularly so quickly, nor that in the process its experience has proved some economists to be too cautious. Rather, its importance is to demonstrate the need for explanatory theories of social and economic change to themselves adapt and change as they encompass the processes underway in China, and not to assume that previous assumptions about either China or social change in general are immutable.

China in Transition aims to participate in these intellectual developments through its focus on social, political, economic and culture change in the China of the 1990s and beyond. Its aim is to draw upon new, often cross-disciplinary research from scholars in East Asia, Australasia, North America and Europe, as well as that based in the more traditional disciplines. In the process, the series will not only interpret the consequences of reform in China, but also monitor and reflect the changes of the future.

China's state sector enterprises have always threatened to be a deadweight on the transformation of the economy in reform. They represented not simply a massive productive force at the centre of the former command economy but, even more significantly, the heart of the political economy of state socialism in the People's Republic of China. A first and crucial stage in the process of reform was to adapt, if not to completely sever, the nexus between politics and economics to allow the diversion of investment funds into light industry and away from heavy industry, the sector where state-owned enterprises dominated. A second stage, which appears to be a major item on China's agenda for at least the latter half of the 1990s, is the reform of state sector enterprises in themselves.

In *China's Enterprise Reform*, You Ji examines this process and its consequences through a focus on the *danwei* – the basic work unit that characterised the former party-state and was an essential part of corporatist state socialism. In particular, he concentrates on the extent and nature of institutional reforms in the development of state sector enterprises since 1984. In contrast to other accounts of those processes he highlights the ways in which enterprise reform has started to transform the party-state as well as the state sector of the economy, not through the purposive action of leadership but through the dismantling of the earlier systems of control in the basic work units from the bottom up. Basic work units within the state sector have already changed beyond the boundaries of their previous existence. In that process of structural change they have not only laid the foundations for their continued development but, as importantly, contributed to political institutionalisation.

David S. G. Goodman
Institute for International Studies, UTS
August 1997

Acknowledgements

This book is based on my Ph.D. dissertation, completed in 1993 at the Australian National University. Therefore I should thank first of all the ANU where I spent five and a half most productive years as an MA and Ph.D. student. During this time I was very fortunate to receive enormous help and encouragement from a large number of people who shared their knowledge with me about China's political and economic development. When I took a teaching position in the Department of Political Science, the University of Canterbury, New Zealand, in 1994, I continued to receive their assistance. Without their help and friendship, it would have been impossible for me to go through this painstaking process of writing and rewriting.

As time passes, the number of people who have extended their assistance to me grows. I would like to begin with sincere thanks to Dr Jonathan Unger, to whom I owe the greatest debt. Dr Unger acted as my sole supervisor, and was a constant source of new knowledge and inspiration. I am grateful not only for his steady and patient supervision at all stages of this research but also for his moral support and confidence in my work. At several points his guidance played a crucial role in keeping the project on the right track. Without it I would have been unable to complete this book.

I am also very fortunate to have had Dr Anita Chan and Mr Ian Wilson as my advisers. During the past seven years, their expert advice has stimulated me to think through many important issues covered by the book. Here I would also like to thank Professor David Goodman. It was he who suggested that I submit my Ph.D. manuscript for publication. He has been most critical of the weaknesses in the original version and given me concrete advice to rectify them.

I also owe a big debt to a number of people who have helped me in many different ways. I would particularly like to thank Chris Connolly, Peter Van Ness, Bob Miller, David Kelly, Barrett McCormick, Harry Rigby, Andrew Walder, Thomas Rawski, Gordon White, Peter Lee and Kate Hannan. My colleagues in the Contemporary China Centre provided a friendly and stimulating environment for scholarly exploration from which I benefited enormously. I would like to convey my gratitude especially to Chris Buckley, Jane C. Y. Lee, Jiang Shu, Scott Davis, Deglopper Donald, Lam Tao Chiu and Wang Hong-Zen. The support from our administrators in the Centre, Dinna Stacey and Heli Petryk, is also highly appreciated.

During my fieldwork at the Universities Service Centre, the Chinese University of Hong Kong, I was very lucky to receive support from Professor Kuan Hsin-chi and Jean Hong. Jane Lee collected a great deal of research data for my Ph.D. dissertation. Their help will always be warmly remembered.

The research was made possible by a scholarship from the Australian National University, which also funded my first fieldwork in China in 1991. I would like to thank Dr Unger for providing a fund from his salary savings to finance my second fieldwork in China in 1992. During my subsequent visits to China the University of Canterbury offered me a generous grant. Acknowledgement is also owed to Beijing University, which granted me a visiting fellowship under the ANU–Beijing University Exchange Program. Particularly, I would like to thank Xue Yongling for her great help.

Finally, I wish to express my heartfelt gratitude to Wu Shanshan with whom I shared happiness and hardship during the toughest years of my postgraduate life.

Abbreviations

ABSP	Administration Bureaux of State Property
ACFTU	All China Federation of Trade Unions
CASS	Chinese Academy of Social Sciences
CC	Central Committee of the CCP
CCP	Chinese Communist Party
COD	Central Organisation Department
CPS	Central Party School
NPC	National People's Congress
NTIS	National Textile Industrial Society
PD	Personnel Department
POD	Party Organisation Department
PRC	People's Republic of China
SCRES	State Commission for the Restructuring of the Economic System
SETC	State Economic and Trade Commission
SPC	State Planning Commission
SSBC	State Statistical Bureau of China

Part I

Reshaping state and society relations

1 Introduction

This book is about changing state/society relations in China since the post-Mao reforms began in the late 1970s. In other words, it is about how the Chinese Communist Party/state is being gradually dismantled at the grassroots level, a process which amounts to a quiet revolution from below.[1] Here the term 'party/state' is used in its general sense, to mean a ruling Communist Party which penetrates into all state agencies and social organisations and dominates their everyday life. Given the very broad parameters of the subject, I have chosen to focus the research on a small but important part of the process: the institutional reforms in China's state-owned enterprises and their lasting impact on political and social change in the country.

THE SETTING OF THE STUDY: A FACTORY AS A DANWEI

Chinese urban society is composed of numerous *danwei* (work units), creating a type of authority relations rooted in a unique social and political order. Indeed, the *danwei* system provides a good case study for an empirically based behavioural analysis which can be used to theorise the fieldwork findings. At the same time, in order to grasp the pattern of authority relations embedded in such a system, it is important to understand the institutions of power through which authority is exercised. For instance, in any political system mobilisation is rarely achieved merely through the use of patron–client networks, but is accomplished more through coercion or commitment to an ideology or a leader and through a set of institutions (Oi, 1989, p. 7). So a study of institutional arrangements is crucial in analysing the nature of authority relations.

A strong political and ideological orientation is the first feature of the *danwei* system. The politicising of state factories began with the establishment of party cells on shop floors in the 1950s. Organisationally, any Chinese workplace with more than three party members had to set up a party branch, while those with more than fifty had to establish a general party branch or party committee. As politicisation deepened, the party created a monolithic leadership structure in state-owned enterprises supervising and very often replacing factory management at all levels. One key element of this was the *nomenklatura* appointment system, whereby the party selected cadres and made them directly responsible for its policies (Burns, 1988, pp. ix–xliii). The party firmly placed the administration, trade unions, security networks and mass organisations under its control and made them transmission belts through which it penetrated into every corner of the shop floor.

Party cells are instigators of ideological indoctrination and propaganda work. They exercise control over people's thought. Ideological work in China's state factories not only is designed to disseminate propaganda but also is an institution for imposing specific patterns of behaviour. Thought control and organisational control are linked by the party in shopfloor politics. For instance, a worker with an allegedly poor work record was commonly regarded in the pre-reform days as hostile to the party and in need of 're-education'.

The command economy is by nature an administrative economy requiring an all-powerful bureaucracy to execute central planning. This has fashioned a unique type of state/enterprise relations. Based on Marx's criticism of the blindness of capitalist production, socialist theorists and practitioners envisaged an economy where all production activities would be organised as if conducted within one enterprise. The ownership had to be 'pure' because such an enterprise could have only one owner. The plan had to be detailed to ensure strict management procedures. Exchange relations had to be curtailed, as they could cause disorder. From this Stalinist model developed the second feature of an industrial work unit – its role as an appendage to state administration.[2]

The cornerstone for such a state/enterprise relationship is state ownership. In China the ownership system has a distinctive political function of control, as it subjects state enterprises to government economic agencies through exclusive property ties. These agencies, as the investors, maintain strong bureaucratic property control. In exercising ownership powers, they wield the authority to appoint factory directors, allocate products, and formulate remuneration and employment policies (Dernberger, 1986, pp. 344–8).

Built upon this state ownership structure is a vast economic bureaucracy. All state factories are embraced in this system and are ranked hierarchically according to criteria such as the amount of state investment they receive, the importance of their products and the number of workers they employ. Depending on their ranking they are granted an official status at the levels of a township government and an army battalion, a county and a regiment, a prefecture and an army division, all the way to the exalted level of the province and the army (Lu Feng, 1989, pp. 71–88). This military-sounding bureaucratisation of factories until the late 1970s was meant to facilitate the fulfilment of central plans, as central decrees could be carried out most effectively within an administrative pyramid like that of an army.

In this hierarchy State-owned enterprises acquire not only an administrative rank but also an administrative superior. Until recently they received guaranteed capital investment and outlets for products through the hierarchy but had little economic independence or identity. Between a factory and its bureaucratic boss, there was space for bargaining over such things as production quotas (Naughton, 1992, pp. 245–9), but under the commanding heights, this space was generally limited and a factory engaging in bargaining could be subject to criticism for 'having a weak sense of organisation and discipline'. It could thus become a potential target in political and economic campaigns.

Direct state control over factory employees' salaries, as embodied in the nationally unified eight-grade industrial wage system, was another feature of the *danwei* system. It served as a key mechanism through which the state exercised control over the economic life of ordinary workers. Under this system, the whole state sector was run like one institution, with the state delivering the wages and the factory management acting as the cashier. In this closed system of the 'big rice bowl' enterprises and workers had little influence on state wage policies.

Created in the 1950s under the formula of 'low wages, low consumption', this centralised, nationally unified wage arrangement reflected the low level of development of the economy. However, it also had a distinctive function of control, forcing workers to remain satisfied with whatever they were offered and contain their everyday pursuits within the limit that the state believed appropriate. The unified wage system served several strategic purposes during the Mao era. Among the most important were a high accumulation rate for heavy and defence industries and an employment policy to keep abreast of the fast growth of the urban population. For instance, in 1978 the per capita income for each city dweller was 26.3 *yuan* per month, while the rationed commodities – the necessities of everyday life – cost 22.74 *yuan*. These included an average of 15 kilos of grainstuff, 0.56 kilos of vegetables, 0.51 kilos of meat, 0.16 kilos of sugar and 0.25 kilos of cooking oil. With other social welfare provisions and state-subsidised items, people could just manage until the end of each month. Throughout the two decades from 1959 to 1979, about 20 per cent of all urban families received less than 20 *yuan* per head. They therefore had to depend on their factory's social relief fund (Cheng Xinsheng *et al.*, 1987, pp. 33–8). In a way the party/state's 'dictatorship over needs' was effectively translated into its consolidation of power and elimination of political opposition.

In terms of politicisation, bureaucratisation and, to a lesser extent, the centrally controlled remunerative system, the *danwei* phenomenon can be found also in collective factories, which are placed under the leadership of party branches within them and under the administrative control of government bureaux. As a result, China's urban industrial sector became part of the infrastructure of the party/state. For factory workers and staff the distance between the state and themselves had never been closer: the institutional establishments of the state within their work units supervised in detail their birth, life and death. Authority relations were built on organisational pressure. This represented a strong tendency towards totalitarianism (Walder, 1986).

Following this historical legacy an industrial work unit, as a cell of the party/state, still serves as the carrier of the party's presence at the grassroots level, as a level of state power, exercising administrative control on behalf of the party/state; it is an economic producer attached to central or local planning; and it is also a state agency providing social welfare to workers. These multi-functional tasks are implemented by a set of institutional arrangements which constitute the core of the *danwei* system. These party/state institutions have transformed the factory into a unique setting that ties workers closely to the state, a setting which has no real counterpart even in other socialist countries.

The significance of this study lies in its analysis of how a workplace became *danweiised* in the Mao era and, particularly, how the post-Mao institutional reforms in state-owned enterprises have *de-danweiised* many of the functions mentioned in the previous paragraph. Through an analysis of this multi-functional framework, we will evaluate how the party/state structure was plugged into the industrial society and was reflected in cadre/worker interactions. By examining the changes generated at the grassroots by the post-Mao reforms, we will evaluate the depth of China's social transition away from communism. The book targets three institutional reforms in China's state sector in the post-Mao era: (1) political reform comprising reforms of the party leadership structure, the cadre appointment system, management mechanisms, and the state/enterprise administrative chains; (2) a series of market reforms with an emphasis on the ownership reform and corporatisation that help state-owned enterprises to emerge as independent economic entities; and (3) reforms in remuneration that have brought about significant changes in the structure of interests in the state sector.

These institutional reforms, the book argues, have pointed to a direction in which state-owned enterprises gradually break away from the tight control of the party/state, as reflected in the phenomenon of the 'two Ds' in China's industrial sector: *depoliticisation* and *de-statisation*. The marketisation of the economy has reinforced these developments. While the following chapters will elaborate this in detail, the theme, as summarised here, is that this development is undermining the foundation of the party/state. It seems that dismantling party/state controls in the infrastructure has accelerated the wider process of political and economic liberalisation in China. In fact China's post-Mao enterprise reform has been instrumental in reconstructing a new social base for political change.

It is happening first at the grassroots and will in due course affect the whole political system.

The essence of this gradual transformation of state factories, from being *danwei* (cells of the party/state) to being *gongsi* (corporations), marks a transformation of state-owned enterprises from political institutions to depoliticised economic entities. This inevitably redraws the boundary between the state and society. At the beginning of the post-Mao reforms many scholars observed remarkable readjustments in state/society relations (Harding, 1987; McCormick, 1990). More often than not they have attributed the political relaxation in China to the concessions made to society by reform-minded party leaders. Few have pointed out that it is the structural changes in basic work units that have institutionalised political relaxation. Since the aborted price reform in 1988, grassroots reaction has been taken more seriously by the leadership. The dismissal of Beijing party boss Chen Xitong, for example, was at least partially a response by the leadership to rising social discontent with corruption among ranking cadres. Indeed, the explosive nature of higher-level corruption might have triggered another Tiananmen incident (You Ji, 1996). This is changing the nature of China's politics, long dominated by the ruling elite. And this factor will become increasingly decisive in the post-Deng era. Only through seriously assessing the change in the social base upon which China's authoritarian structure rests can our understanding of the country's ongoing political and social transformation be sharpened. In this sense a study of the institutional reforms in the industrial *danwei* system will prove particularly helpful.

THE CONCEPTS OF PROCESS AND TRANSITION

The concept of 'process' is the key to analysis of China's second revolution. Its central thrust – socio-political and economic liberalisation – refers to the loosening of restrictions on social activities and expression through institutional reforms within an authoritarian regime. It is important to note that restrictions are being loosened, not renounced. China's process of liberalisation has been largely confined to the social and economic domains. Political liberalisation has been manifested mainly in the form of freedom to escape politics. However, the mutually conditioning interactions between socio-economic liberalisation and political restrictions have generated enormous stress in the political system (Shue, 1988, p. 26) whose resolution will require systemic political change of greater scope. Study of the process of China's post-Mao reforms has taught us that both structuralists and behaviouralists tend towards a static perspective when examining a political and economic system in transition. Many analysts believe that the Leninist system cannot change, that change means collapse.[3] Although this book will not make judgement on this, it draws on, and indeed relies on, an evolutionary approach to assessing

the transition in China. This approach combines elements of both structural and behavioural theories, and extends them along a crucial third
axis, which is that of time (Gaddis, 1992/3, pp. 15–17). Without comparison
of different periods, one may become shackled by a dogmatic perspective.

Yet 'transition analysis' must confront socio-political and cultural dis-
tinctiveness. Scholars working on Taiwan in transition have pointed out
that a hybrid regime, neither fully authoritarian nor democratic, may
persist for a long time. Given its authoritarian political culture and
organisation, China will most probably have a longer path of transition,
and it will definitely take a longer time for the evolution to reach the
point of no return. As always, one can anticipate a dialectical process,
not a linear progression, in this political evolution. Openness and its
excesses will be followed by retrenchment, which will create new pressures and consequent adjustments (Scalapino, 1992, p. 102).

Indeed, in the fifteen years of reform we can see an intensification of
a hard authoritarian image at some given points of time, such as at the
turn of 1986 and 1987 and in the aftermath of 4 June 1989. Yet if one
views the socio-political and economic development of the period as a
whole, one can recognise a trend of 'one step backward and *two* steps
forward' in social and economic relaxation. This has been characterised
by the party's easing of control when it feels confident and reapplying
repression when things threaten to get out of hand (Tsou, 1984, pp.
27–70).

Examining this as an ongoing, ever-shifting process may also help to
prevent the tendency of absolutism, inherent in both idealising the positive signs and dramatising the negative ones. This is very important in
evaluating social change in China. As most China scholars point out, the
country's reform is a 'reform within the system' rather than a revolution.
Social transition as such is pregnant with contradictions. Visible changes
are intertwined with clear continuity of the party/state, as the new institutional establishments are strongly influenced by the old one with its
enduring political culture. On the other hand, in the course of this evolution, reform has produced new political actors. More abundant at the
grassroots than at the apex of power, they readily take chances to enlarge
their realm of freedom. They reconstruct new political culture as they go
along, and make the 'rules of the game' a product, not a precondition
(Winckler, 1992, p. 226). In this light, this book approaches the subject
from the angle of 'what has changed, why and how' rather than 'what it
should change to'.

Thomas Rawski has pointed out the danger of applying stereotyped
criteria to an economic system in transition. When commenting upon the
following sentence – 'The crux of the question is to make Chinese enterprises totally autonomous of government, as such enterprises may operate
independently, lower cost, raise quality and increase sales' – Rawski
wrote: 'Is there a firm in the USA that is totally independent of govern-

ment? Can we see such examples in Japan or in other countries? This is another case of absolutism in economic theory' (Rawski, 1991, p. 9).

Rawski's approach is relevant to this book in that when observing economic reforms in China, it is not enough to judge any phenomenon in terms of what the economic model should be, usually derived from comparisons with the mature market economies. China should be compared first of all with its own recent past. So the central concern of this book is with what has changed in China's state industrial system, both politically and economically – how different the system is now as compared with its past.

For instance, the market reforms may increase either workers' dependence on or independence from their *danwei*. Factory management now has more authority and means in deciding on workers' income and in providing housing and other social welfare benefits. At the same time the fast-growing market has also provided alternatives through which workers can fight for the right to leave their jobs, find opportunities to moonlight, or receive goods and services that were only available through coupons offered by their work units before. Evidence exists for scholars to conclude both that 'organised dependence' has been enhanced and that it has been greatly weakened, depending on the angle from which they view the situation. This not only reflects the complex nature of China's political and social transition, it also makes any generalisation about any developmental trend in China vulnerable to criticism.

Talcott Parsons remarked forty years ago that the social sciences were not sophisticated enough to answer questions posed by social change. My research efforts will present not a single-factor explanation, but a complementary perspective. Social reality is complex. The study of China's industrial reform is not intended to dilute this complexity, but can only try to make it more intelligible. Obviously it will encounter numerous pitfalls.

METHODOLOGY

Research activities for this book were divided between: (1) the collection and analysis of laws, government regulations, research and media reports and other relevant documentary data; and (2) interviews with factory managers, party functionaries and workers. While the first category of research provides the basic framework for my analysis of the institutional reforms in the state sector, the second reveals the impact of these institutional reforms on everyday shopfloor politics. Now access to both official and unofficial documentation on state firms has been greatly broadened. Yet the question of how to interpret the information still poses an enormous challenge. And the problem is further complicated by the ever-changing situation in state-owned enterprises due to the frequent oscillations in state policies.

The interview findings derive from my numerous visits to China since 1991, three in 1995 alone, but the extended field research in China and Hong Kong in 1991 and 1992 laid the foundation. The interviews were conducted in two ways: (1) casual talks that helped me gain a general impression of the state of affairs in various state-owned enterprises – workers' attitudes towards the state and management, and managers' perceptions of both workers and their bureaucratic superiors; and (2) detailed, systematic interviews with a number of workers, managers and government officials about issues of importance in the current transformation of state-owned enterprises. I came across many dozens of people in the first category and engaged them, sometimes on a one-to-one basis and sometimes in a group, with questions reflecting my concerns. Most of them, however, did not know that I was approaching them with any special purpose in mind. Any situation could be a useful venue for a discussion, whether going on a long train journey, queuing up to buy something in a shop, having my hair cut or having dinner with old and new friends. Although these talks were not neatly structured (I never took notes during chats), they served my intention well as tools not for the purpose of acquiring a quantitative picture but for an understanding of the general trend of change and the assumptions behind the process. The biggest advantage of interviewing in such a manner is its casualness, so that people talk with no reservations.

If the casual chats offered me a good amount of peripheral knowledge about how a state firm was changing over the course of reform, the detailed interviews with about fifty workers, managers and government researchers and officials provided me with systematic descriptions of the changes. During these discussions, I repeatedly raised a number of questions, such as what was the state of relations between party secretaries and managers in the factory where they worked, how active were party cells and non-party-member activists, what was the percentage of their products allocated by the state plan and sold in the market, and how were wages distributed to workers and managers and so on. I am certain that the information obtained from these interviewees is reliable to a fairly high level because most of them are my relatives, former classmates or acquaintances introduced by mutual friends. There is no convincing reason why they should not have told me the truth as they perceived it.

In many cases, observation through these regular and casual contacts yielded good insights and a background against which I could read official documents and media reports. The combination of primary sources in the form of official documentation and formal interviews allowed me to explore in depth a number of specific questions, while informal chats provided material to digest information concerning changing state/society relations. More importantly, the empirical basis of this book is intimately related to my own experience of thirty years of living in China and working in a number of *danwei* there. In fact, compared with what I experienced when working in a state factory for a month in 1974, the changes in state-owned enterprises are revolutionary.

The time frame of this book covers the period from the beginning of China's post-Mao reforms in 1979 to the latest developments that the manuscript can possibly incorporate. Yet since China's industrial reforms are the focus of the book, more attention has been devoted to the period after the urban reform commenced in 1984. Because of limited space, discussion of the situation in the state-owned enterprises before the reform is kept as brief as possible. Needless to say, this has limited the analytical perspective.

The book consists of five parts. Part I consists of an introduction (Chapter 1) and a theoretical chapter (Chapter 2). Part II comprises three chapters and concentrates on political change in China's state-owned enterprises. Chapter 3 deals with the institutional reforms that affect the leadership structure in a factory with a focus on party/management relations. Chapters 4 and 5 analyse the reforms of the party's industrial organisations. Part III comprises Chapters 6 and 7, which examine the changing state/enterprise remuneration relations and the impact of wage reform on shopfloor politics. Part IV, which comprises Chapters 8 and 9, evaluates changing state/enterprise relations with an emphasis on owner-ship reform and government organizational reform. Chapter 10 is a conclusion.

2 A quiet revolution from below

The study of China's industrial reform is a study of changing state/society relations. Traditionally such study has been a central aspect of the west's academic efforts to comprehend the realities of socialist societies. Numerous insightful books have given us a fuller grasp of authority relations in China between the party/state and social groups, such as peasants, intellectuals, urban youth, university students and bureaucrats (Goldman, 1996; Chan *et al.*, 1992; Watson, 1984). Walder (1986) has put forward a theory of communist neo-traditionalism that serves as one of the most useful paradigms for studying pre-reform shopfloor politics in China's state-owned enterprises. From a different angle, Womack (1991b) has proposed the concept of work unit socialism: this has also been useful in sharpening our understanding of China's state/society relations in transition (Womack, 1990, 1991b).

COMMUNIST NEO-TRADITIONALISM AND WORK UNIT SOCIALISM

The communist neo-traditional image depicts a strong totalitarian tendency inherent in China's party/state, as reflected by the party's efforts to turn virtually all Chinese urban work units into state *danwei* and make them the political base for party control. Walder's (1986, p. 45) analysis of a Chinese firm as an institution (less an economic than a social and political institution) distinguishes it from a normal western one. The very nature of a political institution is explicated in terms of the party's ubiquitous penetration into workers' everyday lives and the state's historically unparalleled reach into every aspect and level of society. Within the framework of neo-traditionalism, the delivery by an enterprise of social welfare provisions, such as unit housing and scarce everyday necessities, was no ordinary mission as compared to welfare states in the west. It effectively subjected workers to 'peaceful coercion'.[1]

As a logical development, two distinct features strongly influenced political life in state-owned enterprises. The first, says Walder, was the organised dependence of workers on their employers and the second was the politicised clientelist ties formed between workers and their immediate bosses. The workers' dependence on their *danwei* was pervasive: employment did not mean simply finding a place of work and receiving wages, but obtaining a political and civic identity and a whole set of social welfare benefits; sometimes workers could even pass their job on to their children. This dependence gave workers an ingrained sense of vulnerability towards their employers. Moreover, because workers' right to leave their job was largely denied, their dependence on their *danwei* was a lifetime phenomenon on account of which they gradually came to regard themselves as equivalent to other factory assets.[2] Politically, this implied that a factory itself was an embodiment of the party/state.

Organised dependence and politically oriented clientelist networks paved the way for the creation of a peculiar institutional culture in China's state-owned enterprises. Walder's evaluation of politicised clientelism at the basic level is an important advance on traditional thinking on communist politics which was characterised by impersonal domination by state power and ideology. In fact, no authority relations can be entirely impersonal but in non-communist societies these can be non-political. Industrial relations in the market economies are regulated by rule of law, which simultaneously constrains employers and employees. However, politicised clientelism in a *danweiised* firm centred authority relations on 'principled particularism', which rewarded a group of loyal followers with goods and services not readily available to everyone. This practice separated activists and non-activists and thus split the workforce by creating different status groups in state-owned enterprises. Criteria for selecting those who were more equal than others were both political and person-specific. The political demand echoed the impersonal requirement of the party/state on workers, while the personal dealt with everyday attitudes of workers towards their immediate bosses. Skilfully employed, political favouritism was more cost-effective than naked terror as a means of subduing workers' passive resistance (Walder, 1986, p. 43).

The sweeping post-Mao reform has significantly altered the environment in which communist neo-traditionalism is practised. In a way, fast-growing capitalism in China has made it difficult for politicised clientelism to adapt to new circumstances. The old criteria for political favouritism based on ideological correctness and political activism had lost touch with the general social and political mood of the population. With money in command, people have increasingly become apolitical. Although the personal network remains important, it is oriented much less towards political favouritism.

To a large extent communist neo-traditionalism is the product of the command economy, whose by-product, a scarcity of goods and services, strengthened the hands of factory cadres *vis-à-vis* workers. Now the market provides alternatives for workers for both consumption and employment. In a large proportion of state-owned enterprises it is the management which pleads with workers to leave rather than the other way round. Gradually, the base of party/state control through clientelist, organised dependence has been eroded. Organised dependence is best applied to a situation of autarky in a closed system and becomes less effective when the system is opened up.[3]

Recently, some China specialists have proposed new theoretical approaches for studying this evolution. One representative argument put forward by Womack uses the concept of work unit socialism (Womack, 1991b). What is valuable about this concept is that it deals with the welfare benefits provided by a work unit in a positive fashion. According to Womack, state-owned enterprises as social welfare providers both attenuated the gravity of the short supply of goods in shops and underlined the practical need of workers to rely on the *danwei* system. As a permanent community, a work unit is part of a rational, future-oriented, differentiated and technological structure in search of modernisation. Womack tries to show that a work unit in socialist China, be it a factory or a hospital, is not just designed to ensure the state's control over society. It also constitutes a mechanism that delivers goods to members of a community. As long as work unit socialism can deliver goods, it remains a social experiment in state-run industrial communities that integrates the state and society with people's 'active consent'.[4] And permanent employment in state-owned enterprises imposes effective restrictions on the exercise of state power, thus distinguishing work unit socialism from both totalitarianism and neo-traditionalism. Implicit in the concept is a denial of the totalitarian approach that envisions a socialist country in which 'the interests of state and society are so dichotomised and juxtaposed that the state is assumed to be the enemy of the people' (Womack, 1991b, p. 320).

Womack analyses the tension between the irresistible power of the state and the immovable permanence of work unit membership. As a result of this tension there has emerged a visible gap between formal powers and actual control. This touches the nerve of the study of state/society relations in China under Mao, where we see an all-powerful state machine on the one hand and its less than effective functioning at the grassroots on the other (Peter Lee, 1991a, pp. 153–79). This is particularly true in China of the Deng Xiaoping/Jiang Zemin era where the centre's policies became distorted bit by bit in the process of implementation at each and every level of its functioning bodies. The conflict between the centre's preference and the sectoral and regional compartmental interests has visibly eroded the former's authority. Given time, this may even lead to some kind of policy paralysis (Goodman and Segal, 1994). These compartmental interests often took the form of distributions of mass welfare at the state's expense, a facet of social change that China accomplished without too much polarisation of society (Womack, 1991b, pp. 320–3).

Walder and Womack touched upon two key features of a contradictory phenomenon in China's basic-level politics: the overt control in the neo-traditionalist *danwei* system caused enormous grievances among workers but the concomitant job security and welfare provisions have certainly alleviated their difficulties in life. Their entering into the clientelist network as followers was often a self-protective act, reflecting their appreciation of their patrons' dominant status. This was logical behaviour in an uncertain environment where political and social pressures were high but provisions of goods and services were short. On the other hand, factory cadres also had to solicit cooperation from their subordinates. Sometimes this meant that they seriously catered for the needs of the majority of workers, owing partly to mass pressure from shop floors and partly to repeated political campaigns. Theoretically at least, they were not owners of the property, so they did not care too much about labour costs and the growth of productivity when making welfare decisions. Yet the balance of power was clearly in their favour rather than the workers'. For workers, it paid better to submit to the rules of a clientelist game than to challenge them, even though submission entailed a level of humili-ation. This characterised a peculiar institutional culture in state-owned enterprises throughout the PRC's history, despite spasmodic eruptions of discontent.

While neo-traditionalist control over workers has its institutional roots in the communist system, work unit socialism has its historical roots in the industrial development of modern China. In other words, from a historical perspective work unit socialism was not just an invention of the party/state for the purpose of control (Perry, 1989, p. 582). China's indus-trial workforce originated mainly in bankrupt peasantry in the last century. Large numbers of poverty-stricken peasants were brought to the cities by contractors. As these peasants turned workers had no urban roots, it was a normal practice for employers to offer them primitive shelter and limited welfare services. Their biggest problem was lack of job security. This was the reason why the struggle for job security was a central agenda in workers' movements before and after 1949. As far as welfare is concerned, the practice can be traced back to military communism in the 'red areas' where everything was distributed fairly equally to members of civilian and army units. This became institutional-ised later in the 'big rice bowl' system after the CCP came to power.

Both concepts – neo-traditionalism and work unit socialism – have significant practical value in our study of political and social transfor-mation in the former and existing socialist systems. On the one hand, depriving workers of basic freedom was a fundamental reason why oppo-sition movements such as Solidarity emerged in Eastern Europe. On the other, once a level of freedom had been achieved, workers strove to protect social security rights left over from the socialist system. Indeed, the sudden loss of these benefits with the collapse of the previous regimes may be the reason why many workers voted for a communist comeback in Russia and Eastern Europe (Kramer, 1995). Between the thirst for democratic freedom and the need for 'big rice bowl' security is the prevalent mentality of wanting to have one's cake and eat it too. This has been an obstacle slowing down the ongoing transformation in the former and existing socialist countries but popular response is based on genuine concerns. The socialist ideology of people's entitlement to jobs created entrenched vested interests in the state sector.

To some extent, work unit socialism recognised the need to protect the basic social rights of workers through an institutional framework: the work unit-based social welfare system which lessens financial and economic strains on the majority of urbanites in an underdeveloped economy, not just on pro-regime activists. Walder numbers these incentives as the third structural source of regime legitimacy in China and Hartford regards them as the party's second mass base of support (Walder, 1986, p. 248; Hartford, 1991/2, p. 49). Even today, more than a decade after reform, the majority of urban workers still see socialism as superior to capitalism as a provider of public housing, lifelong employment, free medical care and retirement benefits (*Gongjing neican*, no. 23, 1992, p. 12). Clearly the built-in dependence of the system has been instrumental in exacting worker compliance. However, permanent employment has diluted its impact. Granting outright power to factory cadres to fire defiant workers would have served the system more effectively.

One drawback of the work unit socialism approach is probably that it projects the image of an idealised welfare community onto a China which is still under firm authoritarianism. Work unit socialism does not occur in a political vacuum, and welfare benefits are not just benign handouts. The hidden inequalities of the 'big rice bowl' among different work units and within the same one have generated acute tensions which may make the shop floor an unpleasant battleground. There are thus discrepancies between an ideal form of state–society relations as envisaged by work unit socialism and its actual operation in the party/state *danwei* system. For instance, factory cadres still assume political and ideological missions on behalf of the party. It is their job to ensure that workers' attitudes conform to the state's requirements. So they do not run social welfare affairs like a charity. Without adequate checks and balances, the enormous power entrusted to factory cadres inevitably blurs the boundary between individual authority and the authority of office. As a result, the cadres may not give out goods and services according to the rules of work unit socialism. For the subordinates, in a society dominated by status differences, it is rational to act according to the premises enforced by the privileged (Jowitt, 1974, pp. 1171–91). From the 1950s onward, workers' 'active consent' gradually gave way to passive submission to a powerful 'new class' of cadres.

Work unit socialism can, however, provide a practical answer to the contradiction between freedom and security, if the politicised authority relations in the *danwei* system can be fundamentally transformed. Many large firms in Japan and Taiwan provide a prototype for a materialistic model of employer/employee relations. Apart from the way it creates politically oriented organised dependence, a Chinese work unit shares many features of management/worker interactions with a Japanese firm. Functioning like the traditional social group in which members share a sense of belonging and exclusiveness, a Chinese *danwei* is perceived as an enterprise family where the factory and workers are bound together by fate. For better or worse, this enterprise family consciousness is nurtured and reinforced by the welfare policy of the employer who has to take care of the personal lives of employees and their families (Hanami, 1979; Yamamoto Hanami, 1993). This cultural element in *danwei*-based labour relations was well captured by Professor Child in his systematic survey of a number of Chinese state firms under reform (Child, 1994).

Therefore, the first precondition for work unit socialism to work properly has to be depoliticisation of the workplace so that factory cadres are deprived of political and ideological power over workers. The second precondition is effective rules to govern social welfare provisions. This implies a profound political reform in the state sector: state-owned enterprises must be transformed into purely economic entities. While some of the key features of the social welfare system must be preserved to protect workers' interests, this is principally for the purpose of maintaining work morale and staff stability rather than for political control. The state sector transformed along these lines may function like a kind of state corporatism that accords state-owned enterprises a high degree of autonomy in the party/state power structure and creates mutual obligations between the *danwei* and its staff members. In this perspective the state is compelled to share its monopoly over industrial production with state-owned enterprises in order to improve effectiveness. And it makes material concessions to ensure compliance. These inevitably forge segmentary interests, despite the state's call for submission to the centre (Peter Lee, 1991a, p. 153). What is useful about this concept is that we have for a long time focused on the commanding heights but paid little attention to the differentiated roles and interests of the state and producers. Now this gap is being increasingly appreciated by both Chinese and western scholars.

Within a work unit mutual obligations under a rigid pattern of remuneration and lifelong employment constitute the institutional pillars supporting the bilateral ties characterised by bargaining and strife. State corporatism recognises the workers' role in maintaining the rule of a socialist government. It places constraints upon factory cadres through a set of institutional arrangements. Under such a corporatist framework

the relationship between workers and management is centred on a collectivism that reinforces mutual obligations.

These features are close to Vivienne Shue's concept of a 'honeycomb'
(Shue, 1988). To a considerable extent, corporatism is seen in the
autonomous and effective role of a work unit that stands between
the party/state and individuals (Peter Lee, 1991b, p. 162). To many
observers, the degree of this autonomy is a matter of controversy. Yet
this measure of autonomy may constitute the starting point for state-
owned enterprises to initiate a metamorphosis from totalitarianism to
corporatism. Together with Womack's concept of work unit socialism, this
provides an angle from which to analyse Chinese industrial reforms.

CONCEPTUALISING DEPOLITICISATION AND DE-STATISATION

The large-scale *danweiisation* of work units since the 1950s has increasingly blurred the boundaries between the state and society, and at the
same time each *danwei*, being a small closed society, has atomised
the whole of society.[5] The politicised clientelist ties inherent in the *danwei*
system serve as a hotbed of corruption, causing widespread discontent
among workers and the decay of the party's grassroots cells. They have
helped to breed disruptive social forces that may one day bring about a
breakdown in government institutions and social organisation. Such forces
had driven the dynastic cycles of ancient China for thousands of years
(Jin Guangtao and Liu Qingfeng, 1990, p. 89). Since the 1970s the dynastic
cycles have shown clear signs of revival in the PRC, stimulating the post-
Mao leaders to launch the reform in the interests of the long-term rule
of the Communist Party. As pointed out by Nathan, a transition begins
when the ruling elite, or a substantial section within it, perceives that the
potential advantages of giving up some control outweigh the risks
(Nathan, 1990, p. 54). Indeed, the perception of such advantages has
led to reforms that have given state-owned enterprises unprecedented
breathing space, making it possible to ease political tensions between
workers and factory authorities.[6]

The post-Mao industrial reforms have, in short, curtailed the totalitarian
control embodied in the *danwei* system. The Party's autonomy in formulating key decisions without being made accountable to the public still
constitutes a major feature of China's powerful state. However, its policy
has seldom been implemented effectively, causing scholars to infer that
the Chinese state is weak (Kim, 1995, pp. 46–64). The failure in policy
reinforcement is actually the failure of state/society integration, or a
reflection of an increasingly weakened organised state. The following
chapters deal with some specific reform measures that have institutionalised such a tendency. If we define China's pre-reform state/society
relationship as one in which a strong centralised state dominated a highly

organised but less than integrated society, the present relationship may be seen as one in which a gradually hollowed-out state confronts a chaotic society. The slow bankruptcy of the *danwei* system has served as the catalyst for the evolution. In a way this transformation can be conceptualised, as briefly stated in Chapter 1, as the evolution of depoliticisation and de-statisation. To a large extent, this involves two interrelated and interdependent processes: transition from a command economy to a market economy and transition from communist dictatorship towards liberalisation (Hasegawa, 1992, p. 62).

Depoliticisation is a process that reverses the efforts to turn a work unit into a political institution. The central part of the process is the reshaping of those establishments responsible for totalitarian controls at the grassroots level. The key to this, according to Chinese party theorists, is to alter the organisational functions and leadership mechanisms of party cells in the industrial work units so as to make them go along with a general social change that is increasingly apolitical (Li Ming, 1992, p. 23). It is a process of redefining the power of the party at the social base, as will be further explicated in Chapter 3.

Most importantly, depoliticisation means phasing out direct political intrusions into economic activities (Hartford, 1991/2, p. 46). At the macro level, depoliticisation demarcates the new relationship between the party's political pursuits and the government's socio-economic management, which entails a separation of the economic agenda from political impulses. As the reforms unfold, this separation entails two basic changes in the economic system: marketisation and privatisation. These have been largely the initiative of the party, which recognises that tight political control may not guarantee its monopoly of power if the economy fails to deliver. Creating rational-legal mechanisms in governance may actually prolong its hold on power (Harding, 1987, p. 184). The party's omnipresence may perhaps obstruct this goal. This more sophisticated understanding of control has been behind the party's recent efforts to deepen government reform (separation of party and state administration) and ownership reform (separation of government administration and property operations). At the enterprise level, depoliticisation requires the party leadership to retreat from business management and attend to its internal affairs. Consequently, there have been profound changes in the relations between party cells and management, in the way political activities are conducted, and in workers' perceptions of the party. In fact depoliticisation has been the key factor behind the paralysis of large numbers of party cells in the state sector.

Depoliticisation is accompanied by de-ideologisation. These two notions can be seen as two sides of a coin. They underline the dismantling of 'politics in command' in the workplace, both as a mentality and as a mechanism. To the CCP, Marxist ideology has long been at once a theoretical guide to action and a practical means of control. Without either, it is believed that chaos will ensue.[7] This dual function of ideology has given the party justification for suppressing dissenting political views. With the belief system now largely bankrupt, the ideology has been reduced to inculcating in workers a sense of compliance to the existing order, and thus functions more as a control system. But with the deepening of depoliticisation – for instance, as seen from one of its indicators: the phasing out of political campaigns at the grassroots – the control function of the ideology has increasingly lost its relevance.

At the same time the official ideology in state-owned enterprises has been effectively reduced to 'economism' (*jingjizhuyi*), a body of ideas related to material incentives and profiteering. Ideological work is now seen as an attempt to enlist cooperation from workers and ensure harmony between workers and management. In other words, ideology has been neutralised to suit general management purposes. For instance, ideological education has been devoted to promoting a sense of common interests among workers and staff, and creating an 'enterprise culture' to bind the factory community together. But in a common struggle for more income for community members and business autonomy, these efforts can facilitate emergence of a collective identity conceptually independent of the state (Fan Zhu, 1991, pp. 190–213). To a degree, this development is a blow to the unified culture embodied in the *danwei* system which emphasises conformity to the party centre. The newly advocated enterprise culture stresses the individuality of a factory and its specific values, a clear departure from the party's ideological dictates.

This book argues that depoliticisation means restoration of the work unit to an institutional status more strictly related to its specialised functions in the division of labour in a society. Still under the party/state, this does not necessarily mean that a state firm frees itself entirely from the government's official bondage. The concept describes a process in which specialised organisations, with enhanced business autonomy, gradually shake off the core tasks imposed on them by the party/state in its efforts to control the population. For instance, a fairly independent industrial unit will become a business firm in the basic sense that it no longer functions as a political and ideological mobiliser, or a level of state administration assuming a wide range of duties of state control, or an agency of public security monitoring the everyday activities of its members. It will have full power over production and sales, responding more to market signals than government decrees. Moreover, it will have its own remuneration and employment policies, though still responsible for a large amount of social welfare for workers on behalf of the state. In sum, depoliticisation in state-owned enterprises is about removing most party/state political functions that an industrial *danwei* is now performing.

De-statisation describes three crucial aspects of changing state/enterprise relations in China's state sector that constitute the base for the industrial *danwei* system: property links; bureaucratic ties; and remunerative controls. Each is decisive to the nature of state control over state-owned enterprises and to the redistribution of interests between them. This book argues that the alterations in these three systems will provide the institutional foundation for a new state/enterprise relationship to emerge, and that this new relationship will accelerate China's general social transformation.

Hartford employs the term 'de-statisation'. To her, the notion means the reduction of the state's regularised, direct role in the economy as owner, producer, planner or organiser of production. This can occur either through the outright surrender of that role, or parts of it, or through the growth of other sectors (Hartford, 1991/2, p. 46). The scope of her definition mainly covers the mechanisms through which the state regulates the command economy, although it touches upon the issue of ownership.

De-statisation regarding state ownership is analysed as opening up a process in which state-owned enterprises move towards privatisation (*minyinghua*). This constitutes a profound political reform in China. The Chinese concept of ownership is a political and ideological consideration rather than an economic and legal one. The term implies an overall system of governance based on the ideological principles of socialism, such that the state acts as the custodian of this public ownership (Child, 1994, p. 20). So politically, the term 'de-statisation' describes the dismantling of the state's hierarchical controls over state-owned enterprises. A property analysis clearly points to the efforts to transfer property rights and control from the state to producers. This process has been broadly defined as privatisation (Hemming and Mansoor, 1988, p. 1). For instance, Shackleton's definition of privatisation covers the whole range of reforms that subject administrative activity to the discipline of the market (Ng and Woon, 1992, p. 46).

It is inadequate, though, to regard privatisation as merely a transfer of control. At least at the outset, decentralisation in which the state contracts out factories may not turn them into private concerns. However, the process may change their ownership structure as contractors inject into it property acquired through their own investment. To the extent that monolithic state ownership is diluted by such hybridised ownership and to the extent that contractors obtain more power over income distribution, privatisation of the state sector *begins* with de-statisation. The experience of privatisation in Eastern Europe shows that it is crucial first to de-statise state-owned enterprises by granting them property rights. Dilution of monolithic state ownership of state-owned enterprises is instrumental in making them fairly autonomous entities so that a smooth path can be laid for any real, large-scale privatisation.

In China reduction of the state share in the national ownership structure has been gathering momentum since the mid-1980s. Within the state sector various forms of ownership are emerging. The recent leadership consensus to remodel state-owned enterprises through corporatisation has quickened the pace for the dilution of state ownership. Since corporatisation is often carried out through grafting non-state stocks and shares onto state-owned enterprises to create limited liability companies and joint stock companies, the reform will decisively reverse the state's longstanding commitment to 'purifying' state ownership (Gao Shangqun, 1993a, pp. 7–11). The logic inherent in this reform implies a constant decline in state property shares within an enterprise which is being converted into a joint stock company. As analysed in Chapter 8, this process has gathered momentum. In particular, the recent central policy to let go the majority of medium-sized and small state-owned enterprises is an indicator that de-statisation has cut into the foundation of state ownership.

De-statisation in the administrative sense describes a gradual process in which state-owned enterprises break away from the traditional bureaucratic command chains and become, to borrow the buzzwords currently most popular in China, *wushangji qiye*, or firms without administrative 'mothers-in-law'. To this end, the concept assesses the emerging new set of institutional arrangements between the government and state-owned enterprises. Out of these arrangements a new model of corporate governance is being constructed from the ongoing reform of China's economic administration system. This new model will undercut the foundation of the old industrial administration built upon the branch *tiaotiao* and region *kuaikuai* systems.[8] Under the formula of separating government administration and management of state ownership, some industrial bureaux will be transformed into general shareholding companies and some into sectoral associations. For the former, their new relations with their subsidiaries will be more monetary, that is they will receive dividends as the owners of state shares (Wang Xiaoguang, 1995, p. 5). The latter, sectoral associations, will act as the medium for state supervision of state and non-state enterprises in the sector in accordance with its industrial policies. The design is to shift the state's direct (administrative) control over factories into indirect guidance. Here the state monitors state assets operations by producers rather than interfering with their everyday production and management. And it uses sectoral industrial policies as key macro-economic levers (Gao Zimin, 1993, p. 3). When industrial bureaux are gradually stripped of administrative functions and are ultimately removed from the government structure, the industrial ranking hierarchy will be phased out. The rationale for this reform is that if the economy is modelled on market deregulation, there is no need to maintain a vast bureaucratic machine whose chief mission is to *allocate* goods, funds and quotas, which is now the job of the market.

The process of de-statisation in the industrial remuneration sphere means the abolition of the state's nationally unified wage system. In its place there has emerged a variety of wage forms formulated independently by producers themselves. Currently, the 'linkage wage system' is the mainstay, which partially links the rewards of workers to the levels of profit and turnover achieved by their firms.[9] In the future a mechanism of regional/sectoral wage guidance will become the main form of state wage regulation, a reform which will move China's wage settlement into line with international practice (Zhu Jiazhen, 1992, p. 6). Under this system state-owned enterprises will have full autonomy in deciding how and when to reward workers. The system has been legally confirmed by the Labour Law. In addition, the locus of remuneration has been brought closer and closer to the shop floor, with sub-factories and workshops now playing a key role. As a result, state macro wage policy no longer directly affects workers, whose lot is more intimately linked to the market performance of their employer. This effectively enlarges the perceived distance between them and the state.

The state sector wage reforms have created a new structure of interests with the retreat of the state from its direct involvement in micro remunerative matters.[10] This transition has exerted tremendous impact on state/enterprise and management/worker relations. Industrial wages are now much less at the mercy of the state. Moreover, because the industrial wage reforms allowed state-owned enterprises to increase workers' income from their own resources, their status as economic entities has been enhanced.

The direct outcome of these institutional changes has been a visible trend towards *de-danweiisation* in China's state sector. Essentially, this trend means a redefinition in state/society relations: *de-danweiisation* serves as a strong centrifugal force driving workers away from the arms of the state. As mentioned earlier, the *danwei* system assumes multiple functions. Many scholars tackle the phenomenon by focusing on its unit-based welfare functions (Wong, 1994). From this angle their subject of research concentrates mainly on enterprise/worker relations. This study argues that the *danwei* system is first of all an embodiment of special state/society relations. So the *danwei* phenomenon is reflected more by its political functions and state control functions. The nature of its political functions is reflected by the CCP/worker interactions and the party's ideological indoctrination. The nature of its state control functions is reflected by state administrative ties (hierarchy), state ownership structure and state remunerative controls. So the *danwei* is first of all a political institution and the word itself has political connotations. Unit-based welfare mechanisms may have remained intact, or even been strengthened since the mid-1980s or so, but this is not unique to China. Japanese firms have many of these welfare functions and so do many Taiwanese firms. The word *danwei* is Japanese in origin. With the party/state controls withering in state-owned enterprises, the *danwei* system is decaying. In other words, as the *danwei* system decays, a new social base is being reconstructed at the grassroots: this remoulds a state firm from being a cell of the party/state into being a fairly autonomous social entity. In time this new social base will breed political change in the superstructure.

RECONSTRUCTING A NEW SOCIAL BASE FOR POLITICAL CHANGE

The *de-danweiisation* process has been the result of a series of economic reform measures in the state sector. It amounts to a profound political reform in China at the grassroots, even though it is proceeding quietly. On the other hand, depoliticisation and de-statisation in state-owned enterprises have taken place as part of a huge social engineering project which has paved the way for the emergence of social and economic pluralism at the base of the state edifice, although at the apex of political power the party/state remains strongly authoritarian. This dialectical political process is forging some form of authoritarian pluralism in China, a term that Professor Scalapino has used to theorise about social transition in East Asia (Scalapino, 1989). As South Korea and Taiwan have proved, economic relaxation creates pluralistic economic interests such as private concerns, autonomous entrepreneurs, joint ventures. And protracted economic growth gives birth to a freedom-seeking middle class whose members perceive that it is in their interests to struggle jointly to enlarge their political influence. The dynamic of authoritarian pluralism is that once rulers relax control over society in pursuit of economic development, they release a powerful force for political change.

Whether China can transform its party/state will depend crucially on whether it can remake the authoritarian infrastructure embedded in the *danwei* system. Without *de-danweiising* the urban workplace, expansion of the 'buffer zone' between the state and society will be inhibited, entrepreneurs and intellectuals will be reluctant to resist state intervention, and political change will incur at higher human and economic costs. To a great extent the two decades of reform have moved the country firmly in the direction of authoritarian pluralism. Despite the efforts by the party to hold on to authoritarian control nationally, at the grassroots depoliticisation and de-statisation have increased the space for social institutions to pursue their own interests. Any government attempt to suppress this development will jeopardise the economy and thus impede the party's efforts to hold on to power. The constant softening of authoritarianism is thus just a matter of logic: every time the rulers resort to harsh means, they pay a higher price and shorten their rule in the long term. At the social level an environment favourable to growing pluralism has been emerging to challenge state domination. The following are some of the factors that have facilitated the quiet revolution from below.

The role of the market

China's dynamic change is intimately linked to the assertion of market forces. The experiences of the ex-socialist economies have shown that, as soon as the command system is open to the market, new economic mechanisms will inevitably emerge, undermine the authority of central planning, erode state ownership and cause conflicts between the government and state-owned enterprises. The two different sets of economic imperatives during the transition give rise to 'a confusion of traffic, as some vehicles drive on the right, some on the left'. State-owned enterprises then experience what Kornai describes as 'double dependence', namely focusing one eye on the state for subsidised goods and the other on the market for profits (Kornai, 1985, pp. 10–15).

Somewhere in this transition, the point of no return will be reached. In the market, interest groups acquire enhanced collective identities and employ political clout to influence government decision making. Behind the conflicts of interest represented by these different groups, new types of political competition become ever more active and even penetrate into the factional infighting at the apex of power. At the same time, the market generates powerful consumerist pressures which undermine communist ideology and defy efforts at reversal by the party (Van Ness, 1989, p. 19). Indeed, with hindsight it will be seen that it is not the desire of the Chinese for legal democracy that brought down the communist regime, but the desire for consumerism (Glassman, 1991, p. 19). Moreover, with the expansion of market transactions concepts such as property rights, individual choice and fair competition have become more pronounced, inducing people to make new kinds of political demands.

Consequently, workers as well as managers begin to position themselves in the clash between two logics apparent in the coexistence of planning and the market. In a dual-track system, managers acquire more authority to make investment, sales and distribution decisions. However, the more of these powers they obtain, the more intolerant they become of state interference. As the expansion of the market increases their business powers, through use of these powers managers develop a kind of entrepreneurialism that gradually changes their self-perception as cadres of the state. For workers, the opportunities to favour their independent interests offered by the market progressively diminish their sense of being 'state workers'.

As the reform deepens, the operations of the state sector are dominated more and more by the market as regards obtaining capital, raw materials, services and pay rises. The state's capacity to satisfy the needs of its firms has shrunk to the point where state-owned enterprises are increasingly forced to choose between relying more on the state or more on the market. In facing the 'squeeze' of market competition from the fast-growing non-state sector, most state-owned enterprises come to regard the state as increasingly unreliable, and begin to call for the elimination of their bureaucratic 'mothers-in-law'.[11] In sum, the market serves as a cutting edge between the state and state-owned enterprises and provides unprecedented opportunities for society at large.

The role of privatisation

What further drives state and society apart is privatisation – an inevitable outcome of marketisation of the command economy. State ownership becomes hybridised as state-owned enterprises are corporatised. Fast-growing private concerns gradually become a key force in the national production structure. As a result, private property rights require the vesting in individuals or freely constituted associations of individuals of very broad rights as to the use and transfer of property and the drawing of income from it (Prybyla, 1989, p. 9).

For example, the privatisation process breeds a new generation of entrepreneurs. As Szelenyi argues, individuals become entrepreneurs in order to gain the independence denied to them in public employment. Entrepreneurship is by definition an active strategy of resistance against state control. Politically, the market economy in general and private business in particular promote horizontal links of business associations independent of the state. Entrepreneurs seek alliances with other entrepreneurs to enhance their collective influence as a political interest group. In due time they help to forge civil society within an authoritarian system (Szelenyi, quoted in Wank, 1995, p. 58).

Organisationally, privatisation is a fundamental blow to the industrial *danwei* system. It is very unlikely that the privatised state firms will be able to maintain an effective party presence. If anything, the party cells in privatised state-owned enterprises have either become paralysed or been made to service the new private owners.[12] Then the function of state administration collapses, as these firms lose their bureaucratic ranking and bosses. Few political staff remain to perform the functions of state control, such as reinforcing family planning quotas. As discussed in great detail in Chapter 8, the non-state sector in fact employs the majority of the workforce in the country. In a decade or more, the state sector will look like a shrinking island surrounded by seas of private concerns. The totalitarian patterns of state/society integration are then bound to be overhauled and this will significantly affect the country's political and social system.

The role of decentralisation

China's new social base for political change will also be shaped by the main thrust of the country's post-Mao economic reforms – decentralisation, which has transformed Chinese society in the following important ways: (1) the trend towards regional economic pluralisation has become irreversible; (2) the weakening of economic centralisation has also encouraged the nation's 'political pluralisation' – relative local autonomy from the centre; (3) the relative autonomy of local government constitutes a stabilising mechanism for the local economy and for social stability (Jia

Hong and Wang Mingxia, 1994, p. 37). What should be stressed here is that local autonomy is largely driven by individual economic activities, often under the protection of local governments (Oi, 1992).

This new social base is being created as a result of the breakdown of the old hierarchies in the command economy. Its consolidation goes hand in hand with the consolidation of a new central/local relationship shaped by market forces. In this sense, the real challenge of economic reforms is a political one (Shirk, 1993, p. 6). The flourishing pluralistic social structure is clearly reflected in a pluralistic decision-making process at various party/government levels. This has led some scholars to argue that there has emerged a new political system in China, namely market-preserving federalism. From the perspective of the political relationships among the different levels of government, China's political and economic decentralisation has much in common with western federalisms (Montinola *et al.*, 1995, p. 52).

In a liberal federal system, well-defined constitutional powers protect individual rights. Chinese-style federalism may have a long way to go to reach this destination. However, the growing market-preserving federalism has established institutionalised arrangements of power sharing between the centre, the locality and social organisations. The changing political relations among major players impose a number of limitations on the central and local governments' authority. It is no coincidence that the course of decentralisation parallels the progressive expansion of the private sphere in which people manoeuvre to stretch the state's 'zone of acceptance'.

In summary, the above-mentioned are just some of the external catalysts that have liberalised the relationship between the state and state-owned enterprises and within state firms. Grassroots political and economic changes will seriously shake the superstructure in due course and will further stimulate the transformation of the political system as a whole. Since 1978 we have been witnessing a trend to do away with the Maoist revolution. With the rolling back of the state's totalitarian reach, Martin Whyte's concept of 'totalistic logic' – his analysis of traditional state/society relations in China – enables us to project how the country's state/society relations will evolve. The concept depicts a state which tries to exercise all-round control over everything in society but has to scale down this ambition to concentrate on thought control over the people, on account of limited human and financial resources. And it is capable of effective control only at the national level. So autonomous groups emerge at the grassroots, although they are expected to pay homage to official values (Whyte, 1991, p. 256). The current regime may be able to muster enough human and financial strength to suppress society in the short run. Yet the heavy cost will force it to seek alternatives. Increasingly, it will be satisfied with control in terms of totalistic logic, as social forces become more assertive with their augmented economic power.

In the not too distant future, economic progress will bring in its wake democratic inclinations and a healthy surge of pluralism, which in time will undercut the foundations of the authoritarian rule common to developing countries. Analysing the course of socio-political change in Northeast Asia, we see the interaction between economic development, leadership and social forces. While one should not assume that authoritarian regimes will give up their monopoly of power willingly, they attempt reforms under pressure from the growth of people's power. As a result of economic growth and social liberalisation, owners of firms, intellectuals, students and workers will all raise their stake in the country's political transformation. Over time the balance of power between the three forces shifts away from state domination. In other words, political change at the grassroots level represents a time-bomb for dictatorship. Therefore, authoritarian pluralism is very dynamic. Before a revolution from above occurs, there has to be a quiet revolution from below.

Part II

Depoliticisation: diminishing party controls

3 The reform of the enterprise leadership structure

Party cells in state-owned enterprises form a parallel governing hierarchy to management. In fact, party control over shopfloor politics has been much tighter in China than in any other socialist state. For instance, restrictions on the setting up of party committees in factories in the USSR prevented party command being established in those with less than 300 members. Under the one-man management system, most of the Soviet industrial party cells were not power holders. According to the Party Charter (1986), industrial party committees could exercise some supervisory role over managers in certain areas of work, but on the whole they were mainly caretakers of their internal affairs (Li Mu, 1989, p. 46). In contrast, party branches in China's state-owned enterprises until recently formed the leadership core. For more than three decades they constituted the elite of elites and monopolised ultimate policy- and decision-making authority (Barnett, 1967, p. 429).

In relations with government, party command has crossed both vertical and horizontal lines of public administration, from Beijing to remote villages. It has firmly interlocked into all government agencies and social organisations (Lieberthal, 1995). As a result, the chain of party command has become thoroughly bureaucratised. Because party organs at every level of the social fabric now serve as the key hub of communications and tools of policy implementation, it is no exaggeration to state that the running of the country would come to a halt without them.

Party cells in state-owned enterprises have maintained an active 'organisational presence' that is routinised in daily factory life, with party members being constantly reminded of their political duties. One of these duties is to disseminate to workers around them what they themselves are being indoctrinated with. Furthermore, to perpetuate the party's 'life', always in search of 'new blood', a system of recruiting and training activists has been institutionalised. During the Mao era, 'revolutionary struggle' was seen as the basic lifeline of the party, ranging from class struggle to production struggle. Shop floors became battlefields for such non-stop struggle. To cope with a highly politicised environment, survival for many workers, especially those from 'a bad family background', required much more than labouring eight hours a day. They also had to appear politically correct to cope with the pressures of the tense atmosphere.

Even in today's China, the party still regards state-owned enterprises both as productive units and as the setting for political and ideological control. The party industrial cells are therefore accorded a core role in leading the factories' political life, paralleling the management's central position in leading the factories' economic life. The extent to which these 'two centres' coexist in state-owned enterprises shows that the political function of *danwei* is still upheld by the party. However, the post-Mao reform has introduced numerous mechanisms that have seriously eroded the party's presence in state-owned enterprises and paralysed their political function. All this is an outcome of a profound political reform in the mid-1980s that abolished the monistic leadership (*yiyuanhua*) at the enterprise level.

THE ORIGIN OF THE PARTY'S MONISTIC CONTROL[1]

Politicisation of a factory started with the creation of a party branch. In 1950, there were 2,858 state-owned enterprises, with a workforce of 750,000, mainly confiscated from the Kuomintang government. Party organisations existed in only a small number of these factories and in an 'underground' form.[2] In the spring of 1949 the party Central Committee (CC) passed a resolution that industrial party cells should be gradually brought into the open in the liberated areas. This policy was a response to the tension developing between party members, who led activists from behind the scenes as a new centre of power, and management and ordinary workers, who were under constant pressure, as they could not be certain who represented the party and what functions they performed. It was hoped that public listing (*dazibao*) of all party members would ensure proper supervision by the masses, who would have to be more watchful (Zhao Shenghui, 1987, p. 235). Soon all party branches openly set up office. Although this may have alleviated the fears of many people concerning a mysterious force at work behind the scenes, it also legitimated a parallel power centre to management, marking the beginning of politicisation of plants. The heads of party branches could now wield power in an open manner.

Politicisation deepened further when party cells began to recruit new members on a large scale. By the time of the founding of the PRC in October 1949, party membership among workers was very small. Nationally, such members numbered 112,000, or about 0.5 per cent of the urban workforce (Zhao Shenghui, 1987, p. 235). This small representation slowed the consolidation of communist control in the newly captured cities. In factories in particular, the traditional gang-boss networks persisted, adversely affecting the communist takeover.[3] The 'opening up' of party cells was meant to address this problem and indicated a change in the party's focus from rural struggle to urban control. To this end, according to An Ziwen, deputy chief of the COD, the party would recruit about one-third of all industrial workers in the five years from 1950 (Brugger, 1976, p. 86).

The large recruitments played an important role in the successive political campaigns in the next several years, e.g. the 'three-anti', 'five-anti' and Suppressing Reactionaries movements.[4] New party members were organised to carry out propaganda and struggle meetings, mobilise the masses to report 'special agents' of the Kuomintang, search for more activists and promote production. Workers began to sense a different atmosphere. Some benefited from the new political relationship that the revolution brought to the shop floors, others suffered as a result. This gradual politicisation furthered tensions between the party and managers, and between party members and ordinary workers. Most workers could no longer afford to be apolitical.[5]

Party committees soon ran into conflict with management. Until the party centre approved one-man management in late 1953, most state firms were run by a committee comprising managerial staff and trade unionists with managers as the head. In private concerns development of trade unions was accomplished by a state decree which required factory owners to sign a collective contract with the unions and forbade them to dismiss workers at will. Yet as far as the party's policy was concerned, enterprises were supposed to be run as economic entities, even though they took orders from the state. This for some time still allowed managers substantial autonomy in running production (Zhang Zhailun, 1985, pp. 3–6).

The trade union debate, 1950–3

For a number of years after 1949 party leaders had been unable to determine the ideal model for political control at the level of the work-place. The subsequent consolidation of party control at the basic level prompted two extensive leadership debates: over the issues of trade unions and of the relations between party cells and management. In July 1950 Deng Zihui, Secretary of the South China Party Bureau, wrote to Mao, stating that the state, factory management and trade unions all had specific and separate missions and interests. It was not correct to mix them up under a single political agenda. While the basic standpoint (*jiben lichang*) of all these groups was the same, party branches, management and trade unions might differ in their 'concrete' standpoints (*juti lichang*) owing to their division of labour. This difference should be recognised as legitimate. On 4 August Deng's report was disseminated to the whole party as a 'good' report with Mao's approval (Zhang Zhailun, 1985, p. 57).

Deng's view was disputed by Gao Gang, Secretary of the Northeast

China Party Bureau, who claimed in a letter to Mao on 22 April 1951 that in socialist enterprises the state's interests *were* the interests of workers and that the goal of the party, government and trade unions was the same. To stress the difference of interests represented by the state and trade unions was to blur the distinction between public and private concerns (Zhang Zhailun, 1985, p. 54).

Other key leaders were drawn into the debate. Li Lisan, Deputy Chair of the All China Federation of Trade Unions (ACFTU), argued that trade unions in a socialist society had two functions: to protect worker interests from being encroached upon by the state and to organise workers to protect the state. The key to resolving the contradiction between the state and individual interests was what Mao had advocated, namely that 'public and private interests should both be given attention and factory management and workers should both benefit from production'. With Liu Shaoqi's support, Li argued that it was naive to think that if workers had political consciousness, they could work hard without food and clothes. That was why trade unions must not be the tail of the administration (the state) (Zhang Zhanbin, 1988, pp. 59–64).

Neither side of the debate questioned the CCP's leadership over unions. The discord involved how much space the party should allow a social organisation to have for its own initiatives, even as a 'transmission belt'. Those who called for better recognition of workers' interests did so in a belief that over-zealous party interference in the wake of its 'opening up' and the bossy attitudes of management had stifled the workers' enthusiasm, thus being counter-productive for the long-term rule of the party. However, those with the opposite view held that more breathing room for social organisations might help foster anti-government interests, leading to challenges to the power of the party.

Mao intervened in the debate in October 1951 with the statement that the ACFTU had seriously erred. His decision to side with Gao quickly settled the wrangling among top leaders. Soon Li Lisan was purged (Lin Yunhui *et al.*, 1991, p. 323). Earlier Mao had expressed concern over the worsening relations between the party and workers. He wrote on 31 December 1950 on a report on the labour movement submitted to him:

> The Fourth Plenum must discuss the trade union issue, with the focus on how to administer trade unions. In the past the work of unions achieved merits but many problems remained to be solved. In many enterprises the relations between the party and unions and party members and workers are abnormal. Workers are fearful of party members. They would stop talking as soon as party members come in. They are afraid of being reported and see party members as 'special agents' (*tewu*).
>
> (Mao, 1990, p. 753)

Under such circumstances Mao's instinctive reaction was to tighten party control. An explicit emphasis on different interests of the party, management and trade unions could undermine party authority at the grassroots at a time when Mao was to initiate the 'three-anti' movement. Consequently, advocating workers' interests was now interpreted as 'narrow economism' and stressing the autonomy of trade unions in relations with the party was labelled 'syndicalism'. In fact, 'economism' spelled the dichotomy of interests between the state and workers and 'syndicalism' was indicative of workers' resolve to campaign for their own interests. These were seen as anti-party activities. With the regrouping of the ACFTU, all trade unions were ordered to establish a party cell within their leadership, and union work was formally placed under the party system in factories (Du Yaohua, 1987, p. 299). As a result, more direct party control started to take root in shopfloor politics in the wake of the clampdown on unions. However, as long as the workers' interests were solidly structured in the differentiated articulation of interests between the state and society, they continued to make their demands known whenever there was a chance.[6]

The rise and fall of one-man management, 1953–6

At the same time tensions between party branches and factory managers came to a head. Between 1950 and 1953 several forms of leadership were exercised in state-owned enterprises in different regions of the country, for example one-man management in northeast China and the director responsibility system under the leadership of party committees in north, east and southeast China. With the conclusion of the three-year economic restoration, the need to standardise the industrial management system across the nation became pressing. This triggered another leadership dispute over which, party committee or management, should play the central role in a state firm.

In the early days of the PRC, with no expertise in running the economy, the Chinese had adopted a Stalinist model. The agreement between Stalin and Zhou Enlai in 1950 required the USSR to provide China with industrial plants to lay a foundation for its industrialisation. The Soviet experts brought with them Stalin's idea that industry had to be managed by professional managers without interference from the party (Bo Yibo, 1990, pp. 10–11). One-man management was the direct outcome of this idea, which exerted the heaviest influence in northeast China (Schurmann, 1968, pp. 239–40). Yet, as will be illustrated later, the Soviet approach to industrial management based on experts ran into conflict with party cadres from the very beginning.

About 800,000 non-communist government and business administrators worked for the new regime in north, east and south China in October 1949 (Lin Yunhui *et al.*, 1991, p. 70). Under Mao's instruction 'not to destroy the old management structure', most factories were still run by these retained personnel between 1949 and 1954 (Bo Yibo, 1991, pp. 89–93). In order to have them carry out party directives, the newly established party branches were required to play a supervisory role. For that reason the director responsibility system under the leadership of the party committee (hereafter referred to as the party command system) was instituted in most areas of China. Under the party command system, party secretaries controlled the overall political and production agenda while directors carried out in their daily administration the decisions reached by party cells. To strengthen the party's role, the restoration period had seen, in addition to an enlarged party membership among workers, a massive transfer to industry of party cadres from the People's Liberation Army and rural government.[7] These brought to the shop floor a distinctive style of work, characterised by a preference for political and ideological priorities. Although this work style was rejected by many urban staff as a guerrilla approach, there is no doubt that party cadres carried enormous weight in the management process. Therefore, the first step in implementing one-man management in late 1953 was to ask them to surrender many of their powers.[8] Resistance was a natural outcome.

From April 1954, when the CC approved the universalisation of one-man management, to its abolition in late 1955, many factories practised it only in name. Managers failed to carry out their responsibilities for fear of party secretaries. They complained to the investigation teams dispatched by the centre in 1955 that 'they did not even know what the leadership system in their factories was' (Special writing group of Heilongjiang, 1984, p. 17). In order to overcome party cadres' non-cooperative attitudes, many provinces and ministries found it necessary to appoint factory managers with higher party and administrative ranks (Beijing POD and Beijing PS, 1990, p. 305).

The resistance of party personnel to one-man management had presented a familiar scene. There were heated debates among party cadres and managers over such issues as whether a manager who was a party member should abide by the party's principle of democratic centralism, and on how extended a manager's authority should be in handling production versus non-productive affairs. Very often managers were blamed for not seeking advice from the party and, as a result, their management decrees were blocked in the process of implementation (Du Yaohua, 1987, pp. 304–5).

At the same time controversies in the top leadership also worsened. In February 1954 Gao Gang, the chief campaigner for one-man management, was purged. The one-man management system had attracted severe criticism for its alleged effects in undermining party leadership. At a central conference held in October 1955 many participants argued that, in a period of transition, the country's class struggle highlighted the necessity for stricter party control. Pending a decision by Mao, a compromise was worked out, which at once confirmed the continuity of one-man management and stressed the central position of party branches. A dual leadership structure soon emerged and most state-owned enterprises leaned towards party command. This structure was actually the precedent for the 'two centres' phenomenon in Chinese state-owned enterprises in the reform era, which illustrates the long history of tension between factory party cells and management. This will be discussed in more detail in later sections (p. 56).

Mao intervened personally in early 1956. He commented repeatedly that the running of state firms should follow the long tradition of the CCP, not the practice of the USSR. That is, all major issues must be discussed first by party committees and then executed by directors (Zhang Zhanbin, 1988, pp. 78–9). A few years later he remarked: 'All capitalist countries implement the director command system. The socialist principles of management should be fundamentally different, as reflected in our system in which directors undertake management responsibility under the collective leadership of party committees.'[9]

Thus in July 1956 the party command system was formally adopted at the party's Eighth National Congress. This marked the beginning of a unified party leadership, which provided an institutional framework for the party to penetrate into every corner of the shop floor.

Party domination and politicisation

In review of this dispute between advocates of one-man management and the party command system, one may ask: what was the difference between them, since factory management also basically comprised party functionaries? The difference can indeed be sought through several angles. The two systems had created different mechanisms of control and reflected different organisational principles and mentalities. Schurmann summarised this as follows:

> The manager thinks in terms of techniques, both technological and organisational; he prefers rational organisation, for he has the confidence that he can manipulate it and use it to achieve his own ends; he likes rules because he knows he can bend them to his will, to enforce compliance from his workers. The cadre, however, is a leader who thinks in terms of human solidarity. He knows how to solidarise men so that goals can be achieved; he knows how to manipulate their thoughts and sentiments; he operates not with ethos but with ideology; he strives for a different kind of mechanical solidarity, namely that of the combat team.
>
> (Schurmann, 1968, p. 251)

Structurally, one-man management was based on the principle of individuation of management, as opposed to the collective leadership preferred by party cells. The system of production-unit areas was in operation, ranging hierarchically from the top to work sections. Each production unit was headed by a single leader (Schurmann, 1968, p. 264). As a result, in the name of production, factory managers took control over virtually all sub-systems – production, social welfare and even political control – leaving the party to provide moral leadership only. This induced criticisms against managers that one-man management diminished the functions of party committees. If this effect was not very evident in the mid-1950s when one-man management was only partially practised, in the 1980s it became a striking feature of the renewed director responsibility system that increasingly marginalised party cells. Under the party command system, however substantial the authority of a manager, he was only an executive.

At the core of the dispute between advocates of the two systems was the preferred level of politicisation in state-owned enterprises. Mao always believed that political control was most effective when conducted through administrative control over people's everyday lives because 'management was also socialist education' and a factory was a 'revolutionary school'.[10] Under one-man management, however, directors tended to be preoccupied with production. Political tasks often enjoyed only nominal priority. In contrast, the party command system subjugated managers to party secretaries and production to politics. Party cadres were asked to keep an eye on production performance, but they were more inclined to follow political preferences set by their party superiors. For instance, they were judged by whether they had achieved a sufficient level of ideological indoctrination of workers and had held enough struggle sessions against 'class enemies'. In other words, the party command system was the concrete embodiment of 'politics in command' in the Mao era.

First, in the frequent political campaigns initiated by the party centre in the 1950s, party cells, with tight organisational networks, played a much more effective role as political mobilisers than could management. Second, party cells were instrumental in furthering the party's 'mass line',[11] which institutionalised the mechanisms of political control, such as a populous network of informers and a well-structured body of activists. The difference between political mobilisation and a mass line is that the former highlighted periodic political impulses, while the latter, the corollary of the 'mass dictatorship', was meant to routinise political impulses in periods of non-political campaigns. Combined, the party command system politicised the workplace and turned it into the base of the party/state.

So the different mechanisms of control to be used in running China's state-owned enterprises had lasting consequences for state/society relations at the outset of industrialisation. In practice, control is a function any organisation must use to induce expected behaviour from its members. However, the degree of control becomes a significant factor that varies when carried out by different mechanisms. The control exercised by one-man management was more designed to maintain order in production, while the party command system was intended to keep people under a political organisation, an official ideology and a special way of life. From the party's point of view, the party command system was more suitable for its purpose of revolution. And to achieve this purpose over three million party branches were established in China's social and economic organisations (*Zhongguo qingnianbao*, 14 October 1994).

When everything was put under the party command system, the party initiatives were reinforced outside the sanction of legal and administrative procedures. As a party branch assumed all major decision-making powers, the factory became not only the appendage of the state in terms of property relations and administrative networks, but also an appendage of the ruling party, providing financial support for party operations and locations for its pervasive activities. The insertion of party cells into all work units tightened political integration of social organisations and vertically unified decision making, execution and control into one all-encompassing and centrally administered hierarchy (Feher *et al.*, 1983, p. 106). As all work units became political institutions, it became increasingly difficult to answer the question of where the state began and ended.

DENG'S RATIONALE FOR ABOLISHING THE PARTY COMMAND SYSTEM IN STATE-OWNED ENTERPRISES

By the late 1970s the damaging effects to both the party and society of politicising work units were fully appreciated by the post-Mao leadership which attempted a major overhaul of the enterprise leadership structure. Deng was a firm campaigner for this reform. His explicit concern over poor management and implicit concern over defects in the political system underscored his determination to phase out the party command system in state-owned enterprises. To some extent, while his explicit concern stemmed from economic considerations, his efforts also implicitly reflected his motivation to preserve the long-term rule of the party.

The economic rationale

First of all, the excessive political control embodied in the party command system stifled the normal operation of the state sector. Few people cared about economic performance: managers did not have authority to make policy while party secretaries were little interested in everyday management. Production suffered as a result. Ultimately economic stagnation posed a serious threat to party control. Shortly before the epoch-making Third Plenum of the Eleventh CC in 1978, Deng raised the point that the party command system in factories disguised the fact that state firms were largely left unattended. He questioned in particular whether party cells in workshops and sections should assume any leading role at all (Deng Xiaoping, 1983, p. 234). In August 1980 Deng categorically instructed the Politburo:

The PCS must be abolished. I am for some experiments but it should not be delayed. Clearly, eliminating the PCS will resolve not only the problem of a lack of talents in state-owned enterprises but improve the overall management. The PCS is a big obstacle [for production] and represents the inability of our party in managing the economy.

(Chi Fulin and Huang Hai, 1988, p. 55)

Deng's dissatisfaction with the party command system can actually be traced back to the late 1950s when he was instructed by Mao to formulate a central document for industrial management. In order to draft it, a special team was dispatched in 1961 to the Beijing No. 1 Machine Tools Factory for a field survey. Led by Ma Hong and responsible directly to Li Fuchun and Bo Yibo, the team submitted a report to the CC in July in which it summarised eight defects of the party command system:

1 The party command system decided everything, seriously encroaching on the responsibilities of management, trade unions and the Youth League.
2 Leadership was seen as the personal prerogative of party bosses. Without their approval, managers' decisions had no legitimate base.
3 The party command system generated a mobilisational approach to production.
4 The party command system generated too many political meetings. On average factory party secretaries had one meeting a day, general branch secretaries two, and branch secretaries two to three.
5 The party branches in administration exercised the same control over the technical and administrative offices (e.g. approving their technical plans) as party cells did in workshops. This breached the Party Charter, which stipulated that party cells should not lead these offices directly (*xingzheng jishu jiguan*).[12]
6 The representation of specialists on party committees was reduced to a minimum, causing problems for committees attempting to formulate management decrees effectively and creating a gap in communication between the party and management.
7 Managers were not duly respected, personally or organisationally. Personally, managers' decisions were ignored or delayed. Organisationally, factory managers could not exert sufficient authority over workshop party secretaries who listened only to party bosses above.
8 In workshops and sections a mini party command system emerged whereby small party groups were in control. Serious defects arose: first, party members were always given leading posts, whether qualified to take them or not. Second, most party members were young unskilled activists who exerted pressure on older skilled workers, arousing antagonism between party and non-party personnel, sometimes to the point of disrupting production (Ma Hong, 1980, pp. 1–8).

Using the report of the survey team and other findings from the field by central work groups sent to eleven provinces, Deng organised the drafting of the '77 Articles on Industries' in August 1961 (Deng Liqun, 1985, p. 154). In addressing the problems of the 'one-man command of the party boss', Deng tried to promote what he held to be the correct line at the time of politics in command. Five years later when he was purged, the '77 Articles on Industries' was used as evidence of his crime of taking the capitalist road and undermining party leadership in state firms (Liu Guoguang, 1988, p. 665).

When Deng re-emerged on the political scene in China in the late 1970s, all the above-mentioned flaws inherent in the party command system had been exacerbated to a point that called for thorough reform. This time Deng was under constraint not from one particular leader like Mao but from China's political system *per se*. Apparently it was his series of instructions, mentioned earlier (p. 40), that set in motion a chain of reforms in the factory leadership structure. Of deeper interest is the rationale underlying this retreat of the party from its ubiquitous presence in China's industrial society. Shirk defined this political concession as a transition from virtuocracy to meritocracy. According to Shirk, virtuocracy is a central feature of a revolutionary regime committed to bringing about social transformation, mass mobilisation for economic development, political consolidation and legitimation (Shirk, 1984, pp. 57–60). The essence of virtuocracy was politicisation of factory life, which was inherently unstable and left workers and staff alienated from one another and from the state.

Deng's effort to undo virtuocracy was meant to boost economic development, upon which hinged the legitimacy of the party/state (Stavis, 1986, p. 26). What Deng might not have anticipated at the time was that redefining the party's role in economic management would also effect a basic change in state-owned enterprises' organisational mechanisms, ideological orientation and production objectives. The abrogation of the party command system constituted a substantial stride towards establishing a rational-legal order in state firms, as the country's politics moved away from charismatic authoritarianism (Harding, 1987, p. 184).

Such a shift was the result of 'expert' prevailing over 'red' in a protracted and highly politicised debate between China's pragmatic reformers and dogmatic ideologues. Meritocracy recognises the indispensable role of professionals in running firms. As a country modernises, bureaucracy inexorably proliferates in response to the administrative needs of the state and society. The type of managerial bureaucrat that is needed is not only a skilled administrator capable of managing policies and people, but is also well versed in the technical aspects of the economy (Shambaugh, 1984, pp. 117–18). So meritocracy means institutionalisation of a rational-legal framework for experts to perform in. The abolition of the party command system helped pave the way for a managerial command system to emerge later. Deng not only was the first to blame poor management upon the party command system but also became a most powerful advocate for granting central authority to managers. This is one of his major contributions to China's modernisation.

The political rationale

Deng's implicit motive for abolishing the party command system was that it had accelerated the party's internal decay, as unchecked power in the hands of party cadres increasingly enabled them to defy party discipline, worker supervision and higher-level commands. Deng had pointed out as early as 1941 that the best way to make a party corrupt, decadent and alienated from the people was to allow it to take over state administration (China Social Survey Institute, 1990, p. 1007). When in exile in Jiangxi Province from 1969 to 1972 he worked in a small state factory and observed at first hand the abnormal situation around him (Maomao, 1986, pp. 91–9). Deng's personal suffering during the Cultural Revolution and close contact with workers made him more aware of the truth that 'water can carry a boat and can overturn it too'. He considered that the enormous power of party cadres to control people's everyday life had gradually become greater than the centre's ability to oversee its own organisation (Deng, 1983, pp. 190–2). As this threatened the party's long-term monopoly of power, Deng realised that efforts had to be made to inhibit the growth of forces of corruption, mainly through limiting the power vested in the party's grassroots cells. In his famous 1980 speech, Deng noted:

> Under the slogan of strengthening the party's unified leadership, all power was improperly and indiscriminately concentrated in party committees and exercised by a few secretaries. Everything was decided by the first secretary. Ultimately the party's unified leadership became personal leadership.
>
> (Deng, 1983, p. 288)

He stated that without sound political institutions good people may become corrupt, but with sound political institutions even bad people would have to behave in a required way (Deng, 1983, p. 293). Deng's prescription to prevent grassroots party cadres from abusing their power was quite dramatic. In 1979 he outlined a blueprint for the reform of the factory leadership structure:

> Party committees should be preserved. But they should be elected from among managers, vice managers and workers. The committee is a party organ. With one or two clerks handling its daily affairs, there is no need to set up other functional offices. Its task is to manage party affairs only.
>
> (Chi Fulin and Huang Hai, 1988, p. 64)

In practice Deng's reform was implemented through a process of power sharing in the leadership structure in state-owned enterprises. The managers were to take control of all matters related to production and administration. A workers' congress system was erected to play a part in setting remunerative and social welfare policies. The party's role was increasingly confined to minding its internal affairs, as prescribed in the formula of separating party and management functions by the party's Thirteenth Congress in 1987. The previous unified party control structure was split into three components: the party system, management and trade unions; and each supposedly discharged its own functions.

Numerous books and papers were written to explain why such a redivision of labour was necessary for better economic management. However, few scholars in China offered a rationale for the reform from a political angle. Yan Jiaqi gave an interesting account of why the party command system should be withdrawn from the leadership structure in state-owned enterprises. He commented that, from the institutional point of view, the power of a manager could be fairly easily checked and balanced by other political interests, as compared with the support a party cadre could obtain from a powerful organisation (*Jiushi niandai*, no. 12, 1986, p. 40). This is an important point. In terms of power, managers' network of loyalists until recently could not match the party's network of branches and shopfloor activists (Walder, 1989a, p. 147). Generally speaking, when encountering factory heads, workers would have different calculations *vis-à-vis* a manager and a party secretary. They saw the difference between a person who exercised power on an individual basis from a top management position and one who exercised power on behalf of a powerful ruling party. In their interaction with firms' leaders, it was conceived to be less dangerous to resist a manager, a matter of discipline, than to resist party cells, a matter of political attitudes. When outside checks and balances were involved, it was easier to dismiss a manager appointed by government than a party secretary because the state's legal and supervision agencies had less authority to hold party personnel accountable.

Another political rationale was the CCP's concern about its image if it became entrapped in everyday clashes of interests among workers (Yan Shiqu, 1987, p. 20). As mentioned earlier, a Chinese firm assumes major social welfare and remuneration functions. When the party was in command, its cadres had to be in personal charge of distributing housing, medical care and wage increases. Very often this engaged party cells in conflicts among workers owing to short supplies of these benefits. As a result, party cadres' image as biased arbitrators became widespread, greatly damaging its legitimacy.

Those in favour of separating party and management functions construed Deng's proposal to revoke the party command system as a response to the worsening alienation of workers that it had aroused. They believed that if the party was not directly involved in the routine conflicts of workers competing for limited social benefits, it would become less of a target for workers' discontent. As an outside arbitrator, the party would have even more levers in its relations with management and unions, which would now have to deal with the headaches of benefit allocation. Most importantly, to free party cadres from their duties of dictatorship over workers' needs would remove a major source of corruption and thereby prolong the party's monopoly of power.

The legal and market rationale

In addition to Deng's explicit concern over management efficiency and his implicit concern over a popular backlash against party corruption, the reform of the factory leadership structure was also dictated by the need for a new industrial management system harmonised with the evolution of the market in the wake of the post-Mao reforms. Although Deng raised the question as to whether China should practise a market economy as early as 1979,[13] about the same time as he advocated that the party command system be phased out, it is difficult to establish any correlation between the two proposals in his mind. However, the deepening trend to marketisation showed the increased discrepancies between state-owned enterprises' internal leadership structure centred on the party command system and their economic pursuits aggressively dominated by market exchange. The legal and market rationale for a new management structure articulated itself in the evolution of reform.

The party command system best suited a command economy, where planning was reinforced by both state decrees and party mobilisation. As a government appendage, a state firm had little concern for profitability as long as it fulfilled the production quotas (Kornai, 1985). Since the urban reforms in 1984, the market had aggressively exerted itself in the operations of state-owned enterprises. Within a firm's leadership structure, party cells and management tended to respond to different imperatives. A struggle intensified, as party cells were mobilised whenever the centre decided to retrench, while managers demanded autonomy in market activities whenever the leftist rhetoric subsided.

Friedman has suggested that in the late twentieth century Leninist regimes could no longer cope with the world's technological advances owing to their rigid political and economic systems (Friedman, 1991, pp. 162–82). High-tech achievements are dependent on people's imagination, a function that central planning leaves little room for, and thus a fundamental reason why the Soviet bloc lost out in the economic race with the west. At the micro level, the party command system had proved itself to be anachronistic. Its abolition became inevitable not only as a result of the insistence of some top leaders but also as a result of the logic of marketisation affecting state-owned enterprises (Ying Hao, 1987, p. 151).

First, the party is organised on the principle that a lower body must obey its immediate bosses and ultimately the party centre. In this top-down vertical command system it was natural that party secretaries were held responsible to their party superiors. This was at odds with the horizontal and spontaneous competition of the market. Party/management interaction in a firm was caught between the demands of the commanding heights and the self-interest of an enterprise.

Second, in terms of the internal relations of the party, the party command system had two distinct features that were inherently contrary to the trend towards marketisation.

1 The system tended to bring everything under its control. This tendency was at odds with the status of a factory manager as the legal person of the factory under the Enterprise Law.[14] If the manager was accountable first to the party secretary in the factory, how could he take legal responsibility for management decisions?
2 The requirement for collective party leadership made it unlikely that anybody could be held responsible for policy failures. Collective decision-making processes also took time, preventing managers from responding to fluid market opportunities.

Third, the party was still committed to its socialist ideology, one of its four cardinal principles, though to a decreasing degree. One key ingredient of this ideology was egalitarianism in the form of a 'big rice pot' – permanent employment and relatively similar incomes regardless of any variations in input. In state-owned enterprises party committees tended to see themselves as the guardians of this principle.[15] This not only inhibited market-generated competition for greater efficiency but also created difficulties for reform of the employment system according to market principles.

All these barriers to marketisation associated with the party command system were deeply rooted in a politicised industrial *danwei*. As a party secretary stated:

> The party committee must play a decisive part in the management of socialist enterprises. This is because a socialist enterprise is not simply an economic entity that is only directed by the market. It is also 'a small society' taking care of a number of political and social welfare functions. Even though managers can take overall charge of production and sales, they can in no way deal effectively with the other functions a factory is endowed with. These are our responsibility.
>
> (Yao Lantang, 1989, p. 33)

Indeed, it is exactly these other functions that make party responsibilities work against market forces and underline the rationale for a thorough reform. Without getting rid of these functions it is difficult to depoliticise state-owned enterprises in a meaningful manner. In other words, the persistence of the non-economic functions would always legitimise party interference.

THE CHANGING ENTERPRISE LEADERSHIP STRUCTURE SINCE 1979

As the party command system was the cornerstone of party/state control at the basic units, it was predictable that any attempt to dismantle it would encounter severe resistance from both the party's industrial lobby in Beijing and its power base at the grassroots.[16] This was demonstrated during the protracted process of translating Deng's determination to dismantle the party command system into reality. At the very beginning, he was fighting almost single-handedly for a change in the factory leadership structure.[17] Yuan Baohua, former Minister in charge of Industry, disclosed to a national conference in 1984 that, when Deng decided to replace the party command system with the director responsibility system he asked Peng Zhen, his former deputy who had been rehabilitated in 1979, to work out the implementation. Later Deng reiterated this in his famous speech on political reform in August 1980. However, owing to difficulties in reaching a consensus on the suggestion, not only was Deng's plan shelved, but when *The Selected Works of Deng Xiaoping* went to press in 1983 he had to agree to alter the manuscript, deleting the sentence about his preference for the director responsibility system (Yuan Baohua, 1985, p. 8). It was not until 1 July 1987, when the piece was republished, that the manuscript was restored to the 1980 version.

Since 1979 the leadership reform in state-owned enterprises went through ups and downs. In view of changing relations between the party and management, the whole process can be roughly divided into five phases: 1978–82, 1982–6, 1986–9, 1989–92, and 1992 to the present. The guiding thread of this periodisation is seen from the promulgation of major official documents which reflect a succession of changes in party policies. This illustrates how the party had to balance the demands of different lobby groups such as its central propaganda and organisational elites, its industrial organisations and the state industrial administration. At the micro level it revealed complicated political interactions involving the web of interests in factory leadership, whose response to the reform could best be described as a tug-of-war.

The first phase (1978–82)

This phase can be viewed as one of transition to some degree of normality in factory leadership politics following the extreme practices of the Mao era. The guidelines for the transition were what the 'revisionists' had advocated before the Cultural Revolution, such as the Dengist '77 Articles on Industries'. In April 1978 the central document, '30 Articles on Industries', was published, and it abolished the Revolutionary Committees in state-owned enterprises. The position of factory manager was restored and its responsibilities specified, representing a small move away from monistic control by the Revolutionary Committee. However, leftist ideas persisted through inertia; politics was still in command, and party cells remained the ultimate authority for virtually everything.

Deng wanted to change all this. He ordered that the State Enterprise Law be drafted in early 1978 to institutionalise factory management. In addition to his series of instructions on abolishing the party command system (see p. 40), he suggested that a system of director responsibility under a factory management committee be established. The new committees would be composed mainly of specialists such as chief engineers and accountants. The draft law based on Deng's ideas was tabled in the State Council in September 1978 but was rejected on the grounds that the conditions were not ripe for the reform (Song Guohuang, 1988, p. 16) Yuan Baohua explained in 1987 that most comrades balked at Deng's proposal in 1978 because they were not prepared to change their ingrained model of party leadership. The fundamental disagreement was over the system of leadership that a state firm should adopt, party centred or director centred (Sha Ye, 1987, p. 2).

Despite this disagreement the first phase did see experiments with the director responsibility system in Beijing, Shengyang and Anshan. In terms of party and management relations, Deng's insistence on establishing strong management *vis-à-vis* party cells gained some currency (Deng, 1983, pp. 124–9). The proposal to reform the party command system was *per se* significant, as the country was about to move out of the vicious circle of politicisation which had lasted since the early 1950s. Meanwhile management was granted more power, and trade unions were restored after having been done away with in the Cultural Revolution. The collective interests of workers and a degree of autonomy for union operations were again recognised. By the end of 1982, 440,000 unions had re-emerged, with a membership of about 75 million (Zhang Zhanbin, 1988, p. 146). The party's monistic control started to lose ground.

The second phase (1982–6)

The second phase of restructuring enterprise leadership saw management gradually rising to challenge the domination of party committees. It began with the promulgation in 1982 of a set of official documents on the work of the party and management. These included the Provisional Regulations on Factory Directors and the Provisional Regulations on the CCP's Basic Units in State-Owned Enterprises. The two regulations confirmed the leading position of party committees, but gave specific powers of control to directors to run administration and production. Hence the economic functions of an enterprise were to be highlighted. Factory managers were authorised to make independent decisions on the allocation of management personnel, funds and productive materials, on production plans and sales, on discipline, promotion and remunerative measures concerning labour, on matters of workers' training and major technical innovations. They were empowered to set up their own staff network to facilitate daily management. This system was to be implemented by a management team made up of deputy managers, chief technical staff and middle-level managers, all made responsible to factory managers rather than party secretaries. Of particular significance was the inclusion of an article that in 'emergency situations' managers could have the power to decide matters outside the prescribed areas of their authority. Since the 'emergency situations' were not defined in clear terms, managers could interpret this article according to their own judgement. Theoretically at least, with these enlarged powers granted to managers, a new power centre slowly emerged, starting to shake the 'party's empire'.

In contrast, the provisional regulation on party units restricted the power of party cells. For instance, although party committees could continue to discuss and decide upon key production and labour issues, the regulation for the first time stated that they should not be directly involved in the work of management and trade unions. One far-reaching stipulation concerned a major reform at the workshop level, which created a structure equivalent to the one-man management system, characterised by vertical line management with the shop director possessing the final authority in the everyday running of shop affairs. In contrast, the position of party branch secretary was made part time, tenable either by the director or by any party member through election (Zhang Zhanbin, 1988, p. 167).

In accordance with the design for an orderly transition, the regulations still provided enough scope for party secretaries to intervene, though again over specified issues and to a reduced degree. The position can be exemplified by reference to their power in two important areas of control. The first was the requirement that all major administrative decisions should be submitted to party committees for clearance. The second was a conditional continuation of the cadre appointment system, which was reduced in scope, now applying largely to the higher echelons of management. However, because of the retention of these two crucial powers, party cells remained the overriding authority in state firms. This contradiction compromised the purpose of the reform and underscored the anxiety of the party about the prospect of losing control over the urban population. Indeed in practice, owing to these two powers, it was hard for party cadres not to interfere with daily management. As for managers, their earlier experience of Maoist politics based on party domination continued to make them reluctant to decide anything independently. The efforts to institutionalise the decision-making process only went half way: the functional duties of the party and management lacked clear lines of demarcation. For these reasons, this round of reform yielded only marginal results, although the general trend pointed to a weakened party role *vis-à-vis* the enhanced authority of managers.

The unsatisfactory result of the second stage of leadership reform in state-owned enterprises was confirmed by a survey conducted in 1984 by the Research Institute (Tigaisuo) of the SCRES. Fewer than 15 per cent of managers among 400,000 state-owned enterprises believed that their power in their daily work had been enlarged in an effective way by the regulations. They pointed out that the major obstacles preventing them from taking on the full authority permitted by the regulations had come from the intervention of party secretaries under the name of party leadership. They claimed that unless the party command system was overhauled, party secretaries could continue to wield power without responsibility, whereas managers had to assume responsibility without the power to administer. To many managers, this was worse than the party command system. Earlier they had at least been able to avoid being blamed for anything that went wrong. Now tougher demands for delivery made this difficult (Tigaisuo, 1986, pp. 23–35).

Deng again raised the question of abolishing the party command system in late 1983 when hearing reports from the Politburo Standing Committee on the preparation of the Third Plenum of the Twelfth CC, which was to launch the urban industrial reform. The Politburo finally passed a resolution that state firms should adopt the director responsibility system, though first on an experimental basis. The President of the National People's Congress, Peng Zhen, at last made a survey tour of the pilot factories in south China in 1984, five years after Deng's original suggestion. In April of the same year, Peng put forward three reports to the Party General Secretariat concerning the tripartite system in state-owned enterprises (the party, management and trade union). Although he favoured the director responsibility system, he also demanded that measures should be taken to enhance the work of the other two elements in the system. In other words, he deemed that 'conditions' were not ripe for the universalisation of the director responsibility system.

Disagreement among the party hierarchy on the annulment of the party command system was particularly acute. Premier Zhao Ziyang expressed his disagreement with Peng's report on the industrial party units when he presided over discussion on the three reports in the Secretariat and, subsequently, at the provincial governors' conference. He wanted to shelve the report on the party and issue only the other two. But he was almost isolated in the debate. Under Peng's influence, the General Secretariat was called on to disseminate all the reports to the party (COD, 1990, p. 318). The discord was further reflected in January 1985 when the Standing Committee of the NPC under Peng returned the draft Enterprise

Law to the party for 'more discussion'. The major reason for doing so was the perception that it would too much increase managers' power at the expense of the party. Managers were blamed in late 1984 for loss of control over wage increases and failures in investment decisions (You Ji, 1991, p. 65). The concerns of the party's powerful industrial organisations were explicitly expressed in a *Jingji ribao* article:

> Will the director responsibility system lead to abuses of power and arbitrary decisions by directors? Will they develop personal factions and nepotism with their newly acquired power over personnel? As the reform of the enterprise leadership structure deepens, people now have many doubts about the ability of factory directors to use their authority correctly. And these doubts are not groundless.
>
> (*Jingji ribao*, 24 June 1986)

At the same time, in the pilot schemes resistance from party basic units also turned out to be unexpectedly strong. By mid-1986, the total number of factories in the experiment reached 27,700 (Sha Ye, 1987, p. 3). But party personnel put up strong resistance.[18] As in the 1950s, high-powered working groups had to be dispatched to these factories, where they issued administrative decrees to make party bosses stand aside from the centre of power. For instance, the groups convened all-staff meetings to announce that managers would in future take overall charge of the factory's work with specific authority in key policy areas. Yet as soon as the groups left, the party system staged a comeback, with its supporters making trouble for managers. Many of these factories slid into chaos because both managers and party cells were confused about their new missions (*Zhibu shenghuo* (Shandong), no. 1, 1989, p. 35).

Only now did Deng realise that the reform meant not only a change in management mechanisms but a major restructuring of the web of interests in state-owned enterprises. He called his reform the 'second revolution', precisely because each step addressed problems of substantial reorganisation in political and human relations. Success in abolishing the party command system in plants rested on whether several million party cadres affected by the reform could be provided with a dignified way out.[19] This had to include compensation for their surrender of power.

The third phase (1986–9)

The third phase began when the State Council and the COD promulgated in September 1986 a second set of three documents regarding the party/management/trade unions in state firms. This time the word 'provisional' was removed: the regulations became the final official rules. This set of regulations was later incorporated into the Enterprise Law, which took effect in April 1988 and reaffirmed the director responsibility system in legal terms. This paved the way for universalisation of the director responsibility system. The lengthy seven-year process since Deng first made the suggestion in 1979 was itself indicative of the difficulties in gradually revamping the institutions of the party/state.

However, the strife within the elite over the party's role in the state sector did not stop. The regulation on party work had accepted many of the points in Peng's report and, in Zhao Ziyang's view, still gave party cells too much power. Zhao also complained that the regulation did not specify how to streamline the overextended party bodies in state-owned enterprises. With support from Deng and Hu Yaobang, the party centre issued a supplementary document to address these problems two months later. It accorded more power to managers *vis-à-vis* party secretaries by clearly stipulating that managers were the centre of factory political and productive affairs and party cells should therefore take a supplementary role (COD, 1990, p. 318).

Accordingly, the sentence, 'The leadership structure of China's state-owned enterprises is the director responsibility system under the leadership of party committees', was officially removed, and it was confirmed that an enterprise is a legal entity with the manager as its legal representative vested with all necessary powers (Hua Gong, 1988, pp. 88–104). The new documents contained the following key changes.

1 The new regulations abandoned the process of clearance of management decisions by party branches, stipulating that major decisions should be worked out through an administrative committee chaired by the manager and composed of such people as deputy directors, the chief engineer, chief economist and chief accountant. The party secretary, the chair of the trade union and representatives of the Workers Congress could also join such committees. Here it is worth noting that the party secretary was only one of the committee members. The regulations reaffirmed that when different opinions emerged, the manager had the final say against the view of the majority.

2 A factory manager had the power to select and appoint managerial staff up to the level of deputy manager. While the input of party cells was encouraged, there was no compulsory procedure through which appointments were cleared through party organs. This effectively restricted the second-line veto power of party personnel. Moreover, most appointments became contractual with a definite term. Managers' power over disciplinary, promotional and remunerative matters was enlarged beyond those stated in the provisional regulations.

3 The new regulations emphasised the binding power of management contracts between enterprise managers and their government superiors. These contracts specified managers' authority as legal and principal parties to the contracts that redefined state/enterprise relations. The emphasis on contract relations was intended to apply restrictions on the interventionist tendency of party cells as well as state planners.

4 The new documents made it clear that the chief mission of party committees was to ensure the good conduct of party members in the factory. Although the party's role of supervision over managers was reiterated, this became general and abstract because supervision in terms of adhering to the party's line and policies could be explained in many ways. For instance, according to Deng, the party's basic line and policies were to promote economic development, which meant that managers should acquire the necessary power to run production efficiently.

In 1988 the Enterprise Law was passed. It relieved party committees of their power to formulate the agenda for political and ideological work. The question of whether to make managers the masters of political and ideological work had been the centre of controversy in the process of drafting the law and had delayed its submission to the NPC for a number of years. A draft law was discussed in April and September 1984 and again in January 1985 by the General Secretariat. Each time consensus evaporated because of two major issues. The first was the status and role of managers in plants, whether they should be the centre of production alone or the centre of everything including political affairs (personnel, propaganda and enforcement of discipline), mass organisations (trade unions, the Youth League and Women's Association) and social welfare. The second issue was whether managers' overall responsibility should be carried out personally (one-man management) or collectively, with the manager simply being one among equals, particularly in relations with party secretaries and chairs of trade unions (Song Guohuang, 1988, pp. 17–19). The final breakthrough whereby factory managers took control over political and ideological work showed that the debate had clearly favoured the reformers. It also indicated the extent to which the party centre came to grips with the changed nature of a state firm which, it concluded, was an economic body (SCRES, 1988, pp. 157–80). This being so, the mission of party cells in state-owned enterprises was different from that in national and local government: as a factory was not a level of state power, it should not hold political power.[20]

With the strong top-down push by reformers, this phase had occasioned impressive institutional changes in the leadership structure of state-owned enterprises, marking the end of three decades of the party command system. The dominant role of party cells in everyday factory life was greatly curtailed, as has been effectively documented in many field investigations conducted by both Chinese and western scholars. For instance, while surveying 100 state firms in seven provinces in the late 1980s, researchers from the Chinese Institute of Labour Movement found that when workers had problems in their life, the last person they would contact was the party secretary (visited by only 4.7 per cent of respondents) (Feng Tongqing, 1993, p. 237).

The fourth phase (June 1989–92)

Events in 1989 made the CCP leadership realise that consolidation of its rule needed to begin with the reinforcement of influence of its grassroots organisations. In the party's 1990 national organisational conference, General Secretary Jiang Zemin openly commented that his role as leader of the party would be hollowed out if the party basic units exercised political leadership with no organisational reinforcement. In the wake of 4 June, the party reinstituted a nationwide anti-'peaceful evolution' campaign. Politically, Zhao Ziyang was criticised for watering down the party leadership in general and in the state sector in particular. A national clampdown was carried out within party ranks to oust participants in the protest movement. Ideologically, Lenin's indoctrination method was once again emphasised as indispensable for a Communist Party's hold on power (COD, 1990, pp. 69, 107). As conservatism surged, the whole social atmosphere turned visibly tense.

Against this backdrop, a central document, 'The CC Notification on Strengthening Party Building', was issued in 1990 to give a formal 'kernel' status to party industrial organisations, in an attempt to revitalise them through resolving the problem of the 'abstractness' of party leadership (Wu Zhiqing, 1991, p. 151). This abstractness, as one party theorist commented, was due to the gap between the party centre's broad emphasis on a core party role in the state sector and the absence of any definable and enforceable procedures to fulfil the mission. So party reconstruction in state-owned enterprises concentrated on questions such as exactly what were the major issues on which party cells had to have a say, and what organisational backup the party system should be given to supervise management (Wu Zhiqing, 1990, p. 28). The essence of post-Tiananmen party building was therefore to create institutional channels for the party system to interfere with management.

In the document, a crucial sentence was deleted from the 1988 supplement to the Regulation on Party Industrial Units: 'a party secretary can be concurrently appointed as deputy manager assisting the manager's overall responsibility in a factory's political and ideological work'. This sentence had previously settled the debate of who was the first hand in a state firm. With its removal the situation again became unclear. Party secretaries could now capitalise on this U-turn to claim a central role in factory politics, an apparent regression in the enterprise reform designed to transform state-owned enterprises into economic entities.

The political network was still placed under factory managers by the Enterprise Law. Yet the central document handed it back to the party system, and managers were required to match the party's initiatives to advance a propaganda drive against 'peaceful evolution'. One visible reversal of the party reform in the previous phase was the document's re-emphasis on the principle of the 'party managing cadres', which forced managers to seek approval from party committees before making any important appointments (Yue Xiuwu, 1990, p. 171). This was seen as the most concrete and necessary measure to operationalise the hitherto abstract party political leadership in state-owned enterprises.

Consequently, the enhanced power of managers resulting from the previous phases of reform was eroded, with the tightening of political control by the party. Even in the realm of production management, managers had to resist party cadres who erected road blocks through their established clientele networks.[21] However, managers did not give in without a fight. They made use of the Enterprise Law, which grants them three types of powers relating to political affairs, personnel and production. Legally they were still the 'number one boss' empowered to run this multi-functional 'small society'. There were also grey areas regarding authority over personnel between the two systems which caused endless strife. Soon conflict between the party's 'kernel' political mission and managers' central managerial status came to a head (more on this on pp. 56–64). The ensuing battle showed that reform of the industrial leadership structure was a matter concerning not just individual party cadres but entrenched institutions rooted in the overall political system.

The fifth phase (1992–the present)

The party's response to the Tiananmen events slowed down the tempo with which party functions were being reduced in state firms. Yet it did not and could not remove the motive force behind the reforms, as society became further depoliticised. The post-Tiananmen trend of 'back to the future' was partially rectified at the beginning of 1992 when Deng urged during his south China tour that reform should go further. In his subsequent visit to Shougang (the Beijing Iron and Steel Corporation), he reiterated his idea of autonomous management. He asked Zhou Guanwu, the former general manager, why Shougang had developed much faster than Angang (the Anshan Iron and Steel Corporation, the largest in China). Zhou replied that the low pace of development in Angang was due to the restrictions imposed on it, often in the form of excessive party intervention. Deng agreed, saying:

> The CC should be responsible for this. This is the reason why I toured the south and made a few bold remarks [*fangpao*, meaning 'fire a gun']. State firms are tightly tied up. This is what I heard so much in the south. How can they walk? The key question at the present is to enliven state-owned enterprises. We must act now.
>
> (*Jingji ribao*, 31 March 1993)

Deng's criticism forced the Politburo to address the question of the 'two centres' dispute. One of the measures taken was renewed emphasis on the director responsibility system. This was reflected in a number of central documents in 1992/3. The most important signpost was Jiang Zemin's Political Report to the Fourteenth Party Congress in October 1992 in which he demanded serious initiatives to separate party and management functions in state-owned enterprises. All this encouraged managers to stage a comeback and slowly recapture some lost territory.

However, the struggle continues. Premier Li Peng, who is in charge of the economy, has again presented his three-point guideline for party work in state-owned enterprises, namely that the party's political core function should be upheld; the director responsibility system should be improved; and management should whole-heartedly rely on the working class (unions) (*Liaowang*, no. 28, 1996, p. 1). In late 1995 a central notification jointly signed by the COD and SETC called for the establishment of a suitable governing institution in state-owned enterprises in order to implement the party's core missions and enhance political and ideological work (*Renmin ribao*, 23 November 1995). Thus confusing signals continue to be delivered to shop floors from above and managers and party personnel come up with different interpretations, each favouring their own preferences. For managers it is now less controversial to talk about freeing a factory from its bureaucratic hold, but to mention ejecting the party network remains taboo (*Liaowang*, no. 42, 1992, p. 1). In a conference on Deng's south China speech in 1992 many managers complained about constant interference from party cells. A manager from Dalian City commented that to compete in the market, he was required to streamline management ranks in his firm. But nobody raised the question of streamlining party bodies, whose numerous functions had lost touch with the new situation. Yuan Baohua, former Industrial Minister, answered: 'Nobody says that party bodies should not be trimmed but nobody dares to do so because people are afraid of making mistakes' (*Zhongguo qiyebao*, 3 September 1992).

The evolutionary course of enterprise reform since 1992 has effectively undermined the party's efforts to protect a party presence in state-owned enterprises. The party's consensus for the market terminated a long battle between central planners campaigning for Chen Yun's Soviet model 'with Chinese characteristics' and reformers who saw the market as the only way out for state-owned enterprises (You Ji, 1991). This has resulted in two new developments which have not only accorded more power to managers but also threatened the very existence of party cells in the majority of state firms. The first development involves transplanting 'a modern enterprise system' (*xiandai qiye jizhi*) into state-owned enterprises. Central to this reform, formally launched in 1995, is the so-called *zhuada fangxiao* strategy, or corporatisation of large enterprises and privatisation of small ones. The majority of large enterprises will be turned into shareholding companies where boards of directors dominate at the expense of party secretaries. For the small companies, when over 80 per cent of them are privatised, the party's role will diminish, with party control at the shopfloor level being removed from about 70 per cent of workers. This reform is discussed further in Chapter 8.

The second development involves the changing nature of the party's industrial cells. The prevalence of market profits has meant that state firms' interests do not necessarily coincide in all respects with those of the state. This causes divided loyalties among party industrial members, and sometimes they are forced to lean towards their employers. As new entities of interest party industrial members are forced to lean towards their employers. Gradually, the role of the party is being altered or politically neutralised. One party secretary I interviewed in Beijing in 1992 put forward an interesting notion: the emergence of a 'production and welfare party'. He explained that the function of party cells in his firm was mainly to assist in raising production and workers' income, which would be possible only through market success. What pushed party units in this direction was party members' own interest in the factory's market performance. To benefit from this marketisation process, party cells adopted new forms of leadership. Financially, they should dislodge themselves from the chain of party networks. It is impossible to tell from existing evidence whether this cadre's idea represents the will of the majority of his fellow comrades.[22] It is certainly against the views of the party's industrial lobby. However, he did point out a slow convergence of interests between party cadres and managers, motivating them to work together for common goals. In recent years the notion of a 'production party' has become more and more prevalent in the Chinese media. Political and ideological work is now centred on promoting sales, raising the quality of products, reducing costs, and accepting a level of competition among workers in regard to remuneration (*Gongren ribao*, 24 July 1996). It is safe to say that the CCP presence in state-owned enterprises is being transformed by the market, which is accelerating the depoliticisation of the *danwei* system.

To date, the presence of party networks still represents an obstacle to the transformation of state-owned enterprises into economic entities. The ongoing struggle between party cells and management indicates the tremendous task ahead for the reform of China's factory leadership structure. The party has engaged in much soul searching in the quest for a solution to the dilemma it faces: to grant more power to its branches may strengthen political control and thus temporarily deter social protest. However, granting such power also incurs the risk of accelerating internal decay, alienating the population and jeopardising economic growth, which could breed larger-scale social protest. Even though a 'production party' in state-owned enterprises sounds an expedient measure, there is no long-term solution whereby the party can break this self-defeating cycle.

THE 'TWO CENTRES' DISPUTE: A STUDY ON PARTY/ MANAGEMENT RELATIONS

Chinese state firms have been much depoliticised. Yet some new patterns of political strife have also developed. Here conflictual relationship between factory party secretaries and managers has been in the eye of the storm. This has been described as the 'two centres' dispute, and is affecting not only the reform of the leadership structure of state-owned enterprises but also the trend to dismantle party/state controls in China.

As illustrated earlier in the chapter, the rivalry between the two leading figures, the factory party secretary and manager, is not a new phenomenon. What is new is the very fact that management *can* contend with party cells and as an institutional force rather than in an individual capacity. This reveals a lot about the course of the post-Mao enterprise reform. The old conflict re-emerges against an altered background: economic development is emphasised as the saviour of Chinese socialism as opposed to the leftist agenda of politics in command. This has put party vested interests on the defensive. They are entrenched in the remaining institutional frameworks of control that the current top leadership wants to maintain in case of another event like Beijing Spring in 1989. So the root cause of the 'two centres' rivalry is the concern of the party as to whether it can continue its monopoly of power. The consequences bear witness to the structural barriers that limit China's enterprise reform. Probably, the boundary of functions between party cadres and managers will remain confused for some time to come.

The dispute over supervision

The chief mission of the party industrial cells is so-called supervision over management. However, the meaning of supervision is deliberately left unclear. According to the party's definition, 'supervision' means overseeing the process of major decision formulation (i.e. participating in policy making), implementation (hearing periodic reports from management) and subsequent assessment (to find out what has gone wrong and who is responsible, so as to take disciplinary measures) (CPS, 1991, pp. 98–101). Rifts likely to emerge in the process were well anticipated by the party centre. In creating this bipolar system, it stipulated that where any serious dispute occurred the party secretary and manager should report to the superior government and party bodies for arbitration.

This detailed supervision inevitably clashed with managers' authority in running their factories' everyday affairs. Yet by now managers have gradually built up their own networks of loyalists. This means that managers are in a position to resist party supervision. For instance, although party guidelines give scope to party input into the making of a strategic policy, there is no fine line as to what inputs should be solicited and how these should be taken into account by managers when major business decisions are being made. It is common for managers to press ahead with what they think is appropriate without giving much consideration to the opinions of their party comrades.[23] Even though party committee members are accorded a platform in decision making, very often their inputs carry less weight than those of managers who control the agenda.

In a report written by the POD of Weihai City, Shandong Province, the party's industrial interests expressed sincere concerns about the trend towards depoliticisation:

> In theory, the power of supervision is institutionally granted to party cells in factories. In reality, however, this authority cannot be exercised in many firms. There are several main difficulties. The first, the question of what form of supervision is positive and what is hypercritical, is not clear at all. In an atmosphere of diluting party leadership at the grassroots, a lot of party organisations have not dared to use their power. Second, some units do not know how to use party power. In supervision they raise opinions or suggestions. But without practical powers these have no binding force. All depends on whether managers are 'happy' to accept them. Third, the party system is supposed to supervise only major policies. However, there is no clear dividing line between major and minor. Moreover, it is unlikely that serious problems arise from major policies that implicate the party and state line. Minor issues nevertheless often cause major damage.
>
> (*Zhibu shenghuo* (Shandong), no. 9, 1989, pp. 29–30)

The structural hurdles to smooth party/management relations also stand in the obscured boundaries of the multiple functions of the *danwei* which impose many crossing points where the two systems may clash. For instance, the handling of remunerative and social welfare matters is within the realm of managers, though not regarded as part of production *per se*. However, given the explosive nature of these matters, they are always viewed as major issues that the party system has to supervise. Because actual authority over welfare gives substance to one's decision-making power, it becomes a major source of irritation and strife. This is especially true in the allocation of housing, owing to the big gap between supply and demand. In such areas both systems mobilise every resource available in order to reward their followers in the inner circles. Party secretaries see welfare as a major area for supervision while managers try to safeguard their administrative autonomy.[24] Party secretaries are inclined to get involved even in small matters. There is good reason for this. With the removal of the party command system, they have fewer opportunities to control workers directly and this has undoubtedly tarnished their image as key power brokers. Sometimes one's power depends upon people perceiving that one has power. For a party secretary to get into the disputes associated with the distribution of perquisites may remind workers that 'I still count'. One party secretary told me:

> When workers no longer come to us for arbitration of any disputes, we feel abandoned and redundant. Because of this transfer of the locus of power, not only workers but also we ourselves realise that the notion of party leadership is increasingly only rhetorical. We must fight back exactly because of this.[25]

So they do. They raise objections or alternatives to management whenever possible. It is often opposition for opposition's sake, which they believe is an effective way to make their presence felt. Gradually these voices of opposition become a stereotyped source of conflict between the two systems. Clearly the rivalry between party secretary and manager touches upon sensitive issues of clientelist networks revolving around the two power centres.[26]

The conflict over appointments

Another key area of conflict is personnel appointment. The Enterprise Law has vested this power in factory managers, yet in practice the rules of the game are more complicated. The party has its own regulations whereby managers should make appointments after consultation with party committees. Many party secretaries have regarded this consultation as equivalent to a power of veto. Others have used it as a delaying tactic to block management decisions. On the other side, most managers have envisioned this consultation process merely as a formality. So while strong managers get away with an arbitrary approach, consultation has often become a bargaining process in which both sides try to strengthen their own hands.[27]

The organisational procedures for an appointment are also confusing, adding fuel to the fire. Here again the Enterprise Law clashes with party regulations, which specify the steps of selection, investigation and dossier maintenance for party members holding middle-level or higher managerial positions. Only those managerial personnel who are not party members come under direct control of managers through a factory's personnel department. Since a large number of middle-level and higher-ranking managers are party members in large and medium-scale state-owned enterprises, the overlap in appointment procedures has given rise to constant conflicts. For instance, a firm manager who wants to select a deputy who happens to be a party member has to go to the factory's POD to check on the appointee's dossier, and needs to report the planned promotion to his bureaucratic superior through the POD, which must asks its superior POD whether the selection is in accordance with its cadre promotion quota. It is the factory's POD which is first notified. It is the cadre in this department who first notifies the candidate. After the factory manager finally announces the appointment, the POD, together with the party's discipline agency, will continue to assess the performance of the appointee. In this whole process the factory manager willy-nilly constantly has to deal with the party secretary. The secretary can delay the submission and can also influence his superior by presenting alternative opinions. Under the party regulation that the factory party committee should discuss such appointments, he may also block the motion through members' votes. Although it is a bit easier to appoint a workshop manager, the POD's evaluation and the party committee's discussion cannot be curtailed, thus complicating the appointment process. Because of these rigid party controls many managers have tried hard to circumvent the procedures, particularly as appointments at workshop level do not require detailed reports to government superiors.[28]

Behind this struggle over appointments is the attempt of both power centres to maintain and enhance their clientelist networks. In China's state-owned enterprises the title of manager or party secretary does not deliver authority automatically, and so titulars have sought to rely on the support of their own cliques. When Deng and Zhao Ziyang called for the dilution (*danhua*) of the industrial party leadership, party cadres were under increased pressure, and they rallied behind their secretaries for self-protection. To have orders implemented, managers sought to appoint their supporting staff along the lines of personal preference. Under these circumstances, the 'two centres' conflict reflects the concern of many party cadres over their political careers and, among managerial staff, chances for further promotions.

Some empirical findings

When I visited state-owned enterprises in 1991/2 and 1994/5, I found the relationship between managers and party secretaries varied markedly from one factory to another. Basically, their relations seem to divide into four types. The first was what workers call the 'chummy brothers' type (*geliahao*). Close personal ties have traditionally existed between party secretaries and managers and this has provided room for continued effective cooperation and mutual support in plants. When disagreements arise, they are able to sit down and talk them over. Generally speaking, such friendship guarantees a workable division of labour between them. That is, managers actively counsel party secretaries before making any major decisions and the latter help to clear the way for implementation. The key to such a smooth relationship is personal rather than institutional. The following case describes how a good party secretary/manager relationship works.

At Beijing Wool Textile Plant, Party Secretary Zhang Yuhe and manager Zhou Wenkai were personal friends, able to tackle together difficult issues in both management and party work. For instance, in the early 1990s the problem of a labour shortage on the production lines became so acute that the fulfilment of production plans was threatened. The basic reason for this was that, while work was much harder on the first lines, workers were paid at a lower rate than the supply and management staff. The secretary and manager decided that the only way to solve the problem was to raise the wages of the line workers. When the decision was announced, the supply and management staff became agitated. With the manager busy with other management affairs, Secretary Zhang ventured to take charge of the controversy, which would otherwise fall to the responsibility of the manager. In a short period of time he convened more than a dozen meetings of party members and all staff in the supply and management sections. By combining party discipline and personal appeals first to activists and then through them to all staff, resistance was finally overcome and the new wage package was implemented. As a result the line workers increased production.

Manager Zhou, for his part, gave the green light to conducting party activities during working hours. He also tried to raise the pay scales of party and political cadres, which were generally a bit lower than for management staff. Channels for discussing production matters were extended to party committee members, in order to enlist party organisational support for management plans. All this was conducive to the harmony of the two systems, and in fact benefited them both. The party branch was promoted as a model in Beijing's textile industry, because it 'cultivated' enough party activities to meet the criteria for party cadres' promotion. For the manager, good relations with party personnel helped the smooth running of production, which also served to show how capable he was in the eyes of both superiors and workers.[29]

The second type of manager/party branch relationship involves one power centre dominating the other. The major feature of this type is the overriding ability of one figure, be it the manager or the party secretary, to control the agenda of both centres. The varied strength of their clientelist networks can impose an asymmetry of power in the conflict. Traditionally managers were groomed by party secretaries and subject to their control. Since the end of the party command system, and as many senior secretaries were retired, the balance of power has tilted towards managers. Yet the transition is far from complete, and many party secretaries can still wield considerable power over managers.

A typical example of this type is the Capital Iron and Steel Corporation of Beijing. Officially the corporation is one of a small number of factories still practising the director responsibility system under the leadership of the party committee. However, overall power is concentrated in the hands of general manager Zhou Guanwu.[30] The party secretary acts only as his assistant in charge of the party system within the corporation. But Zhou rose to the status of indisputable authority through the party ladder. He preferred to keep the party command system largely intact because he, as a long-standing party leader, recognised that the party's organisational network could be an effective managing mechanism, provided that he could control it firmly. Yet there is a qualitative difference between the current party command system and the situation that existed before reform. Above the party committee there now sits another powerful committee, the corporation managing committee, something similar to a board of directors. All important issues are discussed first in this committee, with Zhou as chair. Although the party secretary sits on the committee, all he can do, essentially, is vote for whatever has been decided by Zhou, and then transmit his decision to the vast party machine. The party system is completely dominated by a manager and services his needs.[31]

A third type of party/management relationship is said to prevail in the majority of state-owned enterprises. This relationship can be described as evasive, which means that the two centres usually avoid direct confrontation. Normally they deliberately leave some vacuum of responsibility between them. However, this does not mean that there is no rivalry but that the conflict is disguised by a number of personal taboos rather than restricted by any clearly defined institutionalisation of power. This evasion *per se* contains the seeds of confrontation. According to Chinese sources, this evasive type is not regarded as preferable to confrontation, as the vacuum between the two centres often prevents timely management decisions. The level of motivation and discipline among workers tends to be low in these factories, owing to the fact that nobody from the two centres is able to manage firmly and effectively.

The fourth type of relationship is confrontational: whatever one centre decides, the other tries to obstruct. This type exists in factories where the two power centres possess fairly even networks of followers. In this kind of relationship, party heads argue that party cells must still take the 'kernel role' in leadership, in line with party tradition, and on the basis of this premise they interfere in management affairs whenever they see fit. Managers, on the other hand, affirm that they can act in accordance with the Enterprise Law, which gives them all the legal authority they need to run the firm. The following is a good example of how the two systems develop a confrontational relationship.

T Factory is a large factory in Shanghai's mechanical industry. When the new party and management heads were appointed in 1986, the two systems were able to work together smoothly and each system operated with help from the other. The party secretary and manager exchanged home visits on a regular basis. But the relationship soon soured and this eventually ruined both systems' authority as well as the factory's production.

Party Secretary Lu Ming, aged 57, was a cadre of the old generation (he joined the party in 1949 and rose as a generalist). In 1964 he was transferred to the Shanghai factory to take the post of deputy factory manager and then became manager in 1976. He became party secretary ten years later as a step towards retirement. On the other hand, manager Xu Li, a university graduate and a party member, was 45 years old. His career started in the factory's technical department. He was first promoted to be the factory's deputy manager in the late 1970s and became manager in 1986, both times at the recommendation of Lu. Because of this *guanxi*, connection, at the time of their appointments everybody, including the factory's party and state superiors, expected that each would support the other.

Towards the end of 1986 bonuses were increased in the entire state sector. Manager Xu proposed to Secretary Lu to follow suit so as to alleviate pressure from the workers. Lu opposed the suggestion. But Xu insisted that without the increase production would suffer, as workers would become dissatisfied. He took the decision alone and the workers' bonuses were increased. Soon word spread that the new manager was more capable and better at winning workers' loyalty. Upon hearing this Lu was annoyed. A few weeks later the factory received a big order from a foreign trader. Xu announced to the workers that if the order could be completed on time, all workers and staff could have a ten-day holiday. When the order was delivered, Xu made good his word. Yet Xu did not notify the party committee, which scheduled a training programme at the time of the holiday for all party members. When party members failed to show up, Lu criticised Xu as being solely production-minded, with no care for party building.

The tension between the two went from bad to worse in July 1987 following Xu's personnel decisions for the posts of chief engineer and chief accountant. The first appointee was 58-year-old Li Guang, an expert engineer but generally regarded as arrogant. The second was Xiao Jun, a *zhiqing* (educated youth sent to the countryside during the Cultural Revolution), who had entered the factory to replace his mother under the state's retirement substitution (*dingti*) policy. Mr Xiao was thought very clever, with a businessman's mind, but not regarded as steady since he showed a cynical attitude to what he regarded as dogmatic regulations. Lu still opposed the appointments, telling Xu that Li was near retirement and did not have a good 'mass base', and that Xiao was not reliable and did not have a college degree. He suggested the POD review the appointments. Xu, however, insisted on upholding them and issued their contracts himself.

Lu was very angry and convened the party committee the following day. He criticised Xu for using his power arbitrarily and violating the party's organisational principles. Xu argued that what he had done was within his authority as prescribed by the government. He stated that neither Li nor Xiao was a party member, so there was no need for an evaluation by the POD. Since non-party members should be assessed by the factory's PD and the PD was answerable to him himself, he had not done anything outside party regulations. In addition he held that appointments should be based on ability, not on age or paper qualifications. The party committee meeting broke up inconclusively.

From then on their policy disputes became personal. Even the most routine decisions by one side would be interpreted as an insult to the other. Neither management nor party work could go on normally. Towards the end of 1988 Xu suffered a heart attack, supposedly the result of these long personal battles. He anticipated that he would not be able to resume his duties for some time to come, so he convened a meeting of the management system and announced that his work would be entrusted to deputy manager Li. But the next day Party Secretary Lu called a party meeting in Xu's absences, and accused him of abuses of power. Under this pressure, deputy manager Li felt too scared to take over the manager's responsibility, and the factory became leaderless.[32]

During my two field trips to China in 1991 and 1992, the worst example of a struggle for power involved a manager who stripped a party secretary of his cadre status and sent him to work in a workshop under a government regulation providing that managers were responsible for issuing work contracts to *all* staff in a factory. In retaliation, the party secretary suspended the manager's party membership, accusing him of not attending enough party meetings.

How deep does this 'two centres' conflict run in China's state-owned enterprises? The problem must be serious since everywhere I travelled in China, I heard stories of power struggles between the two centres. According to a survey conducted by the State Council in 1987 in more than 1,000 factories in eighteen large cities, one-third were troubled by one kind of contentious relationship or another, including about 10 per cent of the confrontational type and 30 per cent of what I call the evasive type. About 40 per cent ran fairly smoothly, among which the 'chummy brothers' type accounted for 13 per cent (*Liaowang*, no. 48, 1987, p. 19). Surveys by local governments showed a far less promising picture. For instance, among state-owned enterprises in Liaoning Province, easy relations between the two centres prevailed in only 25 per cent of the factories surveyed (*Zhongguo qiye bao*, 15 June 1992), while in Taian city in Shandong Province, among 649 state-owned enterprises, 40 per cent were quite contentious (*Zhibu shenhuo* (Shandong), no. 12, 1991, p. 12). Although China's industrial authorities have tried many methods to get the two centres to cooperate over the past few years, progress is not apparent.[33]

In short, structurally, the coexistence of the two power centres provides a focus for rivalry. Personal conflicts are only a secondary contributing factor, though the type of relationship in any given factory is largely determined by its leaders' personal dimensions. This reveals the dynamic nature of the 'two centres' dispute. This is to say that while the 'two centres' dispute is a permanent feature of factory politics (unless one of the centres is deprived of a leadership function), individual firms move from one type to another at different stages. The trend so far points to management gradually gaining the upper hand.

4 The party's organisational reform

As mentioned in Chapter 1, one of the reasons for a work unit to be turned into a *danwei* is that it contains a party/state cadre system. Prior to the reforms the concept of 'cadre' embraced a wide range of meanings and personnel. By the broadest definition anybody except a farmer and blue-collar worker could be bracketed as one, even a nurse or a monk, since he/she worked for the state, received a salary catalogued as that of state cadre and had a place in the official ranking system.[1] When applied to questions of leadership and authority, the concept of cadre serves as a reference to those who ran party and state offices. Although this significantly narrowed the definition of cadre, it still covered a large number of people. With work units *danweiised*, a factory manager or a school director became a state representative and thus automatically became a cadre of the party/state (Hong Yung Lee, 1991, p. 352).

As a result, the political stance of cadres was regarded as crucial to the stability of the ruling party. The CCP therefore demanded that all cadres be answerable to the party and appointed through party or party-controlled channels. This meant that most 'white-collar workers' acquired a dual status: as professionals, they performed their occupational duties; as state cadres, they had to fulfil the political requirements of the party/ state. And in China's stratified society, they had an obligation to lead *laobaixing*, or commoners, according to their second status. The vastness of this cadre system consequently blurred the boundary between the state and society. For instance, a schoolteacher should also act as a state cadre and see to the interests of the regime by indoctrinating his/her students. Never before in Chinese history had ordinary people had to deal with state officials on such an everyday basis.

DISMANTLING THE INDUSTRIAL *NOMENKLATURA* SYSTEM

Cadres in state-owned enterprises are normally called *qiye ganbu*, enterprise cadres. Generally speaking, the industrial cadre system comprises two major components: political cadres (*zhenggong ganbu*) and managerial cadres (*guanli ganbu*). Each can further be categorised into subgroups. Under the category of political cadres, there are full-time party cadres operating the party hierarchy. Then there are cadres of political work, with or without party membership, who run a factory's political and security departments, propaganda office or militia corps. Cadres from the mass organisations, e.g. the Youth League and trade unions, are also treated as political cadres assuming 'transmission belt' functions. Managerial cadres include administrative personnel running everyday production and technical staff assisting management on technical matters.

This whole cadre system constitutes an integral part of the party's *nomenklatura* structure imported from the USSR. It operates under the close supervision of the industrial departments of the party's local committees, which not only monitor the organisational affairs of party cells but formulate major industrial policies for the locality. Within each enterprise, there is a mini *nomenklatura* system in which most party and political cadres are managed by the POD. All cadres in the management system at the rank of workshop or above are also incorporated in the list of *nomenklatura*. Managerial cadres not directly controlled by this *nomenklatura* system are run by the factory's PD, whose members are normally party members selected by the POD (Yu Zhenbo, 1987, p. 304). Cadres' rewards, promotions, dossier maintenance and transfers are determined by the POD and PD, which direct their career destiny.

In the Mao era all cadres had to carry out political duties and assist with ideological indoctrination. So the first feature of the industrial cadre system prior to the reform was the politicisation of management staff at all levels of state firms. This was realised by: (1) the submission of management cadres to the command of political cadres through a set of institutionalised controls; and (2) deliberate confusion of the division of labour between political and management affairs. For instance, a workshop manager had to assist the workshop party secretary's efforts in political education. When the party secretary was absent, the manager, normally party vice-secretary, was required to carry on these political tasks. Managers in China thus differed from those in non-communist societies, as they not only managed production but were also required to police people's daily pursuits.

In the appointment process, it was common practice for leading party figures one level up to 'discover' candidates for promotion. Although formal procedures were through the appropriate party organs, nomination by immediate superiors carried the heaviest weight. Organisationally, the promotees had to be answerable to the committees that made the appointment decisions, but personally they owed a tremendous debt to those who advanced them. As a result, a network of personal followings was woven at every level, and each level was vertically woven to the one above or below it, thus forging an invisible, top-down transmission belt of power. These patron–client linkages, arising from the personalised appointment process, served as informal chains reinforcing the party/

state's formal hierarchical structure. So the second feature of the cadre system was the *guanxi* relationship inherent in the appointment procedures. These procedures were characteristic of 'black-box' operations and closed factory party leadership. Deeply rooted nepotism, favouritism and factionalised power cliques reflected the 'clientelist rules' in Chinese firms (Burns, 1988, p. xxxii).

Such clientelist networks centred on party leaders were perpetuated by their tenure of office, which was the third feature of the cadre system. Sitting on an 'iron chair' (holding a permanent leadership position), party cadres and management cadres as well as technical cadres needed to worry not so much about the factory's production record under their leadership as about political rectitude, the primary reason for removal from office. So a correct party factional line and adherence to current interpretation of the party's ideology had always been their criterion for judgements and conduct.

This permanent cadre stratum, distinguished by special status and wage ranks, laid the basis for a class-like division between the 'intellectual' and 'manual' labourers. In the eyes of workers, the cadre system provided the upward ladder for opportunists who sought cadres' political and welfare perks. This stratification soured relations between the party and workers. The overt submission of workers to cadres had caused tensions between the two, as had been vividly exposed by the violent struggle against cadres during the Cultural Revolution (Chan, 1992, p. 68). By the time Deng launched the post-Mao reforms in 1978, the tension had again mounted to the point where large-scale eruption looked possible.

Hence, the reform of the industrial cadre system since 1978 has been an important part of an overall reform of the political system, the object being to rectify the three key features mentioned above. The guiding principle for reform is summarised by a ranking official from the COD as follows:

> The requirements for industrial cadres should be different from those for government cadres. So it is necessary to separate the management of factory personnel from the integrated post-and-ranking system now in use for all state cadres. The new system should be based on their specialized duties and carry rewards and benefits accordingly. The leading personnel should be appointed through open tendering. And an individual can choose to take the post or quit by his choice.
>
> (Liu Kegu, 1988, p. 337)

The reform of the enterprise cadre system has basically proceeded along this line since the 1980s, although the mission is far from being accomplished. First, the reform emphasises the different natures of a firm and of a state agency, and thus differentiates between the management of cadres in these two systems. This has brought about a new delineation of categories of cadres, which has had the effect of reversing the

politicisation of the industrial cadre system. Second, the reform introduced a contract and fixed-term system for an increasingly large
proportion of managers (cadres). This is intended to address the two
major problems: tenured positions (iron chairs) and closed appointment
processes. One important effect of this is that the sense of permanent
division between staff and workers has begun to fade. Third, although
patron–client ties still remain strong, they are much less centred on
political loyalty and ideological correctness. New factors such as profits
and performance have exerted growing influence on the leader–follower
relationship.

The new classification of factory cadres

The new delineation of cadre categories went hand in hand with the
progress of the director responsibility system, which allowed the formation of a fairly independent management team. A new formula, *guanshi
yu guanren tongyi*, or 'unifying management of production and management of personnel', provided the starting point for the reform (Wang
Jianxin, 1986, p. 47). This was in contrast with past practice whereby
managers managed production but the party managed managers. With
the new division of labour in personnel management between the party
and management, an explicit reclassification of cadres along functional
lines became the central theme guiding the reform of the industrial cadre
system.

   This process of regrouping began in the mid-1980s, with party/political
cadres, managerial staff and technical professionals each divorcing from
the hitherto 'one big cadre family'. Two separate sub-systems were established in terms of personnel management. Party cadres were still run by
the POD, mainly through an appointment system not too different from
in the pre-reform days. As far as political cadres were concerned, the
POD only appointed the upper echelon through the *nomenklatura* system
– normally the heads of the factory's mass organisations and militia. The
remainder were transferred to the PD under the management system. On
the other hand, with the shrinking of the party *nomenklatura*, the PD has
greatly widened its scope of control. Originally the department only
controlled the personnel affairs of ordinary workers and junior cadres
without party tickets. Now this function has been transferred to a separate
body in the management system: the Labour Affairs Department. The
PD concentrates on running management and technical staff at or above
the workshop levels up to deputy factory managers, and it is directly
responsible to the factory manager.[2]

   In addition to this structural change in the *nomenklatura*, there has
been a further reclassification of management cadres and technical cadres.
This is a far-reaching change, as among 32 million state cadres, 23 million
are technical personnel (*Guangmin ribao*, 5 July 1995). First, the manage-

ment of technical cadres has become separated from that of state cadres.[3] They are treated more as professionals, as they are delinked from the current official ranks of seventeen grades (formerly twenty-three grades). For instance, a chief engineer of a factory at the county government level may be entitled to material perks similar to those of a deputy manager of the same factory who, as a state cadre, receives a state-owned house and the use of company cars, which also are available to a deputy county director. But he would not have many of the political privileges enjoyed by state cadres of that level, such as access to classified reports and state and party documents.[4] Compared to pre-reforms days, cadres' political attitudes are no longer an issue of concern. A notable exclusion in the 'Document of the Central Leadership Group of Professional Posts' is the required commitment to the party and official ideology that every *state* cadre must profess (Zhao Qizheng, 1986, pp. 23–8). The management of these technical staff largely proceeds from their professional titles and the technical wage/rank system. That is, a factory works out a list of the technical staff of different ranks it needs. Then the factory manager hires them on a contract basis. The effect of this reform has been to depoliticise a large contingent of cadres (*China Daily*, 18 June 1992).

The reform of personnel management as regards managerial cadres has been less dramatic in political terms. One difficult question remains unresolved, namely: whose interests should a manager represent, the state's or the workers' in his factory? A manager in a state firm has long been seen as a state representative and therefore a state cadre answerable to the state agency that has appointed him. With mounting internal pressure from workers and staff for more income, managers have been forced to place the factory's interests before those of the state. In 1985 the State Economic Commission surveyed several dozen factory managers on the question of whose interests they believed they represented, the state's or their factories'. Only 10 per cent of them claimed they represented the state's, while 20 per cent said both, and 70 per cent held that they worked for the good of their factory. The answer was a shock to some Chinese leaders. Deng Liqun criticised this as a serious situation where 'the buttocks commanded the heads'. These managers were asked to think whether they were good party members (Guojia jingwei, 1985, p. 28). This new thinking on the part of the majority of managers was indicative of the emerging independent interests of the industrial community in the wake of the market reform. More importantly, it reflected the breaking away of these managers from the mentality that their lot was organically tied to that of the state.

The separation of the managerial salary system from the general wage system of state cadres has helped to foster this new perspective. After the 1985 enterprise wage reform, a manager's wage was determined by the post he occupied in the factory. His former administrative rank in the state's twenty-three-grade cadre payroll system served only as a point of reference. Wages are set rather by individual factories, subject to their profitability, than by the official rank of the factories (Xu Songtao *et al.*, 1988, pp. 104–40). The previous equation of state manager and state cadre started to alter, as a manager's new source of income gradually diminished the sense of belonging to the state, even though he still carries the dual status of being both a state manager and a state cadre in the eyes of the state.[5] In fact the delinking process has benefited factory managers in terms of material gains. For instance, according to a survey of fourteen capital cities conducted by the Ministry of Personnel, in 1994 managers at the bureau level were 300 *yuan* better off per month than government officials at the same level. Other things being equal (official ranking, education, length of service and professional title), industrial managers at senior, middle and lower levels received earnings 21 per cent, 15 per cent and 12 per cent higher than state cadres respectively (*Guangming ribao*, 24 November 1995).

The second precipitating factor is the ongoing reform to decouple a factory's official rank from the state ranking system and to remove the post of factory from the state's *nomenklatura* altogether.[6] Liaoning Province, an experimental area, announced in 1993 that from 1994 all its industrial cadres would be removed from the provincial *nomenklatura* system and, as a result, would automatically lose their status as state cadres. This will affect as many as 656,500 enterprise cadres (*Jingji ribao*, 21 November 1993). Similar moves have been registered in Shanghai where the term 'state cadre' was replaced by 'enterprise cadre' (*Wenzhaibao*, 11 April 1996). One of the key features of the *nomenklatura*, as earlier noted, is that factory managers and government officials are listed under the same cadre-rank system and enjoy similar official status and special privileges. When the new reform does away with a firm's government rank, its ranking as a large, medium or small firm will be assessed in commercial terms, often by its market profits and amount of tax remittance. With this change, a manager will no longer possess a position paralleling a party/state cadre rank, thus losing much of the official capacity of state cadre.[7]

The object of abolishing the factory cadre system is the creation of a new contingent of entrepreneurs in state-owned enterprises. In the words of former Minister Yuan Baohua, this is 'a process of professionalising managerial personnel'. Addressing managers' short-term behaviour stemming from the contract system, he proposed to Li Peng that managers should be regarded as professionals rather than cadres. Li responded by instructing the then Personnel Minister that the category of managerial cadres should be separated from that of party and government cadres (*Zhongguo qiyebao*, 22 June 1992; *Jingji ribao*, 4 August 1995). These rules, as explained by the First Deputy Premier Zhu Rongji, are about selecting firm managers through market competitions (*Jingji ribao*, 26 April 1995). The selection process is an open bidding system that constitutes a fundamental challenge to the 'party running cadres' principle. In a national survey of 9,000 large and medium-sized enterprises in 1995, 42 per cent of respondents supported abolition of the current administrative appointment system and bureaucratic rankings in their factories; 50 per cent of them would not mind losing administrative status; only 8 per cent still saw the value of holding a government rank.[8]

Making state managers professional entrepreneurs will further depoliticise state-owned enterprises, for entrepreneurs pay only lip-service to political missions imposed on by the *danwei* system. Unlike a political cadre who, as an executive of the party/state, is a generalist who has to perform multiple functions and sees successful factory management as a stepping-stone to higher bureaucratic positions, an entrepreneur perceives management of a firm as a profession, a lifetime career. Currently, managers still assume some state cadre's political duties because their firms still retain some elements of a politicised *danwei*. Responding to the party/state's conflicting signals thus confuses a manager's main task and makes it difficult for him to place the firm's interest first. In a half-reformed economic system, many managers still entertain the perception that as long as they make their bureaucratic boss happy, their chances of promotion are guaranteed, regardless of whether their firm is making a profit or a loss. This phenomenon is now seen as a major cause of poor management and a major reason why some state-owned enterprises make a loss. Indeed, in 81 per cent of cases loss making was blamed on poor management, as compared to 10 per cent on policy discrimination (the state's controlling their pricing), and 9 per cent on macro-economic fluctuation (*Guangmin ribao*, 27 April 1995). However, a striking feature of well-managed firms is that managers perform party/state political roles only perfunctorily; regarding themselves as professional managers, they identify their future career with the advancement of their firms. In other words, their outlook is politically neutral. The number of such entrepreneurs is rising with the the deepening of marketisation. When responding to a 1995 State Council survey of 2,674 large and medium-sized state firms, 80 per cent of managers believed that it was very necessary to professionalise managerial personnel, a rise of 20 per cent on a similar survey conducted in the previous year. This change of mentality is significant in that about 80 per cent of managers in large state firms are still appointed by the state (*Guangmin ribao*, 23 April 1996).

The contract cadre system

The contract cadre reform has had a great impact on the cadre system since it was formally implemented in 1984 (*Zhongguo qiye bao*, 2 April 1992). One goal of this reform was to open up the *nomenklatura* system. It was envisaged that state-owned enterprises should have their own channels of recruitment for new staff without reference to the state and existing cadres would have the right to leave their jobs (Pu Guangzhong, 1986, p. 139). According to former Personnel Minister Zhao Dongwan, the contract cadre system would pave the way for people without a cadre rank to compete for positions previously allocated in the *nomenklatura* system and to remain non-cadre after getting the job. This in itself amounts to reducing cadres' influence on China's state/society relations in general and on state-owned enterprises in particular. It also poses a challenge to the practice whereby the state imposed upon state firms cadres whom they did not need or want. For the first time firms have the autonomy to hire their own 'cadres' (Zhao Dongwan, 1991, p. 30).

It should be pointed out that the contract cadre system Minister Zhao talked about is only one of the systems in operation. There is a larger contingent of cadres who were appointed before the introduction of the contract system. By the end of 1990 about 2.1 million contracted cadres had joined the industrial cadre payroll. However, this number was only one-third of the total.[9] This is another 'one factory, two systems' phenomenon paralleling the coexistence of permanent workers and contract workers. By the middle of 1996 the number of contract workers had reached 95 million, or 88 per cent of the entire workforce in the state sector (Howard, 1991, pp. 93–114; *China Business Times*, 9 July 1996).

The reason for introducing this 'one factory, two cadre' system is complicated. According to researchers in the Personnel Ministry:

> The state's control over the industrial cadre quota had been traditionally tougher than that for government agencies. For a long time the practice of 'using workers as cadres without giving them cadre status' (*yigong daigan*) was an expedient measure to make up the shortage. But this was terminated in 1983. At the same time marketisation of factory operations further highlighted the need for a new brand of managers. So the demand for more capable managers became more pressing. Now, we have the conflict between the Enterprise Law which grants firms autonomy to recruit managers and the control of the state over the cadre quotas. The easiest way to get around this is to hire non-cadre-status cadres.
>
> (Wen Wen, 1990, p. 6)

The shortage of capable managers has become increasingly acute in recent years. According to a survey by the Personnel Ministry of seventeen state firms in Zhuzhou City, Hunan Province, there were 6,869 cadre (meaning managerial staff) posts available but only 5,184 cadres currently on the rolls. So these factories hired 1,685 contract cadres, making up 25 per cent of the total. And among the 5,184 'full cadres', there were many who did not meet the requirements of the new situation (Wen Wen, 1990, p. 6). While these unqualified cadres could not be asked to resign immediately, the guideline of reform was that the 'iron chairs' should eventually be smashed and all factory cadre posts should be filled by contract managers, a project similar to the gradual phasing out of permanent workers.

Since early 1992, the drive to abolish the cadre system has gathered momentum thanks to the party's new consensus on the market. By the end of the year state-owned enterprises in Tianjing had put half their state cadres on contract (*Guangming ribao*, 15 September 1992). Shanghai announced that it would remove all its industrial cadres from the state cadre system, abolish those ranks linked to state administration and erase the difference in official status between enterprise staff and workers (*Jingji ribao*, 28 February 1993). So the battle over hiring new contract cadres and putting the permanent cadres on contract has now been joined. Some of the reform methods that are being tried are state prescribed, others have been designated as 'local policy' (*tu zhengce*) by individual factories (*Jingji tizhi gaige yanjiu*, no. 4, 1992, p. 23).

The most thorough method is to implement the all-staff-and-worker contract system. Under this reform all cadres are supposed to lose their state cadre status automatically. Anyone who obtains a management post through competition becomes enterprise management staff. They are still called cadres, albeit enterprise cadres, the kind of title the Japanese also use in their companies. They are required to sign a contract with the factory manager, usually for three years. During this period they are regarded as management staff but when it expires they again have to compete for the post. If they fail they have to go back to the assembly lines (United Survey Team, 1992, p. 33). A second method is to assign a specific number of management posts to contract staff, posts which were previously held by permanent cadres, and whose numbers will rise incrementally. In this way contracted positions will move from the periphery to the core of factory management. In the end all the positions will become contract based. In the transition there should not be permanent cadres appointed by state-owned enterprises or allocated by the state. The third method is still more gradual. State-owned enterprises will contract out any position that has become vacant. The new manager taking it will have a fixed term during which he is under constant evaluation. Failure to meet the prescribed requirements means that the contract can be terminated at any time during this period.[10]

The biggest barrier to the universalisation of the contract cadre system has been resistance from cadres currently on the permanent state payroll who had observed the outcome of the labour contract system in the 1980s. Generally factory management has adopted a soft approach towards these inadequate state cadres, in a formula described as 'feeding them but giving them no work in management'. For instance, there were 428 managerial posts with 385 state cadres on the payroll at the Zhuzhou Iron and Steel Plant. Of the 385 cadres, sixty were thought incompetent. In addition to forty-three contract cadres filling the shortfall between 428 and 385, sixty more contract cadres were hired to replace the poorly regarded state cadres. However, the sixty state cadres were still employed. Some were sent to work in workshops, although they did not do any real work. Others simply fell into the 'floating population' in the factory. But this was believed to be a worthwhile price to pay for the maintenance of 'stability and unity' (Wen Wen, 1990, pp. 6–8).

Another development central to the contract cadre reform has been the creation of an evaluation system to assess the contract staff from firm managers downward. The system comprises leadership and worker assessment, examinations and open tender. It varies as applied to the different levels of staff. Generally, leadership assessment is applied principally to top management posts. It includes both an outside evaluation by a factory's bureaucratic superior, usually with responsibility for appointing top factory managers, and an internal evaluation by top managers for the selection of middle-level staff. Worker assessment is usually channelled through the Workers Congress, which solicits workers' views on given candidates. Examinations are held more often when appointments to the technically related posts are being made. The key contents of the assessment have been de-ideologised, with managerial knowledge and experience becoming the principal criteria. Career security begins to be tied less to loyalty to the CCP and more to the fulfilment of contract terms centred on profits.

The ways in which industrial managerial staff currently enter contracts contrast with the party's previous appointment mechanisms. While the latter represented a strictly top-down process channelled through party forums, the contract system is conducted through multiple selection channels, including tendering, competitive running for office, workers' elections, self-marketing and direct administrative appointments. This has oriented personnel management towards an open and semi-open style of operation. With the burgeoning practice of advertising vacant positions across a sector and regionwide, job transfers at management level have become widespread. Moreover, because the terms of office of contract managers are linked to the profitability of the factory or workshop and apply to their own income as well as that of workers, there are now both incentives and disciplinary pressures on managers to deliver. Therefore, an increasing number of managers have been demoted owing to their poor record in running production and sales. For instance, by the end of 1990, some 7,100 state cadres had lost their 'iron chairs' in Shandong Province (*Guangming ribao*, 17 July 1992). At the enterprise level, among 190 state cadres in the Beijing Piano Factory, twenty-two have been stripped of their cadre posts, including three factory-level managers and seventeen middle-level managers (Xiao Wei, 1992, p. 6). In 1994 one firm manager confirmed to me with some bitterness that he had to go back to the assembly lines after he failed to fulfil the profit quota. Although it is difficult to determine how deeply this reform has already cut into the industrial cadre system, its development has marked the beginning of the end of the system of *nomenklatura* in the state sector.

At the risk of simplification, it may be said that four types of contract-based appointment have been commonly practised. The first is through a process of recommendation by individual workers and election by the Workers Congress. As stated earlier, managerial posts in small firms and low-level managers in large state-owned enterprises are often contracted by this process. The rationale is that first-line posts require strong organisational ability, familiarity with basic machine operations and good *guanxi* with co-workers in order to implement management policies. Because the bulk of contract cadres are at a low rank, they constitute a near-majority of managerial staff in the new system. In the seventeen factories in Zhuzhou City, for instance, contract cadres in this lower group made up 45 per cent of all contracts (Wen Wen, 1990, pp. 6–7). According to Huang Qingyi, director of the Organisation Department of Henan Party Committee, in 1995 485 small state firms elected their managers, a fairly large proportion of the state-owned enterprises in the province (*Gongren ribao*, 25 June 1996). In terms of selection, it is usual for multiple candidates to be put forward for positions of section and work-shop leaders. After due consultation, including taking suggestions from party cells, a ballot is taken and those who win most votes are appointed by the factory's manager.[11]

The second method is the direct appointment system, largely applied to top and middle levels of managers. Often managers at the factory level are appointed for a fixed term by the industrial bureaux, usually in competition with other candidates. The appointment is linked with a contract production and profit responsibility system that the bureaux enter into with the factories concerned. These managers further appoint their deputies. The terms are specified at the very beginning: the appointees will not have an 'iron chair' and their cadre status will last only as long as the contract stays valid (COD and the Personnel Ministry, 1991, p. 2). At lower levels, the shop directors appoint their section chiefs. All the appointees are personally responsible to those who appoint them.

The third method is to appoint managers through an open bidding system at the levels of both factory and workshop. About 40 per cent of state firms practise this reform in one way or another and it is recommended as the basic form of recruitment for professionalised managers in the future (Tang Daiwang *et al.*, 1990, p. 324). Bidding is mainly conducted through two channels: from within a factory and from outside through advertisement. The former is used mostly by large and medium-scale enterprises believed to possess enough competent managerial staff. For small firms, the external system of tendering is often adopted. The procedures for both are similar, usually consisting of seven steps: (1) advertising positions with descriptions of duties; (2) soliciting submissions with detailed plans of management; (3) shortlisting candidates with inputs from the three systems (the party, management and unions) within the firm and from bureaucratic superiors; (4) open debates among contestants; (5) workers' evaluation, vote or administrative decision; (6) the signing of the contract; and (7) the process of notarising the contract by a legal body. The main goals are to open up the competition to as many contestants as possible and to introduce mass assessments, thus enhancing the authority of the successful candidates to run factories.[12]

The fourth method is based on written and practical examinations, including tests for technical and managerial skills. The appointees in this category are normally technical staff. They have to go through a process of application, examination, assessment and entry into contracts. This reform is aimed at raising the competence of managerial and technical personnel.

However, it is too early to assume that the state will relinquish control over this large contingent of contract managers. The COD and Personnel Ministry clearly stipulated that contract cadres in state-owned enterprises must be incorporated into the management of cadres by state. According to the Provisional Regulation of Contract Cadres in State Firms, every contract manager must fill in a contract evaluation form which has to be approved by the factory's administrative superior (COD and the Personnel Ministry, 1991, p. 3). One copy of the form should be kept in the personnel department of the local government. Political requirements should also be listed in contracts both for former state cadres entering into a new contract and for newly promoted managers. Moreover, party committees should discuss the appointment of contract managers at certain levels. The regulation also makes it difficult for contract cadres to seek transfers by unilaterally terminating their contracts. It demands that contract managers in key areas of responsibility and major technical personnel seek approval from their *danwei* before their contracts can be revoked. By this means it is hoped to retain badly needed professionals who would be the most likely to leave. Stipulations for contract managers include a senior high school certificate, a minimum of three years' service and six months' probation.[13]

On the other hand, it is clear that state control over contract managers is much weaker than over state cadres. The question also remains of how enforceable these regulations can be. First, as the bilateral relationship is more contractually centred on economic indicators, the political requirements mentioned earlier (p. 65) become largely rhetorical. In terms of production a manager's business autonomy increases with the shrinking of state plans. So his problem with the dual status *vis-à-vis* a state cadre is greatly eased. Representing the state is no longer an important issue in his mind. Furthermore, the changed mechanisms of appointments from purely party channels to a mixture of open competition and administrative selection have reduced managers' organised dependence on their party and bureaucratic superiors, as the contractual relationship begins to erode the arbitrary nature of the superior–inferior ties inherent in the party tradition. This reduction is accentuated by the changed sources of income contract managers can employ; that is, the bulk of their income is now generated outside state provisions.[14] Also important is the enlarged space that the regulation leaves for contract managers to terminate their contract to take up better positions elsewhere.[15] Among the managerial staff the turnover rate for skilled technical personnel is higher than that for contract managers, who regard their promotion as a big step in their career and are influenced by this. Yet even in large state-owned enterprises where state control is comparatively strong, managers have basically won the right to leave, and this has effectively undermined the rigidness and closeness of the party's *nomenklatura* structure.[16]

To sum up, the 'iron chair' for both political cadres and managerial staff has been disappearing in the current campaign to change the operational mechanisms in state-owned enterprises. Although it is difficult to determine how seriously the contract reform has affected the state's industrial cadre system, its effect is gathering strength, and the days of the *nomenklatura* system in the state sector are numbered. Even though it cannot be predicted that the change will lead to the eventual removal of the difference in political status between cadres and workers, one outcome of the reform has been less fear among workers of cadres on contract, now that these increasingly present themselves as employees of a corporatised firm with weaker links with the party/state. The period of their personal control over workers' life and work has become fixed, too. Yet just as contract labourers may seek to change their status to that of permanent workers, there have been attempts in many regions to make contract managers permanent (Zhao Dongwan, 1991, p. 31), and this has threatened to derail the contract cadre reform. More detailed discussion on this will appear in the following chapters.

THE PARTY'S KEY ORGANISATIONAL REFORMS

In addition to the reform of the party's appointment system, party presence in state-owned enterprises has also been eroded by a series of other reforms, most notably the amalgamation of party offices at the factory level. Of particular significance for the relaxation of pressures on workers was that the party office of security affairs was placed under managerial control in 1988. Furthermore, enterprises' public security functions were abolished according to a state decree in 1995.[17] Indeed, these reforms removed the teeth of a *danwei* in its control over workers. At the same time the party's vertical industrial command system has been scheduled for restructuring. Under the principle of *shudi guanli*, or the localised management of party industrial cells, the command chain of the industrial party system will be moved from its vertical and sectoral bureaucratic agencies to the party's local offices where the factories were situated.

Streamlining party bodies

With party functions in state-owned enterprises undergoing drastic changes, the question of redundant party bodies and excessive numbers of full-time party staff became urgent. In September 1986 Deng Xiaoping, having achieved his goal of abolishing the industrial party command system, brought pressure for party functional bodies in state-owned enterprises to be streamlined. (Deng Xiaoping, 1988, p. 156). On 28 April 1988 the CC issued a circular on implementing the Enterprise Law. The document categorically stipulated:

> From now on party committees and their secretaries at every level in state-owned enterprises should be elected through multiple candidatures. Full-time party cadres and functional bodies should be kept to a minimum. Party bodies that assume management missions should be transferred to management. Large factories may keep full-time party secretaries, vice-secretaries and a few crack offices. Small factories in principle should not maintain full-time party cadres and functional bodies. The medium-scale factories may or may not have full-time party cadres and bodies. It should be decided by the factory itself.
>
> (Zhang Zhanbin, 1988, p. 285)

This central decree initiated a major overhaul of the party system in the state sector. Now that a factory's POD had an ever smaller list of *nomenklatura* members, as mentioned in the previous section, it had not had much to do on a daily basis. The party's propaganda department encountered the same problem, as most workers and managerial staff lost interest in political indoctrination. Consequently party committees in many medium and small firms were stripped of their organisation and propaganda offices: this meant severing the two powerful arms with which the party had extended its influence into major areas of factory management and workers' everyday lives. The numbers of party bodies and functionaries in large firms were also pruned. The case study below demonstrates how this reform has proceeded and affected party presence in state firms.

The Changye Bearing Factory has more than 3,000 workers, typical of a medium-sized state firm in China. Before the party's institutional streamlining, the factory party committee maintained three departments (organisation, propaganda and militia), three offices (the general office, the office for combating economic crimes and the office of mass correspondence and contacts) and one parallel committee (the Party Discipline Inspection Committee). Forty-seven full-time party cadres worked in these bodies. After the streamlining, the party structure comprised only one department and one committee staffed by seven people. Three agencies – the militia department, the office for combating economic crimes and the office of correspondence and contacts – were transferred to the management system.[18] The departments of organisation and propaganda were merged into the party committee's general office which was renamed the Party Work Department. Only the Party Discipline Inspection Committee was preserved, although its staff was reduced significantly in number. All party branch secretaries in the management sections and workshops became part time. The seven full-time party cadres included the party secretary, who also headed the Party Work Department, and three functionaries in the Party Work Department, respectively in charge of organisation work, propaganda and everyday office maintenance. The deputy party secretary was also the head of the Party Discipline Inspection Committee, which included the remaining two party cadres, with one managing disciplinary affairs and the other party member education (*Guangming ribao*, 13 December 1987).

The Changye case gives a good account of institutional trimming at a medium-scale state firm. But in a dozen factories of similar size in Beijing and Hunan in 1992 I found that party offices had cut their personnel less severely than at Changye. This was mainly due to the restoration of party organs after the Tiananmen incident. Generally speaking, the new criterion for whether the party should have departments of organisation and propaganda in medium-scale firms was, according to former Politburo member and Beijing party boss Li Ximing, whether the number of workers exceeded 1,000 (*Zhibu shenghuo* (Beijing), no. 6, 1990, p. 31).

Most large state-owned enterprises still keep a full-fledged party structure consisting of departments of propaganda, organisation and united front work, offices of general affairs, supervision, mass correspondence and contacts, the party school and the discipline inspection committee. In many giant factories, such as the Daqing Oil Field, this structure exists not only at the corporation level, but also at the subsidiary level, thus forming a giant party machine. Despite this, the overall number of full-time party staff has been greatly reduced to conform to the centrally prescribed ratio of 1:100 (one party worker to 100 industrial workers). Some of these big corporations actually have a slightly higher ratio. For instance, the ratio at the Capital Iron and Steel Corporation of Beijing has been 1.4:100 since the late 1980s (*Zhibu shenghuo* (Beijing), no. 5, 1991, p. 2).

It is at the more than 480,000 small state firms, which employ up to 80 per cent of the state workforce, that the streamlining of party offices has most affected the party's control over the urban population. As stated earlier, under the principle that small factories should not keep full-time party bodies and cadres, large numbers of party offices have been abolished. Party work is now done by party-member activists after work, and this has been found ineffective.

Undoubtedly, many factories in this category still preserve a formal party office but there is no uniformity about the party structure adopted.

There are several reasons for this. First, there is a wide range of 'small state firms', a term that covers firms with employment ranging from several dozen to several hundred workers. So the number of party members varies significantly from one to another. Second, under different control mechanisms, such as the ministerial (*tiaotiao*) or the local (*kuaikuai*), the party structure tends to be tighter or looser. Generally, the structure appears tight in the *tiaotiao* system. But even under the *kuaikuai* system the party structure tends to be tighter in provincial capital cities than in counties and townships.[19] I visited five small firms in Haidian District, Beijing, in 1992 and found that each of them had a full-time party secretary. Three of them even had a party branch office with one or two full-time clerks handling everyday work. But when I surveyed another five small firms in Hengyang City, Hunan, I found only one full-time party secretary. Among the other four, two party-member managers concurrently held the post of party secretary, and the final two secretaries were retired workers.[20]

There has been wide coverage in the Chinese media of the streamlining in small state-owned enterprises, to show how party bodies have been rationalised. According to a survey of 121 small firms by the POD of Penglai County, Shandong Province, only fourteen had a full-time party secretary. The rest were all part-timers elected by party members in their firms (Yu Shaoxuan, 1988, p. 36). Another report is even more revealing. In 725 firms in Shacheng District, Hangzhou City, which together employed 16,934 workers, there were only ninety-two party and political cadres of whom fifty-three were only part-timers, with their principal duties falling outside party and political work (they included managers, cooks, office workers and shop assistants). As far as party offices were concerned, 80 per cent of these 725 firms had none whatsoever (Zhou Zhibin, 1990, pp. 55–6).

However difficult it may be to assess the exact situation in small firms, it is fairly clear that the party structure is fragmented in the majority of them; the strength of any political organisation is intimately linked to its organisational context, and a large proportion of the small firms have been contracted and leased out to individuals.[21] One party document stated that party work in leased firms was different from in state-run factories in that party cells in the former did not assume concrete supervisory roles (*Zhibu shenghuo* (Beijing), no. 4, 1990, p. 23). Since contractors have full authority in production, personnel affairs and the disposal of profits, party cells are truly subordinate. Moreover, the party structure there tends to be loose because there is no regular party activity: contractors do not allow such activities to take place during working hours and party members have no interest in engaging in party activities after work (Zhuo Zhibin, 1996, p. 56). More on this in the next chapter.

The streamlining has also badly affected security departments in state-owned enterprises, as mentioned earlier. In the 1960s and 1970s security departments were established in large and medium-sized state-owned enterprises with an official rank of county or district government. Nationally, in 1995 they were to be found in over 8,000 of these factories and employed 150,000 factory policemen (*Guangming ribao*, 6 May 1995). In the past, security departments had two chief missions: maintaining so-called 'political security', namely monitoring the political attitudes of workers; and protecting the firm from criminal offences.[22] The political and public security personnel constitute an effective source of control, as indicated by the numerous cases of political and criminal charges brought against workers. However, the factory-based political and public security system has come to be seen as causing tensions in management and being out of touch with the country's political development.

Therefore, the mission of political security was initially handed over to the local public and state security bureaux. However, the latter's limited resources allow them only to monitor a small number of the blacklisted political dissidents or serious criminal suspects. This resulted in a hole in the network of political control at the grassroots level nationwide.[23] More-over, legal and administrative procedures have become tighter for pressing counter-revolutionary charges against ordinary workers. This means that although factory party cadres are still required to monitor 'abnormal actions' around them, they are not supposed to bring charges against workers at will, as they used to do in the Mao era. Here again, some political cadres still maintain the habit of harassing people (*zhengren*), and violations of workers' political rights continue. This is especially likely when political cadres are required by their superior government agencies to tighten surveillance on those who have already been singled out as dissidents. Yet the removal of the institutional frame-work for persecution from party cells has made a difference to organised oppression.[24]

Public security departments have also reoriented their tasks towards safeguarding production, in keeping with the central concerns of factory managers. Most managers I interviewed expressed contempt for the past practice of seeing everything from a political angle. In contrast to their previous focus on class struggle, the public security people now interpret a potentially offensive act more from the perspective of law and order than as anti-party or anti-government. This has reduced political tension in state-owned enterprises. Workers still show annoyance about security agencies but they agree that they are less fearful when the security agencies approach them because public security matters are no longer politically charged.[25] Indeed, Jiang Zemin's call to 'talk politics' in 1995 aroused almost no interest on shop floors.

In the state sector as a whole, the streamlining reform went quite deep. According to Gao Qixiang, Beijing's deputy organisation boss, since the reform began in the mid-1980s, 70 to 80 per cent of state-owned enter-prises nationwide have been affected one way or another. The number of party and political cadres was halved, and the majority of factories have a very fragmented party structure (Gao Qixiang, 1990, p. 19). Even in large state-owned enterprises the party structure can no longer be compared with what existed at any time before the Dengist reform, in relation not only to what party organs a factory may have but also to what they can do.[26]

The concurrent system

The authority of the party has been further weakened by a reform known as 'the concurrent system' (*jianrenzhi*). Under this system, the post of party boss was made part-time and the secretary's principal job has become non-party, whether in management or in other work. Most commonly, managers take on the job of party secretary. The concurrent system had not been uncommon throughout the history of the PRC. Yet a person now takes both the party and manager posts, primarily because of already being factory or workshop manager rather than the other way round, decisively reversing the situation prevalent before the post-Mao reform.

Usually party heads at factory and workshop levels are elected through ballots of ordinary party members, although the election at the higher level is often a formality, with the outcome decided by the factory's superior. From earlier discussion on the new mechanisms for selecting managers, we see that different procedures may be used to appoint a manager and a party secretary. The party leadership has advocated the concurrent system regardless of this procedural confusion. This means that the appointment of a factory manager has to precede the party election; this in itself indicates the diminished party role.[27] At the workshop level, the elected party head may be either a workshop manager or just a worker. The former seem to constitute the majority in large and medium-sized state-owned enterprises while the latter are mostly found in small plants where managers are often non-party members.[28]

The concurrent system has been carried out in a flexible manner. The party centre provides only broad guidelines that can be applied to different situations. Generally speaking, factory and workshop managers are encouraged to take the party posts if they are 'politically qualified' and full-time party secretaries are encouraged to take the position of deputy factory or workshop manager in order to assist managers better in the areas of political and ideological work (*Zhibu shenghuo* (Shandong), no. 11, 1989, p. 24). The party re-emphasised its control for a while after the Tiananmen incident, adding some conditions to the concurrent system. For instance, it was stipulated that full-time party secretaries should be restored in workshops with more than 100 workers (*Guandao zhenggong yanjiu*, no. 28, 1992, p. 90). In principle, managers in large factories should not assume the party post. But after Deng's south China tour the pendulum swung back again. For one thing, the renewed call for tightening political control was received coldly by the majority of state-owned enterprises. For another, the concurrent system is now considered the most effective weapon for combating the 'two centres' rivalry mentioned in the previous chapter, so it has gained more currency. For instance, the Hubei Party Committee decreed that the concurrent system should be implemented in all large and medium-sized state firms in the province, with factory managers assuming the primary duties. This decision was significant because it was the first hard stipulation on the issue, contrasting with the centre's past decrees which always gave a flexible choice at the grassroots. In China's political system it is unlikely that such a policy would be initiated without the acquiescence of the top leadership. This has heralded a new impetus for advancing the concurrent system. The result is further weakening of the party's influence in state-owned enterprises, as can be seen from what follows.

First, when a manager takes on the two posts, he is normally obliged to regard the party post as a 'sideline occupation', although it is beneficial for him to have control of both powerful systems in running the factory. One such person I talked to in 1992 revealed that management work demanded most of his attention. He remarked: 'Contracted production and profit responsibility is certainly the harder task, into which I have to put most of my energy. To me, the party work is mainly a sort of trouble-shooting that helps me to run management.' He gave an example of what he meant by trouble-shooting:

> When I decided to 'rationalise' a number of workers and staff [have them leave their posts], many of them were angry. They complained that they had been working for the factory for the better part of their lives. It was not fair that the factory wanted to get rid of them now that they had become old. Production was disrupted. So I asked the party and union cadres to talk to them one by one and find ways to allay their frustration. They did a good job. First, they talked to the party members involved and then asked these party members to talk to others. At the same time the party and union systems tried to arrange for some of them to work in the factory's service company. Other measures were also taken to help them adjust to the situation. For instance, the factory introduced some of them with skills to work part-time in a nearby village factory which was our client. In this way the dispute was settled fairly smoothly. All I did was to let the party and union cadres take control of the matter.[29]

Clearly this kind of party work diminishes the traditional mission of the party command system. Yet it is natural that factory managers will reshape the party machine for their own purposes. This approach is more apparent at lower levels of management, as when a workshop manager is also a party branch secretary. When a workshop secretary is merely an ordinary worker, the subordination of the party branch's agenda to the management's is even more visible. This state of laxity in party work has become so widespread that some government industrial bureaux have decreed that managers have to assign a fixed proportion of their time to party work and that this will be one of the criteria in their contract assessment. For instance, the Shanghai Watch Factory's party committee stipulated that all managers who were concurrently party secretaries had to devote 60 per cent of their time to political and ideological work. However, managers with a party portfolio saw that this was simply out of touch with reality and they never took it very seriously (*Zhibu shenghuo* (Shandong), no. 2, 1989, p. 34).

EXPERIMENTING WITH THE PARTY'S INDUSTRIAL CONTROL SYSTEM

The Party's Thirteenth Congress in 1987 put forward a far-reaching institutional reform for the party's industrial organisations, which is called *shudi guanli* or localised management of party affairs in industry. The reform developed steadily, unfolding with every province assigning one prefecture plus a few industrial sectors as an experimental model. The reform was made nationwide when the party centre determined that conditions had became ripe.[30] According to the plan drafted by the Beijing Party Committee, the reform would affect 2,100 enterprises and 400,000 party members in the municipality. In 1988 the reform was launched in Beijing's East City District, involving 333 state-owned enterprises with 165,000 workers, 25,000 of them party members, and in the municipal electronics industry, involving 103 state-owned enterprises employing 107,000 workers, about 20,000 of them party members.[31]

Shudi guanli is a new mechanism for running party industrial cells by the local party committees, which are supposed to oversee party affairs in both local and ministerial factories. It should be made clear here that this 'localisation reform' has little to do with the familiar themes of *tiaotiao* and *kuaikuai*. The concepts of *tiaotiao* and *kuaikuai* envisage the arrangement of administrative controls over a factory along the lines of ministerial branches or local areas, in terms of the centralisation or decentralisation of bureaucratic power. The concepts *tiaotiao* and *kuaikuai* are based on the property relations between state firms and the central and local government, which see these firms as bureaucratic investors. The 'localisation reform', *shudi guanli*, would not change a factory's existing administrative and ownership relations with the state hierarchy. Nor would it affect the top-down government personnel arrangement for managers. It simply means removing the *tiaotiao* party leadership relationship between industrial sectors (bureaux) and factories and placing this leadership relationship under the *kuaikuai* local party offices. As a result, the vertically arranged sectoral party leading bodies will be eliminated once the reform is completed (Yan Zhi, 1988, p. 27).

The procedures are complicated, indicating the depth of the reform and its incremental nature. The first step is to establish industrial offices in the local party committee at various levels. The second step is to distinguish various sizes (ranks) of firms and to transfer their organisation (leadership) ties to the local party offices, e.g. to municipal-level large firms; to the county- and district-level medium-sized firms; and to the township- or street-level small firms. The hierarchical ties of the Youth League and trade unions are to be transferred at the same time. The third step is to hand over to the local offices the list of factory party members and cadres, the list of party-sponsored activists, and the registration forms of a factory's leading party cadres. Then the factory's party cells are to submit a number of reports on the general situation of their party members, on party/workforce relations, and on the state of their firms both politically and economically.

In many ways the reform localising the party's industrial leadership was a significant step designed in the 1980s to separate the functions of party control, government administration and enterprise management. This combination of party and state functions in the government hierarchy had been the organisational base of the party/state through which its totalitarian reach was extended to all social units, as party control was delivered through a top-down administrative process. Indeed, the party's power was channelled through plugging its command into the administrative hierarchy, from which it controlled administrative finance, personnel and material allocations. The logic of the reform goes like this: if a factory's party organisation relations were transferred to the local party offices, the direct party ties subordinating it to its 'mother-in-law', the sectoral industrial bureau, would be severed. This would induce two far-reaching changes. First, the administrative control and party control exercised by the bureau over the factory would be separated, thus removing one tight chain of control (the party's) over it. Second, when the bureau party committee lost all its direct subordinate cells, it would have to confine its functions to its internal affairs, in the form of *jiguan dangwei*, or the party office for internal affairs. As a result, the bureau's party committee would not issue concrete political tasks to the factory. This would make it easier for the bureau to be eventually transformed into an economic institution, either as a holding corporation or as a sectoral association (more on this in Chapter 9). At the same time a local party office that was entrusted with management of party industrial cells could not run the factories in the locality as its subordinates, not being their bureaucratic boss and its leadership ties with the factories not being reinforced with administrative means. This distancing of authority would enhance the efforts of industrial concerns to seek more business autonomy.

This localisation reform was meant to transform direct party industrial leadership to indirect party industrial leadership at the grassroots. While the local party office had responsibility for overseeing a factory's party work, it did not have immediate authority over its management and personnel matters, although it could make suggestions to the municipal and district party committees concerning appointment and promotion decisions. Without administrative ties, it had little say regarding the ranks and pay of a factory's leading personnel (OD of the Zibo Party Committee, 1988, p. 16). Nor did the local party office have a financial hold over the factory, which still maintained its channels of funding with its bureau. Therefore, the institutional linkage was too weak for party cadres from the local office to employ effective levers over a factory's internal affairs. Institutional control would thus tend to be not only indirect but loose. Local party cadres expressed their worry that 'their small temple [local party office] is intruded upon by big monks [firms with higher or similar administrative ranks or administratively under central ministries]'. (OD of the Zibo Party Committee, p. 16).

Factory party cadres were also concerned: the reform presented a potential threat to their political careers due to the separation of the party and management personnel systems. Factory managers are still selected by their superior government bureaux. Party cadres, however, would be mainly elected and under the loose supervision of the local party industrial office (*Zhibu shenghuo* (Shanghai), no. 1, 1988, p. 12). Normally opportunities for cadres' promotion, material benefits and official privileges are generated from their vertically accorded status within each industrial system (*xitong*). Once the reform is fully implemented, it would by and large exclude factory party cadres from this system, as their direct working relations would be linked to the local party office, which belongs to a different system and has its own preferred personnel for advancement.[32]

As a result, the party's industrial cadres began to feel that the reform would undercut their power base, and that the party's organisational backing would rest on a less solid institutional framework. Although the party document concerning 'localisation reform' stipulated that factories should be properly linked to the various levels of local party offices, it was likely that many factory party committees would be demoted in official ranking, thus losing access to their previous administrative status and privileges. According to the reform, the horizontally arranged organisational ties would oblige a factory party secretary at the county level to take orders from a local party office which might be at the same rank as him or even lower. In so doing, His own status would thereby be downgraded. For instance, Weiyang Machinery Factory is a large factory directly run by the Ministry of Machinery and enjoys an official rank of prefectural government. When its organisation relationship was transferred to Baoji City, its status was lowered by at least half a grade.

The designers of the reform regarded *shudi guanli* as an initial step in a profound organisational reform of the party basic units in the state sector. This reform was envisaged and promoted by party research bodies on political reform in both the SCRES and CPS. The guiding principles were adopted from the Soviet model of a localised industrial party structure (Wang Yiqing, 1987, pp. 178–83). According to these researchers, the party presence in state-owned enterprises should in future be through a system of party representatives. Under this system, the local party committees at the levels of province, county and township would send one representative to each state-owned enterprise under their jurisdiction. This representative should not be a formal member of the factory or derive income from it. Nor was he/she supposed to become involved in the factory's routine management. He/she would simply run its party committee, which would be entirely composed of people elected by party members of the factory. His/her main mission would be to take care of the party internal affairs, although he/she could report any unlawful operations of factory management to higher party and state authorities, as required by his/her supervisory role (Wang Yiqing, 1987, pp. 178–83).

These proposals were intended as a bridging step in the transition to the eventual removal of all party committees in non-political units in China, as proposed by the reformers (Harding, 1989, p. 48). Their logic is not hard to grasp. If the leading role of party committees is now non-existent in millions of collective, private and joint ventures, there is no reason why state-owned enterprises should not be the same. After all, workers in large and medium-sized state-owned enterprises represent about 6 per cent of the country's population (*Renmin ribao* (overseas edition), 27 May 1996). Looking into the not too distant future, party control in state-owned enterprises will become even less meaningful when the non-state sector, where party committees play no significant role in overall management, accounts for over three-quarters of China's economy in the early twenty-first century. The party system there has already been operating in a way similar to the party representative system mentioned earlier.[33] In a large number of state-owned enterprises which have been corporatised or injected with foreign capital and management, party committees function in a way that is converging with that in state-owned enterprises that have been leased (*Jingji ribao*, 14 February 1993).

Some of the proponents of this party representative system alluded to a similar party control model used by the Guomindang in China before 1949 and subsequently in Taiwan, where party committees were set up only at county government level or above and branches in basic work units were not a locus of practical power. They believed that this fairly loose party structure at the grassroots did not really weaken the Guomindang's monopoly of power at the apex. In their minds, the trimming of the party's basic cells could reduce the number of power abusers: the biggest threat to the party is loss of control over its own body. At the same time, however, such a reform would not adversely affect the party's monopoly of power at the state level if it could sufficiently control the major appointments in government at various levels. If the localisation reform indeed reduced the level of party corruption at the grassroots, this would help the party to position itself favourably in the open elections which represent the undeniable historical trend which the CCP will have to cope with sooner or later.[34]

The events in 1989 and their aftermath have greatly slowed down the experiment, as the party leadership became more concerned with immediate control of the industrial population. Whether the experiment will be universalised still remains a question at the time of writing, eight years after June 4. However, more relevant for this book is the fact that the philosophical ideas behind the reform have been kept very much alive. The CCP does not seem to have many choices if it wants to see a rapid economic development based on the market. This is vividly demonstrated by the CCP's decision to revoke some industrial ministries at the central level and most industrial bureaux at the regional and local levels. This decision constitutes the catalyst moving the experiment forward. When these industrial bureaux are converted into shareholding companies, it is only a matter of logic that their former party ties with their subordinates be transferred to the party's local office. Another catalyst is the current privatisation drive in China. Local governments are especially enthusiastic to sell their state firms. For instance, when Yuncheng City, Shandong Province, sold all its 243 state firms, there was no longer any need to retain the industrial bureaux. So once the vectors of the vertical party control system – the sectoral bureaux – have disappeared altogether, it is only a matter of time before the party has to place the management of its industrial bodies under local command. Chapters 8 and 9 will discuss this in detail. In the final analysis, *shudi guanli* may not be advocated as loudly as it was in the late 1980s. It will take place quietly and in a big way.

5 Withering of the party's industrial apparatus

Since the post-Mao reforms the cohesiveness of the CCP's industrial cells has been greatly eroded. According to Daniel Katz and Robert Kahn, like any organic body, an organisation may gradually wither, dismember and die. So 'negative entropy' is very important for the health of any organisation (Katz and Kahn, 1966, pp. 19–22). The organisational pathologies that Harding pointed out in his book *Organizing China* (1981, p. 2) have been particularly relevant to our analysis of the CCP industrial cells in the reform era. It is clear that the party's problems of personnel, structure and public alienation have deteriorated to a serious degree. In fact no factor has been so detrimental to the industrial *danwei* system as the withering of the party basic units in the state sector. As mentioned at the beginning of the book, if the key function of the *danwei* system is to exercise daily organisational and ideological control over workers, party cells are the actual instigators of this control. When these cells become paralysed, the *danwei* system can no longer function as the party/state expects it to. This chapter will evaluate the extent to which the party's industrial body is decaying. From the four conventional angles from which an organisation is usually studied – its ability to adapt to a changing external environment, its organisational and ideological resilience, its daily activities and the strength of its reserves – I will present findings that reveal an evolutionary trend of the CCP in state-owned enterprises: it is withering gradually. The consequences of this are far-reaching, as the party will gradually become unable to control the grassroots.

The fundamental reason for this decay is the incompatibility of the political missions assumed by the party with depoliticised economic entities. The party's organisational well-being is closely related to the distribution of resources such as power, income and status in society. Each of these has been significantly affected since the reforms. This is especially true at the grassroots level. The ongoing enterprise reform has posed an unprecedented challenge to the party's dominant position on shop floors. The bankruptcy of communism has left it without any ideological belief system with which to indoctrinate the workforce. Functionally, the very existence of the party industrial cells now seems to be irrelevant in factories' pursuit of the market. And the contradiction lingers on. On the one hand, party cells are still required by the centre to uphold political control. On the other, they are themselves increasingly driven by an impulse for profits. This clash of values and interests between the demands of the party and the reality of socio-economic change puts at stake party members' career security and daily activity, and promises a bleak future for the party in state-owned enterprises.

The resultant atrophy produces widespread lack of commitment among party members to party goals. This is a natural outcome of their perception of being seriously underpaid and poorly judged for what they do from both above and below.[1] At the same time the repeated alterations in the party's political focus, from 'economics in command' to political clampdown and back again, have aroused strong feelings of frustration in party members. As one of my interviewees said to me, 'Whenever the party leadership thinks that it needs us, it will use us, but after such use, they put us aside. You need only recall history to see my point: the anti-spiritual pollution drive in 1983, the 1986 anti-liberalism campaign and then the Tiananmen events.'[2]

MOBILISATION VS. THE PARTY'S VITALITY

The party industrial cells began to wither when they were deprived of the function of mass mobilisation on the shop floor, first with the phasing out of political campaigns at the grassroots and then with the gradual bankruptcy of political study sessions, the two principal means of mobilisation during the Maoist era. The CCP is a mass party and depends heavily on its basic units to rule the population. Its presence has been crucial for organising mobilisation in political campaigns and political studies during 'peaceful times'. Losing these two means of control amounts to the loss of its organisational teeth of repression. Consequently, the decay of the party apparatus in state-owned enterprises has accelerated. The following will analyse how this has happened.

Bankruptcy of political campaigns

In 1978, as a measure of re-legitimation after the Cultural Revolution, the party announced its intention to relinquish political campaigns as a vehicle of mobilisation. This substantially altered the political environment in the country. On the whole both party cadres and workers welcomed the move, since they had become hostile to the intimidation posed by the incessant political campaigns. Some of these campaigns had been designed as 'rectification purges', targeting party cadres in the hope of purifying their thoughts and tightening the organisation's discipline (Teiwes, 1979). Others were directed towards members of the society at large. In these campaigns 'class enemies' were punished, but everybody knew they stood a chance of becoming victims themselves, as the direction of the drives was so unpredictable. The repudiation of political campaigns removed a major source of social tension and mass apprehension. Yet this has generated dysfunctional pressures on the well-being of the party as a political organisation.

The party's determination to give up the campaign method has not been consistent, especially during crises of popular protest. Breaking its repeated promises since 1978 not to initiate any political vendettas, it launched a campaign against 'spiritual pollution' in 1983. At the time many urban and rural party cadres took advantage of the changed political atmosphere to reassert their power. Tensions that had been accumulating during the hiatus in political campaigns since the Cultural Revolution burst forth with party cadres' clampdown on people not on good terms with them (Gold, 1984, pp. 947–74). The persecutions of 1983 seriously damaged not only the atmosphere that the party centre wanted to create to support economic take-off but also its carefully nurtured image of returning to benevolent rule.

An alarmed party leadership adopted a middle course in the design of future campaigns: these were to be launched against dissenting intellectuals at the institutions of the 'superstructure'. At the grassroots – basic urban work units and rural villages – only positive education (*zhengmian jiaoyu*) would be pursued.[3] That meant, according to the official explanation, that when workers and peasants were organised to study party documents about the ongoing drive, actions against individuals should be avoided. Although some party cadres ignored the centre's call and continued to make life miserable on shop floors, this policy did withdraw a key channel through which political persecution on a massive scale could be conducted. In the national political campaigns which followed, party cadres, in the main, could not so readily exploit shopfloor action. Without an institutional sanction and against the dominant social mood, they became increasingly incapable of riding a political tide. This trend culminated in the general failure of the basic party cells to prevent workers from participating in the Beijing Spring of 1989 (Walder and Gong, 1993, pp. 1–30).

The phasing-out of political campaigns in state-owned enterprises has exerted enormous impact in terms of depoliticisation. First, it stifled the organisational vitality of the factory party cells. In the past, an industrial party branch assumed three major tasks: everyday involvement in management, the implementation of political campaigns and the conduct of routine political studies. As mentioned earlier, the director responsibility system marginalised party cells in matters of daily management. The abolition of political campaigns further undermined the party presence on shop floors, as it was through mobilisations in political campaigns that this presence was most fearfully felt. To a large extent the vitality of the party's basic units is closely connected to the function of mobilisation in implementing political drives. Indeed, the growth of party membership and the hardening of its power at the grassroots could not be separated from this second mission. By organising public meetings to denounce 'bad elements', the vigour of a party cell was recharged every now and then, as campaigns were pushed through from above. Mobilisation was the lifeline of a mass party like the CCP. One old party cadre compared the present with some cherished memories of the past:

> In the 1960s and 1970s whenever a political campaign was waged by Chairman Mao, party members would become very busy. Everyone wanted to show that he was a fighter. I remember that our shop was given the task of printing a large number of Mao portraits. All party members were working non-stop for two days. Now look at our party secretary! He organises *mahjong* when the party branch is supposed to conduct political study. He would not dare if there were still political campaigns. In the last several years our branch has had few organised activities.[4]

These remarks expose a second type of dysfunctional pathology in party cells: the dilution of party members' sense of belonging due to the phasing-out of the political campaigns. As Barnett pointed out: 'Each campaign has been a period in which the cadres' loyalty to the regime has been tested' (Barnett, 1967, p. 33). With the loss of organisational sanctions and ideological substance, the loyalty of party cadres has now become questionable. As a consequence, they have lost their fear of being exposed in a campaign. With no other forms of checks and balances, cases of corruption among them soared. Internal decay and external mass alienation have become pervasive. Ironically, however, rhetoric against the use of campaigns has become a protective shield for corrupt cadres. Whenever there are disciplinary or criminal investigations against them, they often accuse the investigators of 'using political campaign methods' against them.

The third effect induced by revoking political campaigns is a reduction in the fear felt by ordinary workers towards the party's authority. Political drives were usually launched at the apex of power to purge a few designated members of the leadership, under the guise of abstract ideological rectification. At the grassroots, where the specific targets became remote, it was the task of party cells to tackle the 'social base' of the disgraced party leaders. So 'followers' of the erroneous party line were ferreted out, often on the basis of a quota which factory party cells had to fulfil. Because it was difficult to establish the exact political and ideological crimes of those targeted, people who had either a 'bad family origin' or a bad relationship with party cadres became vulnerable in these drives. An ingrained fear of party cadres developed in the minds of many non-activist workers whenever there was a change of political wind.

Once such political drives ceased to be effective, it became difficult for party cadres to put a political 'label' on defiant workers. Even though some party cadres still try to identify 'backward elements', the nature of harassment cannot be as intense without real political substance to underpin it. Gradually, workers have learned that they can afford to be not only apolitical but resistant on shop floors, even when a political campaign is unfolding in the 'superstructure'. This will be discussed in more detail in a later case study of the party's aborted investigation drive in 1989 (p. 101).

The fourth consequence has been the collapse of a key channel for cultivating party loyalists. Political campaigns had been employed by party cells to recruit contingents of party reserves. During a campaign, ideological propaganda was intensified and opportunities for upward mobility were offered to activists. Even ordinary workers, if they did not want to be targeted as 'backward elements', had to appear politically conformist. Some true activists came to act as 'big brother' to their co-workers.

Activists' involvement in political campaigns earned them a notorious reputation, and this now inhibits new recruitment. The post-Mao political environment has built up pressure on those who send 'small reports' (*xiao baogao*) to the authorities. It is now the turn of activists to worry about the 'hostile climate' surrounding them. Moreover, the changing patterns of work and reward systems present little incentive for workers to become politically motivated, for political attitudes play an increasingly minor role when perks are allocated, in contrast to the time when the party's 'principled particularism' lured many workers to join the ranks of activists. Indeed, the very notion of activism has already become ridiculous to workers. Many of my interviewees would laugh the moment I mentioned the concept. As one noted: 'What do you mean by activists? If you mean the Lei Feng type of people, I'm sure that there aren't any in our shop. If you mean the followers of shop heads, certainly they exist but they're hardly active.'

Bankruptcy of political studies

If the abolition of political campaigns has neutralised a recharging facility for party bodies in state-owned enterprises, the paralysis of political study sessions has served to undermine a major setting for their everyday activities. In the past, political study sessions became instruments of ideological indoctrination for the purpose of achieving a degree of political conformity without generating explosive tensions (Houn, 1961, p. 4). When a political campaign was about to be launched, political study became a more naked form of suppression, with activists mobilised and victims persecuted. Yet whatever the difference of degree, these were two sides of one coin, used by the CCP to re-energise its organisational zeal.

Political study has become a major casualty of the Dengist system of economics in command. The resulting socially apolitical trend has rendered political study a case of much ado about nothing. In the view of management, economic imperatives call for less time to be devoted to these sessions of 'empty talk', to quote the words of one interviewed firm manager. So the study programmes are largely squeezed out of the manager's agenda. Even when a session is convened, it easily turns into a meeting expressing complaints. Participants use the occasion to express bitterness against management and party leaders. Often the sessions are marked by mutual flattery or attacks: if you say something good or bad about me, I will reciprocate in kind (Wang Haili, 1991, p. 27). Consequently, study sessions either have become a formality, undertaken to please superiors when managers or party cadres have to report on how many sessions they have held, or have simply ceased to be held at all in a large number of state-owned enterprises.

The difficulty of holding study sessions is reflected by the failure of workers to embrace the official ideology as a belief system. The No. 3 Beijing Chemical Plant conducted a casual survey on the question of faith in socialism among sixty workers in 1990. Only 20 per cent of workers expressed some hope for it while 70 per cent had lost their faith. This followed three consecutive rounds of study of socialism carried out by the factory's party cells in the 1980s (Xiao Yu, 1990, p. 19). So it has become obvious that the *raison d'être* for political study is dead, not only for workers but for most of the party cadres who have to preside over these sessions.[5] But why, then, is political study still imposed on the factory floors (the party cadres in the factory mentioned above were prepared to initiate a fourth round)? The answer lies in the control function of the ideology, which is regarded as so important for the party that nobody dares to suggest doing away with it. This control function reflects Schurmann's summary of the relationship between pure ideology (theory) and practical ideology (thought control): without pure ideology, the ideas of the practical ideology have no legitimation, but without a practical ideology an organisation cannot transform its 'world view' into action and policy (Schurmann, 1968, p. 23). The CCP leaders firmly believe that without indoctrination, workers would be open to the influence of alternative ideas, e.g. the independent trade unionism embodied in the Polish Solidarity movement. Deng feared this as the worst thing that could occur among Chinese workers.

On the other hand, it is not correct to think that the party stubbornly sticks to the old-fashioned design of political study sessions. The CCP has made numerous calls to reform the methods of 'brainwashing'. And party cadres are required to learn the 'art of indoctrination'. For instance, they are told to combine political indoctrination and material incentives when organising political study sessions. However, since most of them have simply lost interest in preaching, the party's insistence on continuing these study sessions proves to be an embarrassment for those who have to convene them. Before reform, political study entailed rewards or punishments depending on whether one actively participated or not. Now workers have become so apolitical that neither reward nor punishment can effectively stimulate them to react in the way the party likes. Managers and party cadres have to arrange political study in a fashion that can please the workers, often by organising a social gathering such as a dancing party, at the expense of the factory. On the other hand, when factories are ordered to organise political meetings by their superiors, party cadres still have to comply, as their effort is linked to their career advancement. Under the circumstances, one party cadre whom I interviewed remarked that each time he had to explain the political documents in these sessions, he felt uneasy.

> This is because I know I am preaching something I myself don't have faith in. So you feel you cannot escape feelings of hypocrisy. The best way to avoid this embarrassment is to avoid study sessions where possible, or cut the number to a minimum.

If such sessions could not be avoided, he and his colleagues just relayed the documents as required. As soon as they finished reading, they would let the audience 'discuss' anything they liked.

DEMORALISED PARTY INDUSTRIAL CELLS

The organisational dysfunction of party cells has resulted in their collapse in large numbers of state-owned enterprises, although we are not clear about the exact number. Most of the party documents use only vague language to describe the situation. For instance, Shandong's Party Discipline Commission revealed in a 1990 report that the paralysed or semi-paralysed party cells comprised quite a large proportion of party branches in the province (Shandong Shengwei, 1990a, p. 19). At the municipal level, according to an investigation in Datong City, a model city in terms of party building, more than 20 per cent of industrial party cells had collapsed (*Renmin ribao*, 12 November 1991). One source even suggested that 80 per cent of the grassroots party bodies had become inactive by 1993 (*Zuzhi tongxun*, no. 12, 1994, p. 45). This is plausible, depending on the definition of the term 'inactive'. The official definition of an inactive party branch is one that does not hold regular meetings, whose party leaders are involved in serious factional infighting or are lukewarm about their missions, and whose party members take their membership lightly and do not play an exemplary role at work. The most important indicator is whether or not party cells and party members hold dissenting views on the policies of the party centre (Wu Zhiqing, 1991).

The impression gained from my field survey was that the above-mentioned phenomena existed in all state-owned enterprises, though in varying degrees. In fact, the sorry state of party cells seems worse than has been admitted by the reports of party organisation departments at various levels. Party activity is normally conducted through party meetings at the workshop level where a party branch is set up. The activity is most often in the form of 'three meetings and one lecture', *sanhui yike*; that is, regular meetings of the branch committee once a month, of branch party members once a quarter, of party small groups once a month, and party knowledge lectures (*dangke*) twice a year (Yan Pengyuan, 1990, p. 360). This regulation is seldom observed. One model party branch I visited had held only four meetings in 1991, fewer than half of what is required. Most of the branches held two or three, usually at the middle and end of the year, when the assessment reports of party members had to be drafted. Two party branches had held no meetings since 1990. Meetings of branch party members were even less frequently convened. One-third of branches did not convene even one in 1991. Party small group meetings were more regularly arranged, though mainly for discussion of production matters, since at the lowest level of the shop there were few party members and most of them served as the 'backbone' of the section. So when the section chief wanted something done he would call the members together to work out implementation procedures. Yet by its nature this was hardly a party activity. As far as party knowledge lectures were concerned, these occurred only because a party cadre from above came down to deliver them. During many conversations with a number of party secretaries in the last few years only one said that he had arranged a lecture on his own.

With the paralysis of party organisational activities and the redistribution of powers in the wake of the director responsibility system, the morale of the full-time party cadres has dropped to the lowest point since the founding of the PRC. One party secretary summarised the general psychology of party cadres in the following terms:

> If you work for 30 years in the technical field, you become a senior engineer. If you work for 30 years as a manager, you now have every access to the market (to earn big bucks), but if you are a party cadre for 30 years, you have nothing to show for it but an empty mind and wallet.

(Guan Xiaofeng, 1992, p. 28)

While loss of power and a decline in their political and social status are key factors that have contributed to a dampening of party cadres' morale, a more immediate factor has been that they feel disadvantaged in generating income as compared to managerial staff and sometimes even workers. The wages of managers and workers have now been linked to their plant's profits. Party cadres are not directly involved in production in terms of contract quotas. So their salary is evaluated according to the general wage levels of the factory. Normally their pay is determined around the average, lower than that of the managerial staff and workers receiving quota awards, though a bit higher than that of the logistics staff (Xu Songtao *et al.*, 1988). One party report revealed a telling example. In a large factory in Beijing the personnel and wage department drafted a wage package for political cadres giving them the lowest rates of pay of all the staff. Although the draft package was later vetoed by the factory manager because of strong opposition from the party system, this was insufficient consolation for most of the party cadres. Half of them reportedly expressed the feeling that given a choice, they would leave party work at once. This seems to be the feeling entertained by most industrial party cadres (Xiao Wei, 1992, p. 17).

It is not that the party accepts a situation where its industrial cadres suffer economic discrimination. Rather, this has happened because party cadres have lost touch with marketised state firms: their role in the firms has become superfluous. The party has indeed tried to protect the economic well-being of its factory party cadres. In 1991 the COD promulgated a four-level speciality titles system for political staff in the state sector, which created the title of senior political work specialist, middle-level political work specialist, political work specialist and political work staff. The purpose of the system was to align the titles and salaries of political cadres with those accorded to engineers and technicians and to make political work a profession with a stable morale. However, the technical professionals strongly resented this equation. They considered it unfair to equate their hard knowledge with political 'empty talk'. Neither did party cadres take comfort from the system. They wanted to be aligned with managers, whose income was even higher than that of the technical professionals. Since 1989 rising numbers of party cadres have tendered applications for transfer. Over half of party cadres in Shanghai have done so since the late 1980s, although it is not clear how many of them have been successful (*Zuzhi renshibao*, 30 September 1995). According to workers, they are among the least liked personnel in state-owned enterprises as they are seen as only 'working with their lips'. Party cadres know this well. One of my interviewees noted:

I'm aware that people like us are not welcome by workers and technical staff. But is it our fault? When I had just joined the workforce, I dreamed of becoming a technician. Yet Secretary Liu told me that because I had a 'red' family background and a high school certificate, the organisation [the party] had decided that I should work in the party propaganda department. All these years I have been playing with empty words, many of which sound odd today. Now I have a senior title as a political worker. However, besides talking about stuff which nobody listens to, I am good at nothing. All I can do now is to prevent any of my children from following my path but instead encourage them to learn a real skill.

According to official statistics, 80 per cent of all party cadres still have not received any special training in management or in other technical fields (Guan Xiaofeng, 1992, p. 28). Very likely they share the feelings of my interviewee. Given this demoralised state of mind, can anyone believe that the party's industrial cells really have a future?

THE DRYING UP OF PARTY RESERVES

The paralysed or semi-paralysed state of party industrial cells is also due to the drying up of party reserves. Even in those state-owned enterprises where party cells play a key role at the top level of management, at the shop level they do not. A large number of workshops, sections and small work groups have no party members at all. The party has tried everything to attract young people to join the reserves but its efforts have not been fruitful. Take Beijing as an example. According to the municipality's party organisation chief Cheng Guangwen, party members under the age of 25 constituted only 3 per cent of all party members in the city in 1992. This was in sharp contrast to the 12 per cent plus of party members who had retired. Qiang Wei, chief of Beijing party law enforcement, also revealed that the ratio of young party recruits in the overall intake had dropped from 10 per cent to 1.9 per cent between 1976 and 1990 (*Zhibu shenghuo* (Beijing), no. 7, 1991, p. 7). As a result, the number of work sections in Beijing's state-owned enterprises that did not have a single party member reached about half of the total at one point in the 1980s. Even after a long battle to 'fill blanks' after 4 June 1989, 35 per cent of these sections still did not have any party members as of the end of 1992 (*Zhibu shenghuo* (Beijing), no. 10, 1992, p. 7). Similarly, in Shandong Province, among 2.2 million industrial staff, only 11.4 per cent were party members in 1990 of whom a disproportionate number were white-collar workers. So production line membership had declined steadily as old party member workers retired and the number of 'blank work sections' – work sections where there was no party member – increased (Shandong Shengwei, 1990b, p. 12). In Shandong's Weifang City, for instance, in the fifteen state firms under direct municipal control, 52 per cent of the 1,906 work sections did not have a single party member (Yu Hongji, 1991, p. 28). Such reports are pervasive in China's party journals, illustrating that the problem is clearly perceived. Yet it is only the tip of the iceberg. Ironically, however, with no party presence around them the tension between the ordinary workers and the factory's party committee has been eased.

From the 1950s to the 1970s high political ambition and consciousness were manifested in a strong desire to join the party. By discarding this enthusiasm youth in the 1980s clearly demonstrated their value judgement on the party's role in real life. In a survey carried out by CASS in 1988 in all major cities, of the people polled only 0.33 per cent still regarded joining the party as a priority in life. In the overall ranking of choices for a happy life, party membership came last. Other personal goals, such as a harmonious family, a successful career, becoming rich, etc., are far more highly valued than the desire to obtain a party card (Lu Jianhua, 1990, p. 5).

Behind this fundamental change in people's socio-political mentality lies a fundamental disillusionment with the party (Chi Hsi-Sheng 1991). A party member with a special political status is expected to work altruistically. In reality, however, all that people hear are stories of party corruption. As a result, a hostile attitude towards party applicants has gradually gathered strength. One applicant in Beijing wrote a letter entitled 'What should I do?' to a party journal, expressing his sorrow at having lost most of his friends since handing in an application to the party. All that he was told was that his experience was not uncommon so he should stick to his own choice (*Zhibu shenghuo* (Shandong), no. 2, 1992, p. 36). When workers believe that they have alternative ways of obtaining money and a good job, applications for party membership drop sharply. Beijing, with a population of more than 10 million, registered about 70,000 applications in 1986. The next year, with the market making big strides, the number nosedived to around 20,000 and remained there for the following two years. It was not until 1990 that the number revived to the level of 1986 (*Zhibu shenghuo* (Beijing), no. 7, 1991, p. 35). This was due largely to special efforts by the party to 'mobilise' applications, following the 4 June events. However, 1992 saw the number decline again.[6]

In addition to a general indifference towards joining the CCP, the party's own recruitment arrangements have contributed to the gradual exhaustion of applicants. Since 1978 the party has adopted an elitist approach to recruitment, that is it wants the level of education for the new intakes to be as high as possible. A central document stipulated that new candidates should generally have a high school certificate.[7] According to a survey in Jinan City, the new recruits increased the proportion of party members in management and technological fields to nearly 10 per cent of the total. In contrast, there have been fewer recruits in production line posts, the proportion being just over 2 per cent (Shandong Shengwei, 1990b, p. 12).

This approach has, however, posed a dilemma for the CCP leadership: to admit more intellectuals into the party at the expense of workers may have improved its general educational level. Yet it has also weakened party presence at the basic work units, as seen in the growing number of 'blank work sections' and the drying up of its reserves at the points where the majority of the workforce is concentrated. The Beijing Public Transportation Company recruited 31,000 workers between 1978 and 1984. The number of party members increased in the meantime by only seventy-five, resulting in a drop of the worker/party member ratio to 0.9 per cent. Some party branches have not recruited a single party member for nearly a decade (*Zhibu shenghuo* (Beijing), no. 12, 1990, p. 29). So a cycle has emerged: the fewer workers a party cell admits, the fewer party reserves it finds among workers, a major factor leading to the party's atrophy in the state sector.

This outcome has a lot to do with the tedious arrangements for party admittance. For instance, applicants should seek at least one party member as a regular contact. They should attend a number of 'party knowledge' lectures and participate in prescribed training programmes. They should be systematically assessed once every six months by the party branch committee. They should be involved in the party's assigned social work, some of which is unpleasant and unpaid. This test period, with these hard demands, lasts at least one full year. Towards the end of the test period, meetings will be held to solicit criticism of the applicant from the small party groups and the public. Some of these experiences can be very embarrassing.

The party cell then starts personal inspection procedures. The content of the investigation includes applicants' records in past political campaigns, their attitudes towards the party's line and policy, and the political performance of their close family members. Candidates then join for a concentrated study programme about the party which lasts a week. Besides studying party documents, they are also expected to make a full self-assessment and self-criticism, another embarrassing moment. When they are at last admitted, they face a year's period of probation. During this period party membership can be revoked if the applicant has done something wrong. These requirements are even stricter than had been the case in the 1970s. With an alternative path to better social status, e.g. setting up a private business, these requirements are too much for the majority of people to be bothered with, even if a party card is still regarded as favourable to upward mobility.

Ranking party officials have realised the danger the drying up of party reserves poses to party control over society. Qiang Wei, then Beijing's Youth League boss, warned the Municipal Party Committee:

> The fact that the party has lost its attraction to young people is indicative of how the party's authority and image are perceived by society at large. The rising numbers of 'blank work sections' where young workers are concentrated will certainly produce a lasting adverse effect on our work. Without party members, how can the party's line, policy and directives be relayed to the majority of workers?
>
> (*Zhibu shenghuo* (Beijing), no. 7, 1991, p. 7)

In spite of this recognition, it seems that the party is fighting a losing battle in this crucial area of influence.

THE ABORTED POST-4 JUNE CLAMPDOWN: A CASE STUDY

With party work on the shop floor becoming increasingly inactive amid a deepening crisis of the official ideology, it is clear that daily party controls have been defused for the majority of workers. If workers do not resort to dissident action against the state or engage in organised resistance to management, they can now live their lives with little interference from the party.[8] However, it is mistaken to believe that workers are satisfied with this limited liberalisation – diluted political intrusions and greater opportunities to earn money. Even if workers are little affected by changing politics at the national level, the persistent defects of the party/state *danwei* system, as embodied in the difficulties in obtaining job transfers, tensions from uneven allocations of social welfare benefits and mistreatment of workers by the privileged, are constant irritations. Their actions around and after 4 June 1989 served as proof of their discontent.

The challenge of workers to the party/state

Normally workers would not vent their frustrations with their immediate bosses in a confrontational way, owing to the complicated *guanxi* networks on shop floors. But feelings of anger do accumulate, often to be vented against some target outside the factory walls, such as the policies of central and local government. Workers might join in the euphoria of a local or nationwide protest movement, for instance.[9] This is why slogans against corruption and abuses are not abstract. They are the expression of many concrete stories of discontent. The 4 June tragedy revealed to the party leaders that their design for neo-authoritarianism was subject to how workers felt about their basic freedom. Workers are disgruntled with multi-functional controls of their work units, despite the progress in curbing the intensity of these controls.

As other authoritarian societies in transition have shown, social protest movements go hand in hand with a whole process of political change. China's neo-authoritarian path of change has triggered a dynamic process: if the regime allows a degree of social pluralism for the sake of economic take-off, it sows the seeds for autonomous social forces to emerge. Although these may not appear political at the beginning, they may, at the right time, easily prove to be political, taking the form of organised actions. However, the most difficult thing for social forces to ascertain is whether and when the time is ripe for action. The unwritten limits for protest permitted by political change have to be tested before workers can decide on the level of action they can initiate and get away with. For example, during the Beijing Spring in 1989, China's first autonomous trade union, Gongzilian, was being organised.[10]

It may not be mere coincidence that the first people to rise against the regime were from work units where the *danwei* controls had been dismantled furthest. One official summary of the lessons of 4 June describes these *danwei* as 'disaster zones'. Tight or loose organisational controls in various work units make a marked difference. At the risk of simplification, the university students and *getihu'*, or the self-employed, are good examples. Students are mobile and transient. After four years of study, they leave campuses and change their status. And they are few in number. Although these characteristics restrict their political capacity, the fact that they are not permanently tied to a work unit provides larger scope for action. Among other things, organised resistance of the self-employed to government officials has always existed, as in the form of opposition to taxation, but seldom has this had far-reaching political significance owing to its limited goals. In contrast, once workers are organised as in Solidarity, they may pose a serious challenge to the party/state. These facts explain why the state has been most fearful of an organised labour movement (Chan and Unger, 1991, p. 119).

As far as Gongzilian is concerned, its pioneers started to test the water in late April 1989 and were encouraged by the party's inaction in factories amid the new waves of popular support on behalf of the Tiananmen occupants. More workers joined the movement around mid-May 1989. They constituted the bulk of the human shield in Beijing streets that sought to block the enforcement of martial law. As a show of force, workers marched through the streets behind the vehicles and banners of their work units, clearly imprinting on people's minds an image of rebellion against the state by its basic units, once the front line of state control. It seemed inconceivable that without the consent of the heads of *danwei*, workers could stop work, obtain the banner of the *danwei* and take to the streets of Beijing in the name of their *danwei*. For example, Li Jingqun, a workshop party secretary of the Beijing Instrument Factory, initially bowed to pressure from his workers to go to the streets but he soon began to take an active part in the protest, writing the slogans 'Workers in support' and 'We workers are coming' (*Zhibu shenghuo* (Beijing), no. 5, 1990, p. 20). Perhaps it was this image of organised uprising that prompted people to 'feel' that with the cracks in the foundation of the party/state, the days of the CCP itself were numbered.

This political evolution poses a key question as to how much control the party/state can still exercise in the industrial workplace at any critical moment. One may compare this with the situation immediately after the Tiananmen incident of 1976. Once the popular protest was put down, government and factories quickly responded to the party's call to subdue any signs of defiance. In 1989, however, after 16 April when the Beijing Party Committee convened the first emergency meeting of factory party secretaries, repeated calls for party members not to participate in the *dongluan*, or social unrest, had been issued and continuously fell on deaf ears. Beijing's deputy party organisation chief openly admitted that many party members were taking a lead in joining the human blockade of the streets (Gao Qixiang, 1990, p. 16). Senior party leaders had tried to mobilise party members and activists to intimidate workers, but few seemed to be responsive. For workers, their work units appeared for a time to have lost political power over them.

Resistance to the post-4 June 'settlement'

The post-4 June clampdown in state-owned enterprises demonstrated that, while the organised resistance of workers could be suppressed, the trend towards depoliticisation and the logic it had generated could not. This not only hindered the party's efforts to reassert authority in state-owned enterprises but will continue to shake the foundation of its power.[11]

The history of socialist states shows that the party/state system has the capacity to muster enough strength, whether naked or otherwise, to restore control in a crisis situation. But this ability diminishes with each crisis. What has made China distinct from the Soviet bloc is its resilience in this regard. Different social and cultural traditions are certainly crucial factors which have a bearing on this outcome. However, the CCP's deep penetration into all work units has played a key role in maintaining the party's order at the grassroots where mass dictatorship could be more effective than the operations of the KGB and Stasi.

Yet like that of the USSR and Eastern Europe, China's political system is not immune to the destructive effects of political upheavals. The Cultural Revolution had been a most profound lesson to the party. While the Tiananmen episode clearly exposed a crisis in the party's organisational disorder in many work units, its subsequent failure to pursue an effective investigation (*qingcha*) drive further revealed the depth of this disorder.

The post-4 June 'settlement' comprised two stages. The first was an investigation period of a few weeks immediately after 4 June, the aim being to single out the activists of the 'social unrest' and arrest those who committed 'crimes'. The second was a party membership re-registration period in which organisational measures were taken to purge those involved in the movement. As stipulated by the party centre, both stages were to be conducted not as political campaigns but rather as activities of 'positive education' and both were to focus on the party internally, although selected political punishments were lodged against non-party activists.[12]

Generally speaking, the outcome of the two-stage 'settlement' fell far short of the party's expectation. Two major features are worth comment. First, obstruction of the 'transmission belt' between the party centre and its branches at various levels was evident. The lower that central decrees were relayed, the weaker the response from party cells. One factory party boss I interviewed in Beijing in 1991 gave a detailed description of how his branch had reacted to the investigation imposed on it:

According to the dictates from the Party Municipal Organisation Department, the key targets of the investigation drive were party members who'd taken to the streets. They were to write a report of self–evaluation of their motivation and attitudes during the period. The report should record how many times they'd participated in demonstrations, whether they'd obstructed the martial law troops and what they'd learned from the unrest. Then the party branch was to discuss the report, make its own assessment, and put on the report the seals of the branch and the personal one of the secretary. Then the reports from both the party branch and individuals involved were submitted to the factory party committee and later entered into their dossiers.

In contrast to the party's active involvement in political campaigns in the past, this time nobody in this branch was serious about the investigation. The party secretary disclosed that in his factory of more than 2,000 workers twenty-three cases had been established, although nearly half the workforce had participated in actions at one time or another. These twenty-three people were mainly party cadres and managerial staff who had taken the lead in going to the Square. The secretary assured me that he had never written anything serious against them. One of these twenty-three people was detained for attacking the martial law troops. Even in his case, the factory party committee wrote a report saying that he had no record of serious mistakes in the past. For the rest, the secretary confirmed that no report that might cause harm to their future was put in their dossier. He stated: 'We have shelved the material for now and will wait and see what happens later.'

When I asked what he would do if his superiors came to check on the work of the investigation, he replied with some laughter:

Of course if they are indeed serious, you have to do something, like picking out someone we cannot protect. However, it seems that this time most of my bosses adopted an approach of making the big thing smaller, and a small thing invisible. There have been many meetings but so far no real punishments in our factory. After many political movements we know that anyone criminalised at the height of the campaigns will get a severe punishment. But after a while, the wind will die down. In the meantime the penalty will become ever milder for the accused. To save those who might end up in trouble, we just drag things on and on.

My impression from other interviews on the subject has convinced me that this attitude was widespread, although this party secretary was the most explicit. This kind of approach was not confined to state-owned enterprises but was to be found in other state institutions as well. For example, one of the divisional heads in the Beijing government led her subordinates to the Square to support the students. In late 1990, when she was selected to join a delegation for a foreign visit, this caused some controversy. Her bureau director approved her participation, explaining that in 1989 people became confused and he believed that most of the activists were patriotically motivated.[13] Official news coverage also gave many accounts of the sloppiness of the investigation. When I asked party cadres whether there were cases of persecution in their work unit, the answer was always no, though they told me that they had often *heard* that somebody in some other work unit had been arrested. Usually the arrests were made by the police authorities. There may have been some lists of dissidents held by the state security department, they commented, but their factories adopted protective attitudes towards staff who had thrown stones at the approaching tanks.[14]

Have the party cadres become more benevolent since 4 June? The answer may be both yes and no. What happened in Beijing's streets and across the country in May and early June 1989 aroused a sense of panic in them. When they realised that it was not entirely impossible that the CCP would fall like the Berlin Wall, they began to worry about their own futures. Too bitter a tension between them and the workers might be fatal if next time the tanks did not appear in Changan Street. Tensions between leaders and the led were an everyday occurrence, one worker told me, 'but the cadres would not capitalise on this kind of political event. Moreover, many of the party cadres and managers sided with the students.'

Although it is difficult to present a sweeping conclusion from my encounters with party cadres and workers, it seems safe to state that while party branches still take orders from their superior agencies to further various campaigns, they have become increasingly passive in implementing them. The largely aborted investigation campaign in state-owned enterprises serves as just another indication of the party's withering at its foundation. As the intensity of supervision becomes progressively weaker at each lower link in the chain of control radiating from Beijing, the industrial party cadres gradually lose their own initiative. Millions of activists of the 1989 protest movements have thus escaped the clampdown. While this has saved the party from coming into fierce confrontation with the population, it has sown the seeds for another round of protest in the future. Fault lines have been created along the cracks in the party's 'transmission belt', with far-reaching impact for the future of state control.

The second feature of the failed clampdown in state firms was the reluctance of ordinary party members to answer the calls from the party centre. Even before the 1989 protest movement, many of them had become disillusioned with the deterioration of the party work style and with official corruption (Lu Jianhua, 1990, p. 10). Worsening inflation lowered their standards of living. Anger was pent up. Their non-cooperation in the investigation was thus well anticipated, rendering the party's attempts to tighten control anything but effective. During my fieldwork in 1991, one of the interviewees explained:

> Since the early 1980s, we've received an increasingly less favourable response among workers. So party branches changed their recruitment strategy. In the Cultural Revolution they took in the ideologically faithful. Now they try to lure those who have good skills in work. These people are respected, as they are usually hard-working. And they are also influential because most of their co-workers want to learn skills from them. Prior to 4 June when the party branches pressed them to join the party, they would say 'why not?' But at the crucial moment of late May and early June their position was clearly pro-students.

Many of them had an apolitical mentality: 'I'm not relying on the snobbery of cadres for a meal ticket.' Supporting the students in Tiananmen was seen as a natural act springing from conscience as were the non-cooperative attitudes towards the investigation afterwards. For the first time since 1949, during and immediately after 4 June there were public announcements by party members that they were renouncing their membership.[15] During the party re-registration period still more party members decided not to renew their membership (Shi Jian, 1990, p. 18). This prompted the party leadership to issue an instruction that party members were allowed not to register, and that this was regarded as an ideological mistake but not a political one. Because of the scale of non-registration, the party also tried to assure people that if they did not want to remain in the party they could still do a good job as ordinary citizens (Shi Jian, 1990, p. 18). The gradually changing allegiance of many party members, including those who have not given up their party membership for fear of being blacklisted, did much contribute to the malfunctioning of the 'transmission belt', analysed earlier (p. 105). This explains why the party centre targeted members as the priority of the investigation. However, if party cells could not mobilise any significant following, the investigation was doomed to failure.

In conjunction with internal disorder among rank-and-file party members, the passive resistance of the majority of workers sent strong signals to the authorities that any type of political persecution would result in a backlash against them. The following forms of boycott against the investigation reflected this spirit.

Against pressures to inform on co-workers

During the investigation workers were encouraged to report secretly to the party what their co-workers had done on the Beijing streets. However, according to my informants, few came forward. As one worker commented:

The Cultural Revolution has passed ages ago. This small-report thing sounds so odd now. In my workshop, where different clusters of patron —clients exist, passing gossip around is one thing that everyone does. But reporting on such an explosive matter is quite another. Nobody would want to send his co-workers to jail just because they have some rifts in daily encounters. In addition, the fact that one has sent in information of this kind cannot be concealed for ever. In a hostile climate against such behaviour, one shies away, even if one had the intention.

Another reason for the failure of the tactic of using co-workers against each other was that there was general consensus that the shooting had been wrong. This view transcended the differences of factional affiliations in shopfloor politics. Moreover, since many workers ignored the party's call to stay at home at one stage or another between April and June, an unwritten rule was established among workers that, since everyone was involved, informing on one 'comrade' meant informing on all.[16] This was a kind of collective resistance never experienced before in China's state-owned enterprises. During my fieldwork trip across the country in 1991 the majority of workers and managers gave me unanimous accounts of how investigations in their unit failed to achieve 'real results'.

Boycott of the study sessions

Study of the central documents and the speeches of top leaders has always been an integral part of any political campaign in China. Without such a study programme a campaign falters at the very beginning. The 1989 investigation failed precisely because workers refused to accept the official verdict on what had happened in 1989. This was reflected by their attitudes towards the political study sessions during the 'settlement'. And very often their boycott was matched by the sympathy of the workshop leaders. According to my informants, most of their factories did not make very much effort with the study sessions. The managers excused themselves by saying that with the quota and production responsibility system in place, no worker wanted to spend working hours reading and hearing propaganda. It would affect their income which was linked to the amount of work they did. One shop manager, who was concurrently party secretary, said that nowadays it was impossible to arrange an after-hours meeting. Workers simply did not come. He told me that during the entire period of the investigation, which lasted for about one month in his factory, he was able to organise only one all-staff meeting where Deng's 9 June speech was read. Even that had to be counted as paid after-hours work. Although more meetings were conducted for party members, he continued, none of these changed their position on the nature of the 4 June event.

Some interviewees said that the meetings in large firms were better attended, because of the more sophisticated control/discipline systems there. However, they all claimed that nobody really took the meetings seriously. Very often, as I mentioned earlier (p. 94), these study sessions instead provided a good venue for people to express their anger against the leaders. The meetings were simply counter-productive.

Part III

De-statisation: an analysis of the wage structure

6 The dynamics of the industrial wage reform

In the three decades between 1955 and 1985 China's industrial wage system was the eight-grade regime. This was a highly centralised system, tightly controlled both economically and politically. Economically, this system constituted an essential part of the state's labour and wage policies. First of all, an aggregate national wage bill was worked out by central planners on the basis of the state's financial situation. Then this wage bill was used to determine a national employment quota specifying how many new workers to recruit. A central decision, taken each year, was also embodied in the bill as to whether and when wages were to be increased and by how much, and how many workers were to be promoted. The unified eight-grade wage system was crucial for the overall mandatory economic planning process.

The unified reward system was also used to extract political compliance from salary earners. Under a set of political standards, pro-party activists were rewarded while 'backward elements' were discriminated against. In this way material incentives and ideological attitudes (*biaoxian*) were linked together. These two features were among the most important traits of the industrial *danwei* system: work units were bound by top-down unified wage control. This control was very effective, as it was exercised over workers' means of livelihood. The post-Mao wage reforms have put an end to this eight-grade system and relieved most workers from the direct grip of the party. The autonomy of state-owned enterprises in deciding their wage policies has widened the distance between the party/state and its basic units.[1]

DISMANTLING THE UNIFIED WAGE SYSTEM

Wage reform has been a key component in China's overall industrial reform. Soon after Mao's death the Chinese leadership introduced a series of national wage increases to compensate workers who had been subject to a wage freeze since 1972 (Peter Lee, 1987, pp. 192–202). The bonus system and piece-rate earnings were restored in 1978 and factories could introduce their own bonus grades. In the following year state-owned enterprises were allowed to create an incentive fund from their retained profits which was intended to grant managers some leeway for promoting up to 20 per cent of workers. This limited authority ushered in an new era of state/enterprise conflict. The 20 per cent restriction also generated fierce competition among workers (Han and Motohiro, 1992, p. 245). Facing enormous pressures, management tried hard to circumvent state controls. Bonus payments were used as a means to bypass the restriction, as they could be given to compensate those who had not been promoted. The sudden surge in bonuses outside the eight-grade system resulted in wage expenditure overtaking increases in productivity and profitability (Walder, 1987, p. 22). This soon forced the state to impose an unpopular ceiling on bonuses in all state firms. In fact, the subsequent conflict over this ceiling between the state and state-owned enterprises was the stimulus for the new round of industrial wage reform in the 1980s.

The bonus reform 1984–5

As soon as the focus of reform shifted from rural to urban areas in 1984, the State Council chose the removal of the ceiling on bonuses as the breakthrough point for industrial wage reform (Xu Songtao *et al.*, 1988, p. 105). In May 1984 it promulgated the Circular on the Issues of Bonuses in State-Owned Enterprises, marking the first step towards changing direct state control over the remuneration system to indirect control. The circular stipulated: (1) with the ceiling for bonuses removed, state-owned enterprises could increase or decrease the overall amount of their bonus funds according to whether they had fulfilled state plans; (2) using these funds, factories could decide their own forms of bonus distribution; (3) the bonus funds would be largely raised from retained profits. The state agencies together with their subordinate firms would work out the different proportions of retained profits to be used for reinvestment, social welfare and bonus funds (Ye Guangzhao, 1989, p. 31).

In addition to the issue of bonuses, another key measure was introduced: within certain limits enterprise management could, for the first time, increase or decrease the basic salaries of workers. This was a major departure from the previous wage system. If a factory manager decided to promote up to 20 per cent of workers in any given year, it was no longer necessary for him/her to wait for the state to order a national wage-grade promotion, although he/she still had to report the decision to his/her administrative superior and the Labour Bureau in the region.[2] This was an important prelude to the reform in 1986 that overhauled the eight-grade wage system.

The crux of this new round of wage reform was the removal of the state-imposed ceiling on bonuses – hitherto a small though significant part of a worker's income – which opened the flood-gates of the closed system. From then on at least part of workers' remuneration would be freed from the mandatory state plans and become subject to a number of flexible factors, e.g. the financial situation of their factories. As managers increased their say on wage matters, the first crack appeared in the 'big rice bowl' for workers.

The efforts to open up the closed wage system were important in both theory and practice. All industrial wage reforms before 1984 fell into the category of salary additions and subtractions within a state-imposed limit and did not go beyond micro adjustments. And the adjustments were determined as much by the financial situation of the treasury as by the centre's perception of political need. As a result, remuneration had become completely detached from a firm's performance. Allowing bonuses – a significant part of their income – to rise or fall reduced workers' total dependence on the state for wage increases, for any increase was now also influenced by the level of the factory's profit retention. Moreover, profit was determined steadily less by the state and local government, and more by a factory's own market performance.[3] As the wage bills of individual factories tended to fluctuate, the state wage plans began to lose their force.

At the same time as the ceiling on bonuses was removed, the state imposed a new bonus tax on factories in May 1984 in order to regulate bonus awards. The main purpose of the tax was to create a mechanism of indirect control. The tax on bonuses reflected the recognition that the tightly controlled remuneration system had become incompatible with the operation of the dual-track economic system. For instance, a large number of state-owned enterprises had been experimenting with various decentralisation reforms since the late 1970s. The implication was that factories could sell approximately 20 per cent of their products in the market and retain the profits thus generated. A proportion of these profits could be distributed as bonuses to workers. As profit was variable, so, too, should the bonus fund fluctuate; a ceiling on bonuses was clearly inconsistent with the initiative and had made the profit retention reform hard to sustain. Not only did the ceiling suppress incentives for workers, it also discouraged state-owned enterprises from increasing production. Li Ruihuan, then mayor of Tianjing, proposed in late 1983 that there should be no ceiling on bonus payments as long as they were linked to tax payment and profit remittance (Takahara, 1992, p. 139). Clearly the general market-oriented reforms would be hampered without a corresponding decentralisation of decisions on wages (Jackson, 1990, p. 2).

The gap between the fixed bonus and increased profit retention generated huge pressure on factory managers to abolish bonus limits. The result was that the growth of bonus payments went out of control in many factories (Tigaisuo, 1986, p. 24). Consequently, there emerged a visible discrepancy between the planned mandatory national wage bills and the amount of bonus granted from the retained profits, because the bonus constantly exceeded the limits set by the state. Between 1980 and

1984, in order to make the aggregate bonus actually issued match the figure prescribed in the plan, the SPC hurriedly had to readjust the wage budget in its wage plans at the end of every year (Xu Songtao *et al.*, 1988, p. 107).

The creation of the bonus tax was meant to address these new problems arising from the market reforms. While the state's mandatory plan controlled standard wages, the new progressive bonus tax was supposed to bring the payment of bonuses into line with the centre's macro regulation. At the same time, state-owned enterprises were still allowed some space to increase bonuses if they struck a balance between production and wage plans. The rationale behind this design was that state-owned enterprises should be subject to objective constraints in issuing bonuses. For instance, because the increase in bonuses could not be readily transferred into production costs, large bonus awards would definitely cause losses: this put pressure on factories to balance their immediate enthusiasm for more bonuses against their long-term concern for the development of the factory, since excessive bonus payments could not be sustained under the progressive bonus tax regime.[4]

However, in reality the system did not work as well as the designers of the tax hoped. In the last quarter of 1984 the growth rate of bonuses was 117 per cent more than in 1983; this meant an annual growth in workers' personal income of about 20 per cent, the highest since the founding of the PRC (Xue Muqiao, 1988, pp. 3–5). This sharp increase in bonus payments significantly raised the proportion of bonus income in the overall wage structure of workers. According to an official survey in Hunan in 1985, bonus payments constituted more than 30 per cent of total wages in all industrial sectors. In some state-owned enterprises which yielded more profits, they exceeded 40 per cent. Given the recent introduction of the reform, this result was staggering (Tigaisuo, 1988, p. 139). It marked the beginning of an important problem in China's post-Mao wage reforms: the continuous shrinking of normal wages. This will be discussed in detail in later sections.

The introduction of the 'linkage system' in 1986[5]

By 1986 the wage reform had created a two-tiered structure in worker salaries: the fixed part, composed of standard wages, still based on the eight-grade wage scheme and later called the 'base wage' (*dangan gongzi*); and the decontrolled portion, the bulk of which was made up of bonuses. From the policy-making perspective, the emergence of these two components was a conscious reform choice. In 1984 Premier Zhao Ziyang stated clearly that the enterprise wage reform was meant to free state-owned enterprises from the fetters of the eight-grade wage system. Thanks to his insistence, the proposals of central planners, particularly the Ministry of Labour and Personnel, to consolidate the unified wage standards were largely ignored (Takahara, 1992, pp. 158–9). More thorough wage reforms in the state sector were thus made possible.

This 'half fixed and half open' arrangement was a partial reform that soon ran into difficulties. The state's preference was that the fixed portion should be the larger, operating under effective macro wage controls. In practice, state-owned enterprises enlarged the decontrolled part by using various 'local policies', forcing the state to find ways to control what it regarded as 'unprincipled industrial wage increases'. Towards the end of 1986 a new industrial wage reform was enacted to rectify the flaws. This was called the linkage package: it linked a factory's wage bill to economic efficiency (Peng Maoan, 1991, pp. 3–5). By the beginning of 1989, 70 per cent of all China's state-owned enterprises had implemented the new reform, affecting 80 per cent of the industrial workforce (*Zhongguo gongye jingji yanjiu*, no. 3, 1991, pp. 49–54). A number of provinces, such as Fujian and Heilongjiang, also signed an all-region linkage contract with the central government. In the 1990s the linkage package has become the mainstream wage mechanism for the state sector (Ruan Chongwu, 1992, p. 5).

The linkage wage system, which is still in place in a large number of state-owned enterprises, is a complicated one. It has three key components: the floating wages, the economic efficiency target, and the ratio determining the level of floating wages based on the fulfilment of the target. According to state regulations, the floating wages of a factory fluctuate in accordance with the current year's economic results, as measured by the factory's wage bill of the previous year. They include workers' standard wages and bonuses. Therefore, the aggregate wage of a factory now consists of two parts: the annual wage bill (*gongzi jishu*) usually approved by the government, and the floating part determined yearly by the factory's production situation.[6]

The increased part of a factory's yearly wage bill can be shown in the formula:

$$A = B \times \frac{D}{C} \times E$$

In this formula, A represents the increase in the wage bill to be awarded to workers; B, the wage bill base (ascertained normally from that of the previous year); C, the targeted gross value of sales; D, the actual increase of the gross value of sales; and E, the floating ratio (Su Hainan, 1990, p. 51).

To ascertain the economic efficiency target of a given factory is a difficult task, since the ideal target for linkage – the net sales value – is not always relevant in a semi-command/semi-market economy. However, the whole design of the reform was based on the concept of the net sales value, an indication that the wage determinants were shifting from central planning towards market deregulation. Under such a gauge, the cost of labour and raw materials begins to affect the factory's profit account.

In reality, however, China does not have an accurate statistical system making it possible to calculate the net sales value of a given factory.[7] Moreover, planned allocations of production materials and the 'policy losses' of factories allowed by the state often make the concept inapplicable for many large and medium-sized state-owned enterprises.[8] So the net sales value has not been commonly used as the linkage target. At present different industries adopt different linkage targets to ascertain the floating wage bill (A), including remittances on profit, the gross volume of production, the amount of foreign currency created and so on. Other supplementary targets are imposed by the state to ensure that producers fulfil its requirements, such as the targets of quality and energy saving. Remittances on profit serve as the main linkage target for most of the factories implementing the reform. All the linkage targets mentioned above are components of the net sales value. The formula which is actually practised and which determines the floating wage bill is:

$$A = B \times \frac{D}{C_n} \times E$$

In fact, those unregulated variables under C represent the source of the problems with the wage reform, to be discussed later.

The linkage system represents a tangible departure from the practice whereby state-owned enterprises 'eat from the state's big rice bowl'. One important indication of this is that owing to the reform, industrial workers' wages have been uncoupled from the state's nationally unified wage pool, which before the reform embraced the state administrative wage system, the non-governmental institutional wage system (*shiye danwei gongzi*) and the industrial wage system. Any national wage increase under the former system had to affect all three elements at the same time; increases were difficult owing to the pressure of the sheer number of people in the three systems on the financial situation. The linkage reform separated industrial wage increases from those in the other two sectors and mitigated the control of the central financial departments. Moreover, the reform has effectively erased the regional wage differentials, as these only affect the base wage, whose regional variations have become ever more negligible in terms of overall workers' income.

The linkage of wages to economic efficiency constitutes a linkage between state-owned enterprises and the market. This was and continues to be a key change, in that market earnings have made not only management but also workers aware of the 'invisible hand'. The linkage reform has also increased autonomy of producers as regards the state in deciding workers' income, representing an advance on the bonus reform. While the latter only granted power to factory managers to set bonus scales, the former has granted them a large measure of autonomy in setting fixed wages as well. In fact, the introduction of the linkage system accelerated the phasing out of the eight-grade wage system after 1986. This certainly does not mean that the state no longer holds any control over industrial wages as there also exist other direct and indirect control mechanisms. There is no doubt that the rigidity inherent in the pre-reform state industrial wage system is gradually diminishing with the evolution of the linkage reform.

The wage guidance line: the future model

The linkage reform has generated conflict between the state and state-owned enterprises. State control of aggregate wages contradicts the principle that producers formulate their wage policy according to their market performance. The state cares more about the remittances it receives than anything else, constantly requiring state-owned enterprises to lower labour costs. As a result, workers' normal wages are made disproportionately low compared to other components of their income structure. State-owned enterprises on the other hand are driven by the desire to maximise pay for workers and staff, often regardless of productivity. So they create various channels for increasing earnings, circumventing state control over the wage aggregate. By the early 1990s, the state realised that control through crude administrative means, even though more indirect than before, would no longer achieve the desired goal of macro wage balance. At the micro level, bureaucratic controls over the wage aggregate were basically ineffective (Guan Yonghui *et al.*, 1994, p. 29). This prompted state labour officials to seek new regulation methods more in line with market determinants. Gradually, a new distribution model for the state sector emerged at the beginning of the 1990s and became official policy in 1995/6. This model, claimed as China's future industrial wage mechanism, is called *gongzi zhidaoxian*, or the state wage guidance line.

This wage guidance line was borrowed from advanced market economies where it constitutes a macro-economic lever, serving to provide information, recommendations and limits for formulating industrial wage policies. The line for China's state-owned enterprises takes the form of either non-specific principles or a prescribed range of wage increases. It stipulates both minimum and maximum wage levels for work units in the light of the national economic situation. Under this guidance state firms formulate their own wage grades and non-state factories decide their wages through collective bargaining. This reform constitutes further progress towards the marketisation of China's state sector, because it is conditional on further decentralisation of wage decision power to the micro level (Xu Yanjun, 1995, p. 27).

According to Deputy Labour Minister Zhu Jiazhen, the wage guidance line is determined by two 'belows'; that is, the increase of the wage aggregate of a given firm should be kept below the increase of its profitability (based on tax remittance/profit retention ratio), and the real and average income of workers should be kept below the growth rate of their productivity (based on the increase of the net output value) (Zhu Jiazhen, 1995, p. 13). These two 'belows' are important in that they are closely connected with other factors such as labour costs, the employment situation, the availability of foreign investment, fair distribution and competitiveness. Under these conditions, state-owned enterprises can, in other words, further enlarge their autonomy in deciding wage matters.

In 1993 the Ministry of Labour, the SETC and the SCRES jointly promulgated a provisional regulation that allowed a number of state-owned enterprises to experiment with the wage guidance plan. As long as they observed the two 'belows' principle, they could formulate their own wage aggregate and the floating linkage ratio. Certainly they would have to report their wage plans to the labour department of the local government. To a large extent these reports became more or less a formality and were basically for the purpose of state statistics (Du Mingkun, 1994, p. 9).

The wage guidance line represents further progress towards making state-owned enterprises independent bodies of remuneration and is an evolutionary result of the linkage reform. It was designed to address the problems inherent in the linkage wage system characterised by limited elasticity and overt administrative intervention. The state oversaw the wage aggregate of a region. This was supposed to give a degree of elasticity to producers. However, constant administrative intervention by local bureaucrats limited factories' freedom of action. This led to intensified irregular bargaining over the floating ratio and profit retention between state-owned enterprises and the government. Moreover, the linkage reform may be useful for controlling wage aggregate but it is not useful for promoting the labour market.

The rationale behind introducing the wage guidance line reform is that the two indicators – enterprise efficiency and productivity – may provide hard assessment criteria that leave less room for irregular bargaining. The guidance line is thought to be conducive to increased productivity and net output value, while granting additional autonomy to factory management. And it stresses the role played by the market in the formulation of wage policies by individual producers (Zhang Rongde, 1994, p. 20).

For those factories participating in the experiment, the state has abolished the practice of annual assessment which is an essential part of the linkage reform. Instead, a scheme of periodic assessment is used. Normally each period lasts three to five years. At the beginning of the first year, each state firm submits to the local labour agency its forecast wage plan based on the previous year's record of efficiency and productivity. Then the local labour agency submits its own plan for the locality to the provincial government which subsequently reports its plan to the State Council. After assessing the average growth or decrease of the two criteria in each region, the centre approves the aggregate wage guidance plan. Then provincial and local governments work out similar plans for producers under their jurisdiction. State-owned enterprises make their wage plan for the rest of the period in line with what they achieved the previous year, without going through another round of bureaucratic assessment until the end of the specified period. This has not only greatly reduced the amount of red tape associated with the linkage system but has granted producers the authority they need over wages (Zhang Rongde, 1994, p. 20).

According to Du Mingkun, director of the Hebei Provincial Labour Bureau, the key to understanding these plans is their flexibility. By their very name they are guidance lines, not mandatory decrees. Therefore the state labour agencies cannot enforce these lines as strictly as they can enterprises' aggregate wage bills and the floating ratio (Du Mingkun, 1994, p. 9). Moreover, flexibility is also embodied in the following principles: (1) each region and each industrial sector enjoys wide latitude in formulating its own guidance lines according to its own reality; (2) the central government must use macro-economic levers, e.g. income tax, to ensure a balanced growth of wages; (3) the guidance line must be promulgated by government at various levels and have due authority to serve as the criterion for the settlement of wage disputes (Xu Yanjun, 1995, p. 29).

The guidance line reform is an important attempt to institutionalise indirect state control over industrial wages. It will move China's industrial wage system closer to international practice. It has been decided that government at provincial and municipal levels should work out sectoral wage guidance lines as reference standards for the industrial concerns in their locality, although labour officials are still discussing whether it is possible to formulate national wage guidance lines for each industrial sector (Guan Yonghui *et al.*, 1994, p. 29). Chengdu City was one of the first regions to experiment with this reform. In 1996 the municipal labour bureau announced its first wage guidance line, which fluctuated around 5,886 *yuan*, the city's 1995 average annual industrial wage. It was suggested that profitable factories might set 17 per cent as the base line for wage increases. A growth rate of 22 per cent was set as the upper limit for firms capable of awarding more money owing to their greater efficiency. In contrast, loss-making firms would have to satisfy themselves with a zero-growth line.

Beijing municipal government has also announced that by the year 2000 it will create a new industrial wage system based on this model of guidance. To facilitate the changes, Beijing has promulgated a comprehensive wage reform scheme which highlights the following three components:

• from 1996 the government will regularly announce the average labour cost of the city's major industrial sectors and foreign concerns in order to provide reference points for individual producers to formulate their employment policies;

• for the majority of workers the government has decided to phase out gradually the linkage wage policy and establish a new wage mechanism based on collective bargaining;

• for the majority of managers, the government will introduce a new annual wage package which will remove their wages from the bureaucratic wage pool and disconnect their income from that of workers (*China Business Times*, 26 July 1996).

Deputy Labour Minister Zhu Jiazhen has prescribed the scope for the experiment. The reform will first be introduced in those enterprises whose shares are listed in the two stock markets of Shanghai and Shenzhen, and which have been approved by the government as pioneer enterprise groups to be converted into 'modern corporations'. Pioneer enterprise groups now constitute a large proportion of China's large and medium-sized enterprises. The number of enterprises being turned into modern corporations alone has exceeded 1,000 (100 at the national level and the rest at the local level). The impact will be far-reaching (Zhu Jiazhen, 1994, p. 8).

BARGAINING BETWEEN THE STATE AND STATE-OWNED ENTERPRISES

The series of institutional changes in China's enterprise wage system in the 1980s and 1990s gave rise to new patterns of interaction between them and the state, which can be characterised as intensified bargaining.

All the reforms so far in place have entailed a large measure of expediency. Both the bonus reform and the linkage reform were designed to guarantee the state at least a minimum amount of revenue. State-owned enterprises practising the linkage reform became liable to pay a new state regulatory tax in 1985. According to a central circular, if the increase in floating wages (calculated from the wage aggregate of the previous year) was below 7 per cent, factories were to be exempt from paying tax. If the rate of increase lay between 7 per cent and 12 per cent, a 30 per cent tax would be levied; and between 12 and 20 per cent, a rate of 100 per cent would be imposed. Any increase above 20 per cent was taxable by 300 per cent.[9]

It is easy to understand the state's concern over the control of industrial wages. Thanks to decentralisation, the proportion of state revenue as a share in the national income has progressively dropped to its lowest point since 1949. The reduction in the state's financial strength was manifested in a drop in state revenue as a proportion of GNP from 31 per cent in 1979 to 16 per cent in 1995 (Jiang Liu *et al.*, 1996, p. 19). The central government found it increasingly difficult to muster enough revenue to proceed with its major capital projects, particularly in the transport and power sectors. The combination of increased profit retention, enlarged wage pool and slow growth in productivity of state-owned enterprises created a vast drainage process, taking a great deal of the income that would previously have been available to the state treasury. In the Seventh Five-Year Plan period, the ratio between the growth of the industrial wage bill and the growth of profit turnover and tax remittance had reached 5.23:1 (Ding Xianjiu and Yong Weiguo, 1992, p. 9).

The state was thus confronted with a dilemma. It needed more revenue from state-owned enterprises, which was possible only if it relaxed rigid controls. Yet allowing state-owned enterprises to decide on wage policies would in turn threaten state revenue and macro-economic stability. So the state attached three preconditions to the linkage reform.

1 It was to have the final say in setting the enterprise wage bill. This was an important measure, as any increased factory earnings (the floating wages) grew from this basis.
2 For most state-owned enterprises, the target variables would include a compulsory minimum amount of taxation on profits set by the state.[10] This meant that producers had to increase production to a certain point to generate enough profits to ensure that their income would also increase.
3 The state would adjust the wage bill and linkage ratio annually through administrative decrees (Liu Quintang *et al.*, 1989, p. 69).

However, the desired results were not easily achieved in reality. It has become impossible for the state and state-owned enterprises to work out together solid long-term ratios for the linkage. These variables have thus proved to be catalysts for bargaining. As a result, the state and state-owned enterprises have become bogged down in a struggle for control of wages.

Bargaining over the wage aggregate

The wage aggregate is the primary target for bargaining. As mentioned earlier (p. 114), this aggregate comprises two parts: a largely fixed 'base wage' and a floating wage composed of 'efficiency income'[11] and other wage forms such as new piece-rate awards, overtime pay and national and regional per capita living subsidies. To a large extent the ever-changing variable of 'efficiency' has made the wage aggregate anything but predictable.

The floating part of the wage aggregate thus provides opportunities for producers to bargain with the state. Official guidance is as follows: if a factory's efficiency income increases by up to 15 per cent *vis-à-vis* the base figure of the wage bill (the previous year's), all the increased income can be awarded to workers; between 15 and 25 per cent, 60 per cent can be awarded; 35–45 per cent. 20 per cent; and over 45 per cent, no more than 10 per cent can be awarded (Su Hainan, 1990, p. 25). Obviously, the base figure of the wage bill is a key determinant of the amount that can go to workers. State-owned enterprises choose carefully what items to include in the base figure of the wage aggregate and negotiate with the government for a preferred settlement. Usually the bigger the base of the wage aggregate that enterprises submit to the state for approval, the bigger the floating income they may secure later in the year. Because the assessment is done chronologically on a case-by-case basis with little horizontal comparison within an industry, factories deliberately manipulate their previous year's wage indicators so as to have more room for wage increases in the years to come.

Factory managers have a number of techniques at their disposal in this regard. For instance, the state stipulates that state-owned enterprises should delete from the wage bill items such as per capita living subsidies. Items like energy-saving and material-saving funds, although indicators of economic efficiency, are awarded by the state through a separate bonus fund and, therefore, should also be omitted from the wage aggregate. However, there are many loopholes in the definition of these funds, and it is common for managers to include them in the overall wage bill. Another technique is to incorporate into the bill payment to workers hired independently by state-owned enterprises on a temporary basis (usually people from the rural areas). Such payments should not be listed in the wage aggregate, according to state regulations, but most factories do list them in order to inflate the base for the wage bill. When the temporary workers go, the already enlarged floating income does not shrink but will benefit the permanent workforce. Other items such as labour protection subsidies or danger money should also be excluded but often are not. Generally speaking, false claims may make up as much as 10–30 per cent of the wage bill that state-owned enterprises present to the state for approval (Wang Kezhong, 1991, p. 9).

The bonus fund is a major source of manipulation. It should be counted as the key component in the floating part of the wage aggregate. As each enterprise has its own bonus practices, however, it is not possible for the state to standardise them, so it is generally left up to producers to declare what they have delivered to workers as bonuses. There are many loopholes here. For instance, the state stipulates that the proportion of bonuses that have been paid as state bonus tax (the part exceeding four and a half months' base wages) should be excluded from the wage aggregate when factories go through the first assessment after entering the linkage reform. A labour department official in Beijing told me in 1992 that infringements were widespread among state firms, which either delete only part of it or ignore the regulation altogether.

Bargaining over compulsory remittances

Although the remittance of profits to the state is compulsory, there is no regularised assessment procedure for determining its level. So working this out has become an important part of the negotiation process between the state and state-owned enterprises. Since the rate of remittance is crucial to both sides, it is one of the most contested items in the wage arrangement. The linkage reform is premised on an indirect incentive mechanism rather than on direct intervention. But the remittance requirement does not impose effective constraints on the behaviour of either side (Sicular, 1995, p. 27). For state-owned enterprises, a lower remittance to the state means more profit retention, which means the possibility of more bonuses and more social welfare benefits such as larger housing funds. The current state regulation allows about 25–30 per cent of retained profits to be listed as a factory's social welfare fund.

In striving for smaller levies, state-owned enterprises have a number of advantages in their negotiations with the state. First, the linkage reform was launched at a time when the national economy was undergoing drastic changes. The external economic environment posed risks to factories practising the reforms. Among the risks, the most acute was posed by the distorted dual-track price structure, which unevenly affected the profit earnings of different industries. For instance, the price rises of primary materials meant that a manufacturing firm's production and sales might both increase, but cash returns decrease. The firms then put pressure on their bureaucratic agencies to reduce their original demands. Consequently, reduction in the rate of remittance to the state becomes a major form of preferential treatment used to induce state-owned enterprises to join the linkage reform (SPC, 1991, pp. 49–54). For instance, the three-year retrenchment between 1988 and 1991 significantly reduced the profitability of a large number of state-owned enterprises, and this provided a good excuse for factories to bargain with their administrative superiors for reduced remittance.

Another bargaining chip available to factories has been the impact of inflation on workers. In the late 1980s and mid-1990s, China's inflation spiralled upwards. At the same time, the state could not afford subsidies to compensate workers for its effects. For their employees to keep up with the rising cost of living, enterprises had to assume a role as additional providers. In fact, this became an important aspect of their newly acquired remunerative power. Under these circumstances, managers manoeuvred to hold up remittances to the state and redistributed even more income to workers from profit retention. For its part, the state was forced to make concessions constantly, in order to 'stabilise workers' morale and production'. The linkage reform has not lessened state-owned enterprises' keenness for subsidies. As a result, the original object of guaranteeing a minimum remittance to the state by producers is often compromised.

Apart from the external factors, any internal problems such as a change in a product, the installation of a new production line, or plans for new housing projects can be used by state-owned enterprises to negotiate with the state for a reduced rate of remittance. And the factories which can make the most noise or have the best *guanxi* (connections) with the bureaucratic authorities may get the best deal. Even when factories fail to achieve what they want in the bargaining process, they may adopt numerous measures to cheat the state and submit less in taxes. One popular measure is to launch many technical innovation projects with loans from banks. Before 1988, when most factories entered the contract responsibility system, they had to pay the loans back to the banks before handing over tax remittances. After 1988 the state stipulated that state-owned enterprises must submit taxes first and then repay loans from their retained profits. However, according to director of the Research Institute of SCRES, Liu Shuren, a great number of large and medium-sized factories cannot afford this policy change. The state then has to choose between either allowing them to stick to the old policy or seeing no technical innovation in these 'backbone' factories. Consequently, the traditional principle of eclecticism (*zhongyong zhidao*) has to be used: some factories are permitted to operate under the old rules and some are not, and some are allowed to stick to the old rules one year but not the next (*Gongjing neican*, no. 27, 1992, p. 12). This confusion is exploited by factories, which not only try to reduce the tax remittance, but secretly distribute the bank loans for technical innovation among workers as bonuses.[12]

Bargaining over the linkage ratio

Control over linkage ratios is another means by which the state tries to subdue state-owned enterprises' enthusiasm for higher floating wages. When the linkage reform was first introduced, the state imposed a range of ratios of 1:0.3 to 1:0.7 to different factories: for every 1 per cent growth in economic efficiency, often measured by growth of turnover, state-owned enterprises may raise their floating wages by at most 0.7 per cent. This range of ratios was quite arbitrarily set since there was no reliable theoretical explanation for it. Nevertheless, control over the linkage ratio served two purposes in macro-economic management. First, the state tried to make the growth rate of the aggregate wage lower than that of productivity. The range 1:0.3 to 1:0.7 certainly gives the state an advantage over state-owned enterprises. Through the ratio the state could plan for the increase in the national wage aggregate because the capacity for a meaningful growth of economic efficiency is quite limited for large and medium-scale factories. As one of the designers of the reform remarked, if an average ratio of 1:0.5 per cent could be achieved, the state would surely increase its revenue by a large margin, while workers could also increase their income. Within this limit producers may encourage initiative through wage incentives but at the same time still remain effectively under state control. Here the crux was to restrict the ratio of wage increases as strictly as possible; that is, only to let a limited number of factories have a ratio near 1:0.7.[13]

Second, by applying different ratios to different state-owned enterprises, the state favoured some factories at the expense of others, a phenomenon often dubbed 'whipping the fast ox'. That is, the factories which started with higher levels of economic efficiency would have a low potential for any increase in economic efficiency, so their aggregate wages would be allowed to rise less quickly. Recently, in order to ascertain the various linkage ratios, horizontal comparisons have been used to assess factories in the same sector to determine their average levels of productivity.[14]

The linkage ratio is important in that it constitutes a decisive denominator in the linkage wage formula. Different ratios yield different shares of income to the state, enterprises and workers. Therefore, the state and state-owned enterprises are involved in incessant bargaining over an appropriate linkage ratio. For instance, one leading official in the Ministry of Labour suggested in 1990 that factories with greater economic efficiency could have a ratio slightly higher than 1:0.7; factories that did not make a loss could have a ratio around 1:0.7; and factories with poor performance should have a ratio below 1:0.7 (Su Hainan, 1990, p. 23). Again no sound reason was given as to why this should be the norm. Since the judgement of whether a factory performs well is also very subjective generally, there has been no agreement on a common standard from the factory's point of view.[15]

Indeed, the ratio range was intended to draw clear boundaries for the new structure of interests in which the state and enterprises interact. The state may want to set a lower ratio for a factory whose wage aggregate is already quite large or whose economic efficiency is too low. In practice, this only prolongs the bargaining. Many factories with a large wage aggregate are large and medium-scale. As they play a key role in their industries and in the national economy as a whole, they are in a strong position to bargain with the state and usually win concessions. Factories with a low level of economic efficiency may, as noted earlier, have a good potential to improve and thus to see their floating wages shoot up. Understandably, the state is reluctant to grant them a high linkage ratio. But again, many large and medium-scale factories have a record of poor performance. It may not be their fault that they are not profitable. Even for poorly managed enterprises, if the state does not allow an attractive ratio, workers will have a low incentive to improve labour productivity. Eventually, the burden will still be carried by the state. Caught in this vicious circle, the state has no choice but to grant them attractive ratios. On the other hand, according to the ratio formula of 1:0.3–0.7, if factories want to increase their floating wages at a rate of 5 per cent continuously, they must maintain a growth rate of 16.6–17 per cent in productivity. There is no way that such a high rate can be sustained (Long Xianying and Guo Hanxian, 1990, p. 5). The result is, again, that the state is forced to bow to pressure from state-owned enterprises for higher ratios.

Sometimes the centre allows a high linkage ratio in order to persuade regional governments to enter the linkage reform. In 1988 when Fujian Province was asked to carry out the linkage reform in all its state enterprises, the State Council offered a preferential umbrella ratio of 1:0.8. After the centre and the Fujian government worked out a wage aggregate of 1.7 billion *yuan* for the province, the profit remittance was fixed at 24.4 billion *yuan* according to the ratio. Although this remittance was larger than the previous year's, it was not a high target, given the province's fast industrial growth. Therefore the province could retain a much higher amount of profit.[16]

This is a typical example showing how the plan to bring wage growth under control through a fixed linkage ratio failed to give the expected results. According to a report of 1990 by the SPC, the increases in productivity and in wage aggregates were not proportionate or simultaneous. In 1985, the first year the linkage reform was applied, the actual linkage ratio nationwide reached 1:0.73, breaking the prescribed upper limit but not by much. From 1986 to 1988, the ratios climbed to 1:1.05, 1:1.12 and 1:1.04 (SPC, 1991, pp. 49–54). This negative linkage (*daogua*) between economic efficiency and wage increases vividly demonstrates the shifting balance in state/enterprise relations in the area of income redistribution.

Cooperation between state-owned enterprises and local government

Another factor that helps erode the state's macro wage controls is cooperation between local governments and state-owned enterprises to cheat the centre. Except in a limited number of key enterprises, the state's wage control and assessment system has been implemented by sectoral industrial bureaux in the localities. This is commonly called *fenji guanli*, management delegated to government at various levels. Under this arrangement, the centre allocates a sum of wage aggregates to regions and sectors, which further disperse it among plants (Peng Maoan, 1991, pp. 3–6). Yet the actual distribution policies are formulated by factories according to their production, sales and tax remittances. As both ends cannot meet, the size of the 'cage' designed by the state to contain the 'bird' can never be correct. Supervision over this bottom-up process is very weak.

Moreover, more factory profit retentions, higher enterprise wage funds and lower remittances to the centre may help raise departmental and local income. This interest structure generates great pressure for the state economic watch-dogs at local levels to relax their actual control over the wage proposals put forward by state-owned enterprises under their jurisdiction. Local bureaucrats make concessions to reduce producers' compulsory remittances to the centre, shut their eyes to their wage aggregate evaluation, grant more tax exemptions and readily bow to the demands of factories to raise their linkage ratios, meanwhile requiring factories to pay 'tributes' to local development. Very often part of these 'tributes' end up in the welfare benefits of the bureaucrats employed in local government (Huang Yasheng, 1990, pp. 431–58). Once they approve the wage plans of their subordinates and submit the actual local wage bill to the centre, there is little the centre can do but accept it.

The following is a good example showing the conflict of interests between central and local governments in managing industrial wage awards. In early 1990, the Beijing municipal government raised the base wage for all the workers in the municipal factories by one grade without prior approval from the State Council.[17] The reason was legitimate enough: the economic retrenchment programme had greatly reduced the 'efficiency wages' of the workers in Beijing. The promotion of one wage grade would marginally increase the wage aggregate of the city and thus in some measure compensate workers for the losses incurred. However, the central government did not concur. The Ministry of Labour, the SPC and the Ministry of Finance responded strongly. They issued a document worth quoting at some length.

> The one-grade wage promotion of your city without prior approval gravely infringed the State Council's national wage policy, jeopardised macro wage management and increased the cost of products. It has exerted a far-reaching impact on the ministerial factories located in your city and on other regions as well. This is an erroneous decision. In order to handle this properly, we have, upon receiving instructions from the leaders of the State Council, made decisions as follows:
>
> 1 When the state adjusts the national wage plan for the second half of the year and assesses the plan for the next year, it will not increase the wage aggregate of your municipal firms and, under this principle, the labour and planning departments should strictly assess the wage aggregate plan and the wage aggregate base for the linkage.
> 2 This wage rise should not affect the actual industrial wage level of Beijing.[18]
> 3 The increase in production costs should not affect the remittances to the centre.
> 4 The ministerial factories located in Beijing should not follow your practice of wage promotions.[19]

Naturally, Beijing was not alone in its 'illegal' practices. In the same year, the centre issued similar documents to a number of other provinces.

When I enquired into the case of Beijing during my 1992 fieldwork, people in the Beijing Bureau of Labour confirmed my suspicion that all four of the points in the document were largely ignored by the Beijing municipal government.

THE UPSURGE IN IRREGULAR WAGE INCOME[20]

One significant result of dismantling the state unified wage system has been a proliferation of the means by which state-owned enterprises create their own earnings and distribute them to workers openly or secretly. Increasingly workers and staff depend on their 'extra income'. However, to what extent this phenomenon has affected workers' income structure has remained controversial.

According to Professor Sun Zhen, director of the Ministry of Labour's Research Institute of Labour Science, the national average wage for workers grew from 615 to 1,747 *yuan* between 1978 and 1988, a quite impressive 2.8-fold increase. Excluding the increase in prices, this was a rise of 11 per cent per annum, in a decade of fast growth second only to the First Five-Year Plan period from 1953 to 1957. At the same time the national industrial wage aggregate increased 1.2 times, an average growth of 0.8 per cent per annum (excluding the factor of inflation).

On the other hand, national income increased 1.42-fold during the corresponding period. Its annual growth averaged 9.2 per cent (calculated in constant prices). The ratio of growth between national income and the wage aggregate was 1:0.87 (assuming the growth of national income to be 1) (Sun Zhen, 1990, p. 3). What can be inferred from this group of figures is that the increase in wages did not overtake that of production. It remained within a rational range of proportionate development. And the two years of 1988 and 1989 saw further declines in wage increases. The national industrial wage aggregate and average wages declined by 2 per cent and 4 per cent in real terms respectively.

Professor Sun's calculation was based on official statistics. However, it contradicted many other research reports by academics which showed that state control over industrial wages had ended in 1984. For instance, according to an economist in CASS, only an average 44.7 per cent of the increased national income from 1979 to 1988 was at the disposal of the state, compared to over 80 per cent before the reforms, while most of the rest went to boost personal incomes. In 1987 and 1988, the individual shares from the increased national income were as high as 45.5 per cent and 47.9 per cent respectively (Zhang Jun, 1990, pp. 46–50). Other facts may also be used to support this argument, including ever-expanding bank deposits, nationwide consumption waves and shrinking state revenue at a time when national income has increased. For instance, it is interesting to note that in 1990 the recorded wage bill for all workers (including those in the non-state sector) was 296 billion *yuan* (an increase of 34.15 billion *yuan*) but the same year saw an increase in bank deposits of 145.8 billion *yuan* (Huang Weituan, 1992, p. 187).

The major reason for these vastly differing accounts lies in the different methods used to calculate the data for factory income. The official statistics take into account the income items that the state requests state-owned enterprises to report, which are normally composed of three parts: (1) the wage aggregate, the floating wages according to the linkage ratio and bonus funds; (2) state subsidies, for example for food, transportation and hygiene, subsidies to couples with an only child, and so on; (3) funds that state-owned enterprises deliver to workers from their own income-generating sources, either in the form of nonwage-bill cash in hand or payment in kind. While the first and second parts may be fairly accurately calculated, there is no adequate way to assess the third.[21] In fact, state-owned enterprises are very selective in reporting what they have given their workers outside the normal wage. Researchers said that they could only estimate this vast pool of independent income. Perhaps there will never be adequate data on this, as every factory goes its own way and deliberately makes 'irregular distributions' behind the scenes. It is exactly in this area that the cat-and-mouse game between the state and enterprises intensifies.

The sources of the 'irregular distributions' are very diverse. Some are legal while others are not. Among the legal ones, the most often used item is the labour protection and welfare funds. It is resilient because it is not often counted in the cost of production and therefore it is under looser state wage controls. This fund can be a regular part of workers' income. According to state regulation a factory can allocate an amount equivalent to 11 per cent of its wage bill from its total revenue. In addition, the factory can increase this fund by transferring 25 per cent of the profit retained after paying taxes. In 1989 this fund reached 23.53 billion *yuan*, in contrast to 67 billion *yuan* in base wages.[22] But the fund can also become a type of irregular income. The profit retention changes from year to year, and 25 per cent from retention does not incorporate all that has been awarded to workers. Behind this legal award is an unknown amount secretly transferred from the retained profits. Moreover, the state allows only a few items to be listed under this fund, but over twenty new items have been added without approval. Factories secretly incorporate these items into the cost of production (Huang Weituan, 1992, p. 190). Inevitably, the more autonomy state-owned enterprises gain in remunerative matters, the looser state control over this fund becomes.

There are many other types of irregular income available to a factory. For instance, the government allows state-owned enterprises to create service companies to accommodate surplus labourers. A large proportion of the workers in these companies receive state salaries, operate state machinery and benefit from the enterprise's use of state loans as circulation funds. Yet their earnings are regarded as having nothing to do with the state and are openly or secretly distributed. In addition, it is popular for factories, workshops and individual workers to engage in moonlighting in the second economy. Workers receive cash in hand, factories and workshops establishing their own 'moneyboxes' from which workers get extra pay.

Paying workers in kind is not new in China's state sector. However, it could legitimately escape the state's close monitoring only after state-owned enterprises gained a degree of autonomy in income redistribution in the wake of the wage reform in the 1980s. Since the introduction of the linkage reform in 1986, the practice has become more widespread, as an effective means of avoiding the state macro regulations and income taxes. Receiving money secretly or payment in kind also enables workers and staff to hide their taxable income, the threshold of which now is 800 *yuan* per month (*Jingji ribao*, 26 December 1992). During my visit to the Beijing Capital Iron and Steel Company in 1992, a trade union chairman told me that every month most of the workers in the factory paid a few *yuan* as personal income tax (the threshold then was 400 *yuan*). But a careful calculation of their income at the time, which stood at over 500 *yuan* on average, shows that they should have paid much more. The few *yuan* had become a symbolic gesture to give the workers in this model factory a semblance of honesty.

The enterprises' autonomy in income redistribution is reflected in the fact that there is virtually no limit to secret earnings and payment in kind: anything ranging from consumer goods, public meals and children's education fees to paid travel for staff and their families may be included. Academics estimate that irregular earnings rose from one-third to 40 per cent of workers' total income in the 1980s. At the beginning of the 1990s, they reached 70 per cent and in 1994 they became larger than normal salaries (Zhang Shuguang, 1996, p. 24). In a large number of state-owned enterprises irregular earnings could be twice the regular part or more (Zuo Chunwen, 1995, p. 47). According to a 1991 survey by the SSBC of 2,000 state-owned enterprises under the contract reform, this secret distribution meant that about 70 billion *yuan* was unaccounted for nationally each year. This sum should be added to the 60 billion *yuan* or so of other items of irregular income that could be traced in the bank records, the total figure exceeding 130 billion *yuan* (Huang Weituan, 1992, p. 193). These figures reflect the extent to which the state is losing control over personal income across the board: its mechanisms for regulating normal wages have become less and less effective and it has no sound mechanisms whatsoever for dealing with the irregular distribution. (See Table 6.1.)

Politically, the growth in irregular earnings has effectively reduced workers' dependence on the state. But does this growth also mean a corresponding increase in their dependence on their work units, which in turn would mean enhanced organised control by *danwei* over their

Table 6.1 Annual income per wage earner (formal vs. informal) (in *yuan*), 1978–94

	Formal income[a]	Increased savings in bank	Expenditure[b]	Informal income	Ratio (%)
	1	2	3	4 = 3 + 2 − 1	5 = 4/1
1978	569.8	19.8			
1980	778.6	80.0			
1985	1,435.0	281.0	1,689	536	37
1988	2,441.4	592.0	3,164	1,314	54
1989	2,744.0	1,075.0	3,577	1,909	70
1990	3,095.0	1,458.0	3,861	2,224	72
1991	3,502.0	1,598.0	4,440	2,537	72
1992	4,166.0	1,887.0	5,412	3,133	75
1993	5,292.0	2,949.0	7,040	4,697	89
1994	7,363.0	5,076.0	9,780	7,492	102

Source: Zhang Shuguang, '90 miandai de Zhonggno gaige he hongguan jingi' (On the economic reform and macro-economic situation in China), *Jingji yanjiu*, no. 6, 1996, p. 30.
Notes:
[a] National wage aggregate divided by total number of nationals employed.
[b] Average expenditure of sample city-dwellers surveyed by the SSBC multiplied by the total urban population.

everyday life? Answering this question requires comprehensive investigation. My fieldwork findings tentatively point to the fact that irregular earnings are vital to the maintenance of a decent standard of living. Even though many surveys show that the irregular distributions have mostly been accumulated for buying electrical durables like colour televisions, they constitute an indispensable part of a person's overall income at a time of high inflation (*Zhongguo jiyingbao*, 13 March 1990). To a degree, as the *danwei*-based remuneration increases the importance of work units, state wage control has somewhat changed in nature. It provides only a minimum income for employees to live on rather than a dictatorship over people's needs. It may mean some compensation for inflation. And it may remain useful for the state to level standard wages in the state sector, in the hope of achieving a fairly even growth of income among industrial workers. Increasingly this has become essential to keep people happy at a time of aspiration to keep up with the neighbours. In other words, as the political functions associated with the *danwei*'s welfare functions diminish, the wider use of irregular distributions to workers, usually on an egalitarian basis, has contributed to the process of weakening political individualism.

The tendency to provide workers with irregular earnings reflects the clash of interests between the state and enterprises. Realising that the linkage reform did not follow the original design, the state has tightened up control over approval of the wage aggregates. It has also instituted stricter checks on the submission of regulatory wage taxes since the introduction of the three-year retrenchment programme in 1988. As a result, average industrial wages that year dropped by 0.8 per cent, and the following year by a further 4 per cent. According to a labour official, the runaway expansion of wage funds between 1987 and 1988 was basically brought under control in 1990. However, the expansion of the irregular distributions has worsened.[23] In order to give workers more money, factories have had to circumvent state controls over regular wages.

The irregular distributions by state-owned enterprises can thus be seen as an independent channel for compensating workers in their war over wages with the state. One survey conducted by the Ministry of Labour reveals that while the regular industrial wage aggregate increased three-fold from 1979 to 1988, irregular earnings grew twelvefold during the same period (Sun Zhen, 1990, p. 5). The fastest growth took place after the linkage reform. From 1986 to 1988 the growth rate was 44 per cent. This figure, as admitted by the researcher, was an underestimate because no record at all was kept on the distribution of a large proportion of the irregular earnings (Sun Zhen, 1990, p. 5).

The impact of the irregular distributions on the state's industrial wage policy is enormous. A double-edged sword, they may help temporarily to satisfy workers' growing demands on their factory. However, the practice stimulates open-ended competition among factories for more irregular income. Whatever the state can offer will not be good enough in such a social environment.

In sum, it is largely because of its hidden nature that we have such a confusing picture of China's national remuneration. And this is not con-fined to the industrial sector. I was told that the staff of Deng Xiaoping and Jiang Zemin also depended on irregular earnings to cope with the consumption wave in the country.[24] On the one hand, as noted, official statistics show that the increase in the national industrial wage bill has lagged behind that of national income. It failed to reach the targets of the Sixth and Seventh Five-Year Plans. On the other hand, it is generally acknowledged that the much weakened state control over micro wage initiatives has given rise to a runaway expansion of consumption funds, both individual and institutional, which has eaten deep into the state's revenue. An understanding of irregular distribution helps us to bridge the gap between the official statistics and the real situation. As factories gain more autonomy in remuneration, the state is increasingly put on the defensive. At the same time some officials argue that this development is, after all, the correct direction of the wage reform, which should allow state-owned enterprises to become independent bodies of remuneration. Only when this is achieved will the concept of irregular earnings become irrelevant. The first precondition for this is to phase out what remains of the eight-grade wage system. After all, the role of the state in industrial remunerative affairs is that of guidance, rather than command (Zhang Wenmin, 1990, p. 274).

More importantly, the future of China's reform and stability hinges largely on sizeable increases in people's incomes. Yet the state has been unable to increase the wage aggregate for state-owned enterprises in a satisfactory manner. At the same time many workers are in real need of meaningful compensation for high inflation. If their demand can be met by enterprises themselves, it will help to maintain social stability and save the state a lot of trouble on the political front. For reasons of expediency, the state from time to time shuts its eyes to factories' distribution of irregular earnings to workers. Handed out in an egalitarian manner, these earnings have the effect of narrowing the gaps in workers' incomes within one factory, thus reducing workers' complaints (Zhao Renwei, 1992, p. 61).

7 The politics of the industrial wage reform

In addition to altering remunerative relations between the state and state-owned enterprises, China's industrial wage reforms have at the same time altered relations between factory management and workers and relations among workers themselves. Chinese economists define the 'distribution' of profits between the state and state-owned enterprises as the first distribution, and that between factories and workers as the 'second' (Yue Guangzhao, 1989, p. 67). In the post-Mao era, as enterprises are allowed to generate their own resources to enlarge workers' earnings, the previous unified line of wage allocations through planning has broken down, giving way to a two-tiered distribution process in which the role played by individual producers has gradually surpassed that of state agencies. Within a factory one predominant way of reforming internal wage mechanisms has been to delegate powers of top management to lower units. Again, this constitutes another dual distribution process in which factory management allocates a flexible amount of wages to a collective according to its production performance, and the latter further divides it into different shares among its members. Since the late 1980s, the top management of the majority of China's large and medium-scale enterprises oversees individual workers' wage awards much less directly (Guojia jingwei, 1987, p. 21). Workshops are often more responsible for deciding the form and amount of rewards for each employee. Being the first feature of the post-Mao wage reform at the basic level, the rise in importance of sub-units in the process of the 'second distribution' has led to rising numbers of independent distribution entities in the state sector.

A second feature concerns the emergence of numerous varieties of income distribution as a result of delegating powers to those on the shop floor. According to a Chinese wage expert, there are now more than 200 forms of wage awards in China's factories (Xu Songtao et al., 1988, p. 165). The number is significant in that it illustrates the scope of wage autonomy achieved by firms and their lower operational units. Indeed, in one factory or even in one workshop, there may exist different wage forms that cluster workers in various wage categories. This variety not only points to a complicated wage structure, but also makes it difficult to analyse the current remunerative process on shop floors.

As far as the subject of this book is concerned, these two features are important in that they contribute significantly to the process of *de-danweiisation*. The *danwei* system is supposed to be a tightly integrated mechanism of party/state control. Resembling China's traditional authoritarian state/family power structure, the system requires a high concentration of financial and remunerative power in the hands of the leaders. The newly acquired autonomy of subordinate units in distribution matters fragments the monistic top-down command, control and communication channels. And with autonomous remunerative power, leaders in lower units try to assert varying amounts of financial power as well. As a result, 'independent kingdoms' spring up within a closed 'empire'. This directly challenges the operations of the *danwei* system, which heavily depends on a vertical, undisrupted power flow. The implications are profound.

A REVIEW OF WAGE REFORM WITHIN STATE-OWNED ENTERPRISES

As mentioned in the previous chapter, in 1985 a new fifteen-grade industrial wage system was established to replace the eight-grade one. When the new system was established, all workers were promoted by a few grades. When state-owned enterprises were allowed to devise their own wage forms, this state-sponsored fifteen-grade wage structure was treated as a reference system only. The workers' new grade in the structure became the base grade upon which their employers subsequently designed new wage initiatives. For instance, the base grade has functioned as the standard scale for most state-owned enterprises. When workers seek transfers, their standardised base wages make it easier for them to enter the wage system in their new workplace.

More important than the base grade is an open-ended component of a worker's earnings which 'floats' up and down. In fact, the question of how to float this second part represents the key to all intra-enterprise wage reforms. In order further to break down the 'big rice bowl' system, many state-owned enterprises have also tried to float a certain proportion of the base wages – the fixed part. To enlarge the open-ended part and reduce the fixed part has become the main object of wage reform. This also provides some clues as to why the proportion of the regular part of wages has dropped so quickly in the industrial income structure (Jackson, 1992, pp. 185–90).

Generally speaking, the following forms of wage awards are most commonly practised in China's state sector today.

Quota contract responsibility system

According to an SSBC report, about half of China's state-owned enterprises have adopted the quota contract responsibility system. In this form of income distribution, the main component is the base salary plus bonuses. But many variables have evolved. Those most often used are the following:

1 The base salary + a floating efficiency salary + bonuses. In this formula the floating efficiency salary is part of a worker's income that increases or decreases, depending on whether he/she can meet the assigned quotas. Moreover, the state allows part of the floating salary to be added to the 'fixed' part, if workers can fulfil their contractual obligations for three consecutive years. This means that they will have an enlarged wage base, a favourable condition for future promotion. This practice constitutes the main reason why the base wage of many workers, many of whom are still quite young, reached the top grade in the reference system a few years after the fifteen-grade reference wage system was introduced, leaving no grade for further promotion (Ding Xianjiu and Yong Weiguo, 1992, p. 7).
2 The base wage + partial floating base salary + floating efficiency salary + bonuses. This formula represents another effort to shake the 'big rice bowl' system. Usually factory management requires the lower units to tie 10 to 30 per cent of workers' base salaries to the floating efficiency salary in order to broaden the income gap within the workforce, for the larger the base figure of the floating wage bill, the larger the possible wage rises. The reduced fixed wages mean increased flexibility for additional income.
3 The floating of the entire base salary + floating efficiency salary + bonuses. This is a step further than the partial floating of the basic salary. In fact, when everything is 'floating', the concept of the 'fixed' base salary becomes empty.[1] Some factory managers told me in 1991 and 1992 that this formula was used to encourage a sense of competition among workers. However, I found during my subsequent fieldwork trips that most managers adopted this method only when the sales of their factories were good. Otherwise they only partially floated the base wage, which at least guaranteed a safety net for their workers.

The structural salary

This formula first combines both the fixed and the floating parts of workers' wages and then dissolves these into four components: the base salary, post (skills) awards, premiums for years of service and efficiency pay. The structural salary offers some recompense to workers with more seniority. More importantly, however, it is a design that gives more incentives to the posts with difficult working conditions, particularly in the 'first line of production'.[2] In terms of components, the base salary and the premiums for seniority are static. The post award varies depending on the assessment of factory and workshop managers. After these three have been fixed, efficiency wages may be worked out subject to a pre-determined ratio between the fixed and floating components. The officially suggested ratio for state-owned enterprises adopting the system is 6:4 or 5:5 (SETC, 1994, p. 31).

The structural salary represents a major overhaul of the old eight-grade system. For instance, the Beijing Heavy Machinery Factory, which adopted the structural salary system in 1988, stipulated that the proportion of the base wage would be only 18 per cent, while the proportions of the other components would be 15 per cent for the efficiency wage, 37 per cent for the post and skill award, and 27 per cent for incentive pay based on piece-rates. The seniority premium was included in the base wage, so this played a fairly small role in the factory's wage distribution (Su Hainan, 1990, p. 216).

According to my fieldwork findings, the structural salary has not been an effective means of linking increased workers' income with increased production. (The above-mentioned case was an exception because the factory assigned a large proportion of the salary to awards based on piece-rates.) The reason is that under the restrictions imposed by the factory or shop management on the ratio between the fixed and unfixed parts of wages, if the portion of the awards for seniority and posts is effectively large, this will leave less room for increased efficiency wages, entailing simply a change to a smaller 'big rice bowl'.

The wholesale piece-rate wage system

This system is implemented in industries where individual production can be calculated easily. The system eliminates the grades, and places all workers on an equal footing. In other words, the number of finished products they have made determines how much they receive. However, while this system is attractive to young workers who can benefit from it, the old and weak are disadvantaged for physical reasons. At the same time, worker income may be too easily subject to the sales situation in the market. Furthermore, because the concept of the base salary is no longer relevant in this reform, the workers may have to face dramatic decreases in their pay when the market turns bad.

The post-assigned wages

This system was designed for specialised posts in factories which require certain types of expertise. It has been widely used for first-line production posts as an incentive arrangement. For instance, in 1986 the State Council approved a wage reform plan for the whole of China's textile industry, which established a five-grade post-assigned wage system. In order to attract workers to remain in the first line of production and in difficult jobs, these posts are better paid (Su Hainan, 1990, p. 138). The system is especially attractive for workers with better skills, as they receive pay not on the basis of seniority but on what posts they have the skills to occupy.

THE NEW WAGE ENTITIES AND NEW CENTRIFUGAL FORCES

The post-Mao wage reform has paved the way for state-owned enterprises to seek additional income. Between the state and producers, the effort to increase a firm's wage aggregate is largely a collective one, campaigned for strenuously by factory managers. The workers in a factory often lend their support to managers in the bargaining process, as mentioned earlier (p. 123). However, when the wage quotas are devolved to groups and individuals, the collective effort to maximise factory income is translated into action by individual workers to maximise their personal earnings. Competition becomes more intensified. Institutionally, this helps to create many new entities with *de facto* distribution powers in large and medium-sized factories. As a result, workers have shifted their attention to shop-floor management for most wage deals. The centre of gravity of the strife between the state, enterprises and workforce has moved further down the hierarchy.[3]

In consequence, many workshop directors feel increased pressures from below in conflict with the strictures from above. This pressure now dominates most of their policy considerations. Good cooperation from the workers under their leadership represents the key to fulfilling production quotas, which also means higher income for themselves. One workshop manager told me that in order to satisfy his fellow workers, whenever possible he would open up channels to grant them money regardless of state and factory regulations. Indeed, with the state retreating from direct involvement in distribution affairs on shop floors, the very closeness between workshop managers and their workers has started to reshape the tripartite relations.[4] A survey by CASS among 769 large and medium-sized state factories produced interesting data. While only 12.3 per cent of workers surveyed thought that they carried no weight in the wage policy-making process, 65.9 per cent believed that they could influence the process one way or another and 21.8 per cent were confident that they played a key role (Zheng Honglang, 1992, p. 28).

The same pressure has also driven a wedge between managers at different levels within a plant. This stems from the conflicts of interest represented by the various parties. For the time being most factory managers of large and medium-sized state-owned enterprises are still appointed by the state (*China Business Times*, 20 November 1995). Thus, hovering over the shoulders of factory managers, there is always the shadowy authority of the state. It is widely perceived that the contract

responsibility system and the linkage wage reform have created differentiated institutional interests in relations between the state and factory
managers, and between factory managers and lower-level managers. And
the representatives of these groups must protect the interests of their
constituencies in order to obtain their cooperation (Ma Bin, 1986, p. 74).
But, at the same time, factory managers must also be mindful of the state
bureaucrats who appointed them, while trying to maximise their own
factory's income. This means that factory managers often put a brake on
the wage initiatives of workshops so as to strike a balance. Dealing
with the state is not the business of workshop managers, however. Their
calculation is based more on the pressures from their immediate superiors
and from the workers under them. In fact, all the workshop managers I
interviewed admitted that they had had many problems with their factory
bosses in the area of remuneration. Most of the difficulties occur when
factory managers break the wage deals embodied in the quota/wage
contracts, fearing that lower units are giving too much to workers. The
factory managers claimed that the state would hold them responsible.

The following is a case illustrating the tensions between factory and
workshop managements regarding wage problems. At the beginning of
1991, Workshop No. 3 of the Beijing Wool Textile Factory entered into a
quota contract with the factory manager by which the workshop would
increase the efficiency salary by 6 per cent if it could over-fulfil the
contract by 10 per cent, annually calculated, and by up to 9 per cent if it
could surpass the quota by 15 per cent. The first two quarters saw the
agreement go well, as the workshop paid 7 per cent wage increases in
accordance with the contract. In the third quarter overproduction
exceeded the 16 per cent mark but the factory manager hesitated as to
whether to make good his promise. He realised that the increased
efficiency salary for this workshop and others would far exceed the targeted increase in the factory's floating wage bill. The bureaucrats above
would definitely intervene. So he negotiated with the workshop for a deal
by which the workshop could still get its agreed share for the present
quarter but from the next the increase would be much lower. Under
great pressure, the workshop manager gave in, although there were bitter
complaints from workers.

However, this was not the end of the story. At the end of the fourth
quarter the factory manager wanted to reduce the rate of increase again.
This time the workshop manager did not agree because his workers
threatened to go on strike. The increased wage was eventually paid.
However, the factory manager later refused to release end-of-year
bonuses to the workshop, using the excuse that some of the products did
not reach the quality standard. Nor did he extend the contract for the
workshop manager at the beginning of the new year. But towards the end
of 1992 when the new contract for the factory manager came up for

tendering, the workers in Workshop No. 3 opposed his bid for the job. This time it was the workers' turn to be successful.[5]

For many shopfloor managers, productivity is important, but less important than harmony with their fellow employees. They are constantly caught between workers and company management in rows over wages. Before the reforms, except for a few instances of limited wage promotion, for which a face-to-face group assessment was conducted, workers' complaints about wages were generally directed to the state which was blamed for freezing wage increases or for only allocating a small percentage of workers for promotion. Now, with the new powers of remuneration, the heads of workshops are in the eye of the storm. Their closeness to the production line, however, often makes them adopt attitudes and positions in favour of the shop floor. They are more liable to increase wages in order to obtain worker's cooperation than to worry about labour costs and overall profit. Indeed, the shift towards smaller entities for wage distribution is really the cause of Walder's observation that a tacit alliance has emerged between managers and workers, who share an interest in retaining the highest amount of incentive funds while distributing them relatively equally (Walder, 1987, pp. 22–41). If by the word 'managers' he meant factory managers, the alliance is fairly loose. In many small state factories that have been contracted and leased out on a long-term basis, firm managers have actually had strong incentives to lower wages, extend working hours and reduce welfare provisions. However, the situation is different in large and medium-sized firms where workers and lower-level managers generate enormous pressure on factory managers to deal on their behalf with state bureaucrats. In fact, a much tighter alliance has been formed between shopfloor management and workers to protect their own interests, which often suggests a joint struggle against factory managers. According to a national survey of 2,765 factory managers in 1995, to the question, 'What is the most important thing in your management?', the biggest proportion of respondents (48 per cent) answered that maximising workers' income was their primary objective. In contrast, a smaller proportion of respondents (37 per cent) thought market share was the most important objective (Jiang Liu et al., 1996, p. 59). In terms of macro wage controls, it seems that two barriers have been erected between the state and workers: factory management and workshop management.

The enlarged power over remuneration by sub-unit management has enhanced the influence of middle managers significantly. In the Chinese command economic system before reform, management at the middle level had little influence on decision making, particularly on strategic decisions such as pay levels. This was due to the organisational structure of a factory as an appendage to the centralised decision-making system in the state sector (Laaksonen, 1987, p. 305). Now with the power over remuneration made available to them, middle managers have gained influence in several areas.

First, thanks to the closer connection between workers' income and production quotas and retained profit, the shop managers' control over rewards has strengthened their say in strategic issues about production and sales decided by top management. In other words, when making a production and wage plan, factory directors have to give more serious consideration to the response to the plan of middle-level management and workers, particularly when any major policy change affecting the existing ways wages are distributed in workshops is involved.

Second, the new power over wage issues has strengthened the hand of workshop managers in everyday management. Though they are still unable to dismiss workers, middle managers' authority to set salaries has made it easier for them to tighten work discipline, decide on job allocations and work out many forms of favouritism for their own clientelistic network. For instance, middle managers can now use monetary sanctions to control absenteeism and coordinate sick leave applications (Zhao Minhua and Nichols, 1996, p. 11).

Third, smaller entities of distribution have enabled workshops to create their own channels to generate earnings, so many managers have for the first time acquired independent financial power. This augmented power operates entirely outside the state industrial wage system. According to official Chinese sources, a good percentage of factories and their workshops seek business deals of their own.[6] While a firm may legitimately conduct business as an independent accounting unit, it is legally dubious for workshops to do the same. This is largely because the firm is the basic unit for paying state taxes according to production and sales, and a workshop's income is most unlikely to be counted in the total factory income. A huge second economy has thus been created, generating income for workers which comes outside the state tax system.[7]

This phenomenon originated from the state's tacit consent to allowing enterprises (not workshops) to engage in moonlighting in the early 1980s when central planners had no production orders to give to state-owned enterprises, owing to a three-year retrenchment programme. The state actually encouraged them to produce in order to survive. Therefore, factories tried to seek their own orders outside the state plan. The booming village and township industries and the newly acquired autonomy of state-owned enterprises in production and sales provided ample opportunities for these 'secret account' activities, as mentioned on p. 130.

This collective moonlighting embraces a wide range of activities: from private orders for small numbers of special products to selling parts or even complete sets of equipment belonging to the work units. There are abundant examples. For instance, when a factory is in financial trouble – for example if it cannot pay workers' salaries – it asks workshops and individual workers to market the factory's products through their own personal connections. Each workshop would have a specific quota. One popular form of 'secret account' activity has been using surplus workers streamlined from *youhua zuhe* (the rationalisation and reorganisation programme) to engage in semi-private work outside the factory. Workshops sign contracts with outside customers and take the lion's share of fees after submitting some to the factory and distributing a proportion to the workers doing the work. The reform by which sub-units were made entities of remuneration has cleared up some of the accounting problems for workshops doing business on their own, and the fast-growing second economy has provided an outlet for such pursuits. Although there are no systematic data to show how widespread the practice is, there is reason to believe that this is a pervasive phenomenon. More important politically, this massive collective moonlighting reveals the extent to which workers have lost any sense of the state as the sole provider for their livelihood.

THE WORKERS' REACTION TO THE WAGE REFORM

During my fieldwork in China in the 1990s, I asked about workers' reaction to industrial wage reforms since 1984. Responses were quite mixed. Some believed that these reforms provided more ways of earning money and thus inspired workers to increase production. Others commented, however, that the ending of the previously closed wage system also opened up more opportunities for corruption and abuse of power by unit heads. Industrial disputes were on the rise, too. Generally workers were in favour of the abolition of the old eight-grade wage system and agreed that the best thing about the new system was that it brought in 'extra money'.[8] The fact that the linkage reform was universalised in China's state-owned enterprises in less than three years illustrates its general acceptance by enterprises and workers. This is in sharp contrast to many other reforms that are pursued very hard by the state but have to be abandoned later owing to resistance by those on the receiving end.[9] Whether or not a reform can deliver immediate benefits to the populace has now become a touchstone of whether it can be successfully implemented. Yet beyond the monetary gains offered by the workplace-centred remuneration, workers' generally positive attitudes to the system are also due to mechanisms built into it that enhance their strength in dealing with the management, as shown in the following section.

The embryonic form of collective bargaining

A factory's management always hinges on the cooperation of workers. Before the reform this 'cooperation' was secured primarily through tight controls. One outcome of the post-Mao institutional reforms in the state sector has been that with the erosion of these controls the desired cooperation is achieved at a much higher price. Increasingly, workers' cooperation can only be 'bought' through more material incentives. For instance, the quota system based on personal responsibility has highlighted the importance of the contribution of individual workers because their performance can make the production of a workshop more or less effective.

Spontaneous collective action

In shopfloor politics, these material incentives have clearly augmented the bargaining power of workers on matters of remuneration. The eight-grade system left little room for bargaining. Any attempt at collective action was too risky and thus out of the question, as workers could not directly confront a powerful state. But now, as already noted, the pay of the majority of workers has been linked to a floating rate, which itself entails flexibility for manoeuvring. This makes workers more aware of the connection between their work and how it is reimbursed. At the same time the delegation of remunerative powers to enterprises and sub-units has reduced the gravity of consequences when workers resort to collective resistance to management. Now it is the factory and workshop managers who design the wage deals. If these do not appear satisfactory, workers may resist the policies of these smaller units, a stand which will not necessarily be interpreted as against the state. Indeed, this relaxation of control via the wage reform has triggered a large number of industrial actions which would have been inconceivable before the reform. In Beijing, for instance, the municipal government processed 1,043 such cases in 1994, 2.6 times more than in 1993 and the same number as in the previous six years combined (*China Business Times*, 15 May 1995). In 1995 officially registered labour disputes reached 33,030 nationally, a large proportion of these being wage-related. Reported cases numbered 210,000 and unreported cases could be much more numerous, for both parties to the dispute, factory management and workers, are reluctant to go to the government for a settlement (*China Business Times*, 10 May 1996).

Seen from the angle of a political sociologist, every one of these actions has political ramifications in a party/state. In western countries workers press their wage demands through an independent trade union, which bargains with employers on their behalf. In China, since there is no such effective channel for collective bargaining, many workers take action outside the normal processes in order to achieve their goal of a wage rise. The relaxation of state control over micro wage matters has stimulated workers to insist on having their say in the wage-setting process. However, with no institutional outlet for their grievances, they have no choice but to take spontaneous collective action themselves (Wilson, 1990, p. 59). This strong motive for spontaneous collective action may pave the way for organised opposition movements to emerge during times of political strife, nationally or locally, as shown by the 1989 events.

Through my visits to a number of Chinese factories, I found that spontaneous collective bargaining was widespread in various disguised forms. According to one interviewee, the struggle with management over wage issues is a good way of learning collective action:

> You have to learn the meaning of the contract and your rights associated with it. You have to learn how to arouse and organise your fellow workers who have fallen victim like you. And you have to learn the art of bargaining and compromise.

He acknowledged that after a few 'encounters' with managers, many workers started to develop a sense of solidarity, as they realised that 'workshop directors can bow to workers' pressure over wage demands, if this pressure is heavy enough. Yet such pressure can never be generated by individual efforts. So the victimised workers usually come together.'

There have been few signs that collective action originating from wage claims is politicised. But since wage-related conflicts are prevalent in China's industries, workers have ample opportunity to learn how to organise themselves to protect their rights and interests, as seen from the sharp rise in labour disputes. More importantly, the increase in wage disputes is also due to the depoliticised atmosphere in state-owned enterprises where many party cells have become inactive, as mentioned in Chapter 5. In the past, with the heavy pressure of the party's presence, it was difficult for any informal groups to emerge. But in recent years many such groups have sprung up, commonly centred on a few charismatic figures in workshops who have good technical skill, a following among apprentices, and an uneasy relationship with the bosses.[10] A wage dispute would most probably strengthen their influence among their co-workers. A key question to be explored is how to interpret this phenomenon: will independent worker organisations based on blue-collar constituencies eventually emerge from these organised efforts to achieve wage demands, and if so how soon? Han Dongfang, a well-known dissident trade unionist now in exile in Hong Kong, claimed that the decade of reform had opened up unprecedented opportunities for this to take place (*Voice of America*, 2 September 1993).

On the other hand, it should be noted that the influence of workers over labour/wage issues has not been actively pursued through well-organised collective actions, as was the case with Solidarity in Poland. Rather, workers tend to attribute their wage demands to random violations of contract terms by shop managers or to unfair distribution of income within their work units. In other words, the workers' struggle for fair pay is still in a stage of fitful reaction. To some extent, this situation can be analysed as a transitional phenomenon where workers, though increasingly conscious of their interests, have not acquired a definite status and identity *vis-à-vis* the state and managers. They play a more crucial role in post-Mao industrial relations but their power is more than offset by the state and management, on which they remain dependent. Generally speaking, their rights and benefits are looked after when their employers operate well in the market. Yet they will be the first to suffer if their firm goes bust (Chang Kai, 1995, pp. 46). Despite this asymmetry, the widespread simultaneous collective bargaining represents the workers' desire to fight for their basic rights.

AN EXAMPLE OF A LABOUR DISPUTE

In 1995 a high-profile legal case involving a labour dispute attracted the attention of 300,000 state-sector workers in Kaifeng City, Henan Province. Nine dismissed workers lodged complaints in court against their employer, Kaifeng Automobile Parts Factory. The nine workers had withdrawn their labour because the factory reduced their pay, did not provide them with safety equipment in time, and refused to submit labour insurance for them to the local labour affairs agency. After waiting for one month for an answer from the factory, they sought temporary jobs in another factory. This made the factory management very angry. It reported the case to the Municipal Labour Dispute Commission, demanding a fine of 220,000 *yuan* from the workers. The Commission sided with the factory. The nine workers were asked not only to pay the fine but, worse still, to go home.

These workers were thrown into a very difficult situation. Some of them even thought of committing suicide. Later they decided to take the case to court. Public support for them was mounting through media coverage. The local and provincial governments became concerned. Even trade unions at various levels started to speak for the workers. Under pressure, the local court decided against the management, ordering it to withdraw all sanctions against the workers (Wang Hongming, 1996, p. 12).

The court verdict may be of less significance than the spontaneous action *per se* in such a case. It reminds people in all relevant offices – government officials, factory managers and trade union activists – that the new wage mechanism is breaking the existing tripartite balance between the state, management and workers. The independent action by the nine may have indicated that workers are willing to take risks to build a new balance which can serve their interests. Furthermore, the case also raised the question of where the trade union was in the whole process. Spontaneous action means that workers do not trust the unions. Nevertheless, whether it is organised by the unions or not, collective bargaining has already become a way of life in China's state sector. Suppressing it may only make conflict fiercer.

OFFICIAL COLLECTIVE BARGAINING

Chinese labour officials have increasingly seen the seriousness of the consequences of this trend (Chan, 1993, pp. 31–62). They have proposed allowing collective bargaining to be legally sanctioned, in order to replace the method of handling labour disputes through heavy-handed political power. Zhang Guoxiang, secretary of the ACFTU, argues:

> Under the command economy, industrial relations concerning employ-ment policies, remunerative matters and welfare standards were regulated by state decrees and bureaucratic interventions. There was no need for factory management to negotiate with workers. Now the state has largely retreated from these areas and factory management assumes the right of legal representative of state property. In the market economy labour disputes have become an internal concern with which the management has to deal independently. However, without an effective system of checks and balances it is difficult for them to avoid the temptation of 'what I say goes'.
>
> (Zhang Guoxiang, 1994, p. 5)

Zhang Dinghua, first deputy chair of the ACFTU, announced on 22 July 1996 that in order to make labour relations run smoothly, China would create a tripartite collective bargaining system between state labour administration, trade unions and management. The system should be formulated according to international practice (*Gongren ribao*, 24 July 1996). The institutionalised establishment of collective contract and bar-gaining will accelerate a far-reaching transition in China's labour relations from domination by political interests (the party's control) to domination by economic interests (employment conditions) (Chang Kai, 1995, p. 44). In a sense, the party/state does not normally allow real industrial relations to exist: such relations, as practised in the west, are between employers and employees, and are handled fairly autonomously. In state-owned enterprises the state is the employer and industrial relations are part of state/society relations. Bargaining by workers with their employers is indirect bargaining with the state, and collective bargaining implies organ-ised action independent of the state. But why is an institution so dangerous to authoritarian power given a green light?

Fundamentally, this is because the state now sees the emergence of autonomous interest groups as an inevitable part of China's market reforms. In this process labour/wage disputes are recognised as unavoid-able. To permit the parties concerned to bargain according to a set of rules may actually lessen the intensity of a conflict. The state has tried to divert spontaneous collective actions into certain government-arranged channels for labour disputes, e.g. wage settlement by the networks of official trade unions. In this way the party hopes to remove the necessity for workers to take independent action for remunerative gain. This major policy change represents the end of the myth that in a socialist system workers and the state do not have conflicting interests. Indeed, encouraging tripartism may have prevented a situation in which the state would be caught between two powerful social groups, managers and workers.

Managers as a professional force will decide China's future and workers collectively still hold the key to the country's stability. Whether or not these two powerful groups can stick together affects the ability of the CCP to continue its rule over the population. So party officials argue that collective bargaining is a better mechanism through which to coordinate the different interests articulated in the negotiation process over terms of employment between the state, management and workers (Bianji xiaozu, 1990, pp. 329–48). This means that in a changed social environment the state has to use a more sophisticated approach to achieve the results it desires. Through introducing officially sponsored collective bargaining, the state and the ACFTU hope to instate the Japanese consensual style of management in order to ease rising tensions between managers and workers (Chan, 1995, p. 4). This may prove the extent to which the state is prepared to yield to the demands of new social forces. Increasingly it has to play a balancing game between workers and managers: its days of absolute power over them may be over. However, through its balancing role, the state is still able to preserve its powers to act as arbiter.

Articles 33, 34 and 35 of the Labour Law (in effect since 1995) legally confirm government policy on collective bargaining. However, they place limitations on genuine collective bargaining as practised in industrialised countries. The two key limitations include: (1) administrative approval of any collective contract; and (2) channelling workers' collective efforts through the official trade unions. Moreover, the state has adopted a cautious attitude towards implementing collective bargaining. The labour administration agencies warn that collective bargaining may have a lasting effect on China's labour relations at a time when the country is undergoing enormous change. It is redefining state (state firms) and society (workers) relations. Therefore, the reform has to be carried out gradually and through pilot schemes. For instance, collective bargaining should be introduced first on an experimental basis in those enterprises that are being converted into share and stock companies. And the non-state sector should universalise collective bargaining ahead of the state sector (Dong Ping, 1994, p. 15). This caution is easy to understand. Those 'modern firms' have entered a new type of business relations with the state: bureaucratic control has become much weaker. Bringing workers' collective pressure to bear on managers may actually enhance the state's indirect control, particularly in the non-state sector. Indeed, through encouraging collective bargaining between management and workers, the state may drive a wedge between them. According to a leading Chinese economist, the state has long been fearful of an invisible alliance between managers and workers in dealing with the state (Guo Yanxi, 1995, p. 25). For the time being, however, the state is hesitant to relinquish its direct grip on labour relations in the majority of state-owned enterprises. Yet once the government employs collective bargaining as the mechanism for regulating industrial relations in China, it legitimises workers' direct collective pressure on management and indirect pressure on itself. And sooner rather than later, workers will back up their pressure with strikes and lockouts. Indeed, this is already happening. The genie has come out of the bottle.

THE ALTERNATIVE TO ORGANISED DEPENDENCE

Along with the delegation of remunerative powers to sub-units, individuals have acquired freedom to generate their independent sources of income, mainly through moonlighting. Significantly, this deals a blow to one major feature of the industrial *danwei* system: organised dependence. Before reform, workers received income from the state which could only cover the daily necessities provided by the state through coupons. Generally speaking, four modes of consumption dominated during the entire Maoist period: (1) a rationing/coupons system was instituted to guarantee the essential materials to be supplied to every citizen (including clothing and foodstuffs such as vegetables and a small amount of meat); (2) free provision of high-priced commodities to a number of senior officials; (3) welfare arrangements for state staff and their dependants, such as housing, heating, education, medical care and retirement pensions; (4) state subsidies on rural produce and everyday industrial goods, anything from matches to bicycles.

Under this consumption pattern, an average 80 per cent of a person's monthly salary went on food and clothing. According to Engels Law this was typical of a subsistence economy. On the other hand, the system may serve to hide overt differences in consumption. Without coupons, people had to put their money in the bank because they had few places to spend it. The higher the percentage of the disposable income that is spent on daily necessities, and the fewer the alternatives to earn money, the more dependent workers would become on their fixed income. When they were anxious about satisfying their hunger and securing basic clothing, the state's control through the eight-grade wage system was effective indeed.

Throughout the 1980s the percentage of workers' disposable income spent on basic daily necessities declined. For instance, in 1989 an average of some 50–60 per cent of a person's salary went on daily necessities. At the same time the base salary controlled by the state dropped to below 50 per cent of the total income (Shi Wei, 1990, p. 11). The new alternatives available for workers to earn money have alleviated their sense of being helplessly owned by the state. In fact, never before have so many workers felt they could somehow take their economic livelihood into their own hands.[11]

This feeling has been further strengthened by the opportunities for second jobs created by the wage reform. During my fieldwork in Beijing in early 1991, I asked workers how much a month it cost to provide for a family of three (a couple and a child). The usual answer was about 500 *yuan*. This was in sharp contrast to the average wage they earned, which stood at 200 *yuan* each (for husband and wife). Then I asked them how they bridged the gap. They remarked that they could make ends meet by generating their own earnings. It was much easier now to make money, people added, but it all depended on ability and, more importantly, *guanxi*, connections. These remarks convey a strong impression that the benefits of moonlighting are not evenly distributed. Moonlighting has become more popular in recent years, as the strong growth of the non-state sector provides more channels for state workers.

Apparently moonlighting has become an important source of income for workers in state-owned enterprises. For workers in state-owned enterprises that do not have good 'efficiency', moonlighting has become a matter of survival. In June 1995 40,000 state-owned enterprises had stopped production, affecting 7,450,000 workers. The workers did not need to report to their firms every day and received only a proportion of their base wages (Feng Tongqing, 1996, p. 271). Many of them are actually engaged full-time in the search for moonlighting. As this relieves the state of the need to inject more 'social stability' money to these factories, the authorities have closed their eyes to this abnormal situation. However, moonlighting does worry labour officials and managers. Between 1993 and 1994 there was a heated debate about whether it should be banned under the Labour Law. Managers felt that moonlighting damaged discipline and eroded the profits of state-owned enterprises, so it should be forbidden. However, as moonlighting is the only way for workers in loss-making firms to make ends meet, it is politically unwise to forbid it. Under pressure it was agreed upon that no mention of moonlighting should be made in the Labour Law (Hu Keming, 1994, p. 11).

Perhaps no exact data can be established on how many workers are now engaged in moonlighting. As mentioned earlier (p. 130), official figures put the number at 15 million, or between 20 per cent and 25 per cent of the urban workforce in 1991. My questions about moonlighting to some forty workers at that time revealed that almost all of them had had a second job at one time or another. The statistical gap may be because: (1) many second jobs are done secretly; and (2) most of these jobs are neither stable nor long-lasting.[12] Furthermore, the amount of income so generated is subject to fast-changing conditions. When high, it could be many times the income from a regular job. When low, most of my interviewees agreed, it may merely help to compensate for inflation.

There is no doubt that opportunities for second jobs have weakened the control of the party/state over the urban population. The profits generated by second jobs have also magnified the determination of workers to jump into the 'business seas' (*xiahai*). As one worker put it jokingly, 'The door has opened just enough for us to increase our income through our own resources – our hands and our business contacts. Let's work harder to pull it further open.' These words send out a strong signal, which means more than earning just a few more dollars for daily expenditure. It is to do with the restoration of a sense of personal independence rather than living on state provisions. It is about enthusiasm for enlarging personal property, which was long suppressed by state ownership but has now engaged the entrepreneurial zeal of many Chinese. This constitutes the root of the revolution of consumerism in China. In terms of the damaging effect that private business activities pose to the official ideology and the *danwei* structure, moonlighting triggers a 'quiet revolution from below', as also seen in the Hungarian reform experience (Szelenyi, 1988).

Again, although this is the direction of China's ongoing socio-political transformation, one has to exercise caution not to overstate it at this stage. For one thing, some state-owned enterprises forbid workers to take second jobs.[13] For another, the benefits created by a second job, generally speaking, have not come near those a permanent job can provide. According to some surveys by Chinese academics, in addition to regular wages, a state worker can receive lifetime welfare services worth over 200,000 *yuan*, covering housing or housing allowances, medical care and other state and factory subsidies. Collectively 192 million people (staff in government offices, personnel in social and cultural institutions, and workers in the state sector), or 16.2 per cent of China's population, enjoyed nearly all the state welfare spending, which was 317 billion *yuan* or over 10 per cent of GDP (3,138 billion *yuan*) in 1993. The breakdown of some of these items is as follows: superannuation, 167 billion *yuan*; poverty fund, 8 billion; housing allowance, 35.6 billion; food subsidies, 25.4 billion; awards in kind calculated on 300 *yuan* per head in the state sector, 52.5 billion; and living subsidies (public transport, heating and so on), 13.6 billion. According to the survey, these were conservative estimates but the ratio of 10 per cent welfare spending in the state budget was already much higher than in other developing countries, e.g. India, 3 per cent, Malaysia, 6 per cent (*Jingi ribao*, 31 July 1995). To be more specific, another SCRES report indicated that every worker in the twenty-eight large state firms it surveyed received in 1995 an average of 324 *yuan* for free education, 844 for medical care and 582 for housing maintenance. They spent 1.6 billion *yuan* on workers' social welfare in the year (*Gongren ribao*, 12 June 1996). On the basis of these figures, a worker in the non-state sector earning 10,000 *yuan* a year, not a bad income in China, would have to devote twenty years' income to achieve the same level of benefits available to workers in the state-owned enterprises. The uncertainties associated with the market also inhibit workers in state-owned enterprises from abandoning what they have achieved in a secure job. This is why many of them want to keep their permanent jobs, even though they would do well in the market. They want to benefit from both ends. As long as the 'big rice bowl' delivers their basic needs, the desire of workers to stick with it will remain. This reality limits their choices and, therefore, it may be too early to talk about the 're-emergence of civil society' within the state sector.

Since 1992, there has been one new development in moonlighting, the so-called 'one family, two systems': either the husband or the wife leaves his/her regular state job to engage fully in the second economy but the other continues his/her state employment. The one keeping a state job gets the public housing and other welfare provisions not only for him/ herself, but for the whole family. The other will *xiahai*, or jump into the 'business seas', where, if successful, he/she can earn an income far greater than his/her spouse's regular wages.[14]

CONFLICTS IN THE FACTORY REWARD PROCESS

The industrial wage reform has engendered a new search for a suitable reward system in China's state sector. As is common in other transitional processes, the most striking feature of this endeavour is that it is pregnant with conflicts. Often the wage reforms are carried out by managers as *ad hoc* measures designed to increase the pay of workers rather than productivity. The resultant uneven distribution of income, due to lack of rules and regulations and the lack of a fully-fledged labour market, has heralded a lengthy period of chaos in the remuneration system in state-owned enterprises. In other words, the current wage mechanisms are not at all stable for a number of reasons, as analysed below.

Keeping up with the Joneses

The first reason touches on a fundamental question of fairness and equity in meting out rewards. The new wage arrangements have so far failed to address this adequately. The question of fairness and equity embraces two important concerns. In theory it raises a question of perceptions of what is fair. In practice, it involves the conflict inherent in a web of interests in state-owned enterprises. The two elements are mutually reinforcing and constitute the origin of an over-zealous competition (*panbi*) among all social members towards wage issues. *Panbi* is now driving shopfloor politics in industrial wage disputes. In fact, the huge pressure generated by such an intensified comparison has been a major factor in determining the fate of any wage reform measures enacted in the state sector.

Despite their positive reaction to the overall programme, the feeling of being unfairly treated has underlain workers' prevailing sense of discontent with the reward process: nationally 72 per cent of them believe that they are not paid their due (*Gongren ribao*, 11 June 1996). This contradiction not only stems from the complicated interactions of interests in any factory, but is also the result of deeply embedded Chinese attitudes towards the distribution of wealth. The phenomenon of keeping up with the Joneses is an expression of the traditional Chinese principle of egalitarianism, as embodied in the saying 'concerned not so much over the scarcity of wealth as over the uneven distribution of it'. This egalitarianism has penetrated deep into the general social mentality, with the conviction that despite the scarcity of goods, as long as distribution is even, the smooth operation of society will be assured. Mao's creation of the policy of 'three people's food for five people to eat' in 1953, when pressured by growing unemployment, testified to his understanding of this popular mentality (Peng Xianzhi, 1989, p. 54). The eight-grade wage system was built on such a premise. In the hope of achieving some sort of psychological equilibrium among the masses, a highly egalitarian pattern of consumption was imposed to prevent polarisation of wealth when there was not much to share. The psychological equilibrium, built upon a combination of communist ideology and Confucian egalitarianism, had a value orientation: social fairness meant everyone should have a similar share of social income.

The post-Mao reform has upset this equilibrium with an enlarged wealth gap between different social groups. Within the state sector, state policies and the invisible hand of the market have jointly ingrained a dilemma in the minds of workers: while the wage reform is perceived as much needed, its effects are unfair. As the powers of remuneration have been transferred from the state to producers, no factory wants to fall victim to this fluid socio-economic environment. State-owned enterprises respond by trying to keep up with their neighbours regardless of different circumstances in production and profitability.

Keeping up with the Joneses is deeply institutionalised in workers' search for higher earnings. They make constant comparisons because they started from an identical level of income at the beginning of the wage reform. Now some of them have gone far ahead. So in a way *panbi* results in an emerging stratification within the workforce in both state and private sectors (Li Beilin, 1996, part three). And this stratification is often an outcome of an irregular distribution process that contributes to growing income disparities among workers. In state-owned enterprises, under the remunerative policies of the small work units, one worker may earn over 1,000 *yuan* a month while another earns just a few hundred. The same worker may receive several hundred *yuan* in March but less than 100 in April. According to a survey conducted among 100 enterprises in 1996, the lowest level of monthly income for workers was 240 *yuan*, and the highest was 2,500. The workers' average monthly income for the top twelve firms exceeded 1,500 *yuan* but for the bottom twelve it was below 500 (Wang Xiaolu, 1996, p. 46).

Among different industries the capacity to make profits has varied sharply. The uneven effects of market forces, and particularly the logic of wage reform, which no longer makes a linkage between pay and profit, have left 'sunset' industries in a dire situation. The booming sectors may be wealthy enough to pay every worker more than 10,000 *yuan* a year. For instance, telecommunications is now a golden industry. In Beijing, it costs 5,000 *yuan* to install a private phone. The demand for installation is so high (over one million) that there is a long waiting list. To meet the demand means making 5 billion *yuan* in sales. This has made workers in Beijing's Telecom among the richest in the industrial workforce (*Wenzhaibao*, 25 July 1996). In contrast, a large number of factories in traditional industries, e.g. mining or defence-related, ran a huge loss and relied heavily on state subsidies. However, the state's assistance could at best provide a bare subsistence to millions of workers in these industries.[15] One industry may go quickly through a period of boom and bust within a number of years, its workers the best paid one year and the next receiving only a fraction of their base wages. The electrical durables industry is a good example. Between 1984 and 1986, the retail sales of colour TVs, refrigerators and washing machines increased by 69 per cent, 157 per cent and 77 per cent respectively, and jobs in the industry were keenly sought (*Renmin ribao*, 19 June 1988). By the middle of the 1990s the market for electronic durables has become partially saturated, which has forced the closure of a number of producers. Now the workers in these factories are complaining bitterly about their pay. So the profit-based industrial wage reform has built up the framework for enlarged income differentials between industries, regions, factories and workshops. The workers in the loss-making factories feel victimised, for in a semi-reformed economy it is not often possible for them to choose where to work. Yet they now have to share the misfortunes of their work units. (See Table 7.1.)

Workers are convinced that they have a right to compare or *panbi* because they see a gap between perceived fair standards in wage distribution and those in real practice. A large-scale field survey conducted by some Chinese labour experts in 1993 found that most workers thought capability should be the primary standard for awards, but in reality seniority was the most decisive. Particularly annoying were the discrepant roles played by work attitudes and the relations with leaders in the reward process. The former was regarded as the third most important standard that should be employed. In practice the relations with leaders actually occupied that position. Workers engaged in *panbi* also because of the low level of transparency in the distribution of earnings. In the same survey, 89 per cent of workers expressed a preference for openness in their work

Table 7.1 Annual income for workers in different sectors of state-owned enterprises per person (in *yuan*)

	1995	1990	Growth rate (%)
Banking and insurance	8,197	2,164	279
Telecommunications and transportation	7,904	1,886	319
Building	6,627	2,333	184
Manufacturing	6,239	1,963	217
Retail	5,952	1,793	231

Source: *Zhongguo gongshang shibao*, 30 May 1996.

units' reward process. Yet only half are informed of the criteria used (Feng Tongqing, 1993, p. 99). Decisions taken behind close doors naturally breed suspicion, which in turn intensifies a *panbi* psychology.

The legacy of the command economy, e.g. state-assigned employment, and irregularity in small distribution entities, have combined to cause a popular sense of discontent among workers. *Panbi* is just their bitter reaction to a reward system in which they have found neither the process nor the result to be fair. In this environment their work achieves less than they would expect, but political power brings in easy money for those who do not make any serious effort. So they feel vulnerable. *Panbi* then results in actions such as strikes and stealing factory property, the only recourse available.[16]

Worsening labour management relations

As Walder points out, one major change in China's state-owned enterprises in the reform era is that industrial relations have been grossly monetised, which has further entrenched the web of interests among management and the workforce (Walder, 1989b, p. 30). In the past, the political favouritism granted to the party faithful was not always accompanied by wage increases, as the factory authorities did not possess the power to provide increases whenever they wanted. Now with this power in their hands, factory and workshop managers can exercise favouritism to a much greater extent. They tend to abuse the power over remuneration to their own advantage (*Zuzhi renshibao*, 4 July 1995). Given workers' uncompromising attitudes towards wage disputes, labour relations have become more difficult to manage. The tripartite interactions between the state, enterprises and workers have entered a new period of enormous complexity.

Factory managers are now at the centre of wage conflicts. In large part this is because they now have the power to decide on their own wage scales, although the state does have a reference wage limit for them, which stands at three or four times the average wage of the factory. Workers perceive a widespread misuse of this power by factory managers to increase their own personal gains. For instance, from 1986 to 1988 out of eighty-three factory managers in sixty-one municipal factories of Fuxin City, Liaoning Province, only one did not promote himself to a higher grade of base salary; forty received rises twice and, in an extreme case, a manager raised his base grade six times (Huang Yuan, 1990, p. 138). As far as bonuses and other fringe benefits are concerned, there are virtually no limits. According to an investigation in Anshan City, again in Liaoning Province, in one industrial bureau which has five factories under it, the average bonus for workers in 1988 was 258 *yuan*, while the five factory managers allowed themselves to take 59,450 *yuan*, amounting to 11,890 *yuan* each, forty-six times a worker's bonus. In one factory in Anshan a total of 101 kinds of bonuses were created to reward staff and workers in different jobs. The manager grabbed ninety-six kinds (Huang Yuan, 1990, p. 137). This abuse of power has been in striking contrast to the policy of granting income as equally as possible among co-workers (Sun Zhen, 1992, p. 10).

It is too simplistic to conclude that all factory managers are capable of abusing remunerative power to the extent indicated above. The general trend is that the larger the state-owned enterprises, the smaller the space for income manipulation by factory managers. Pressures have been generated from both below and above. The large and medium-sized state firms are under tighter scrutiny from state agencies. And the influence of the trade unions over wage levelling can also be strong. Many factory managers are aware of the limits to which they can go before enraging subordinates. Unwarranted gaps in income between management and workers will exacerbate already visible passive resistance and may even pave the way for violence.[17] Many factory managers in capital cities exercise self-restraint in deciding how much they receive. This was particularly true for a time after 4 June 1989, when the state stepped up its control over remuneration matters as a key measure for stabilising industrial relations.[18] Yet without an institutional mechanism, abuse of wage power by factory managers has again risen in recent years. It is even regarded as a normal practice within a manager's legitimate authority.

On the other hand, it is equally misleading to state that the managers of large and medium-sized companies are cleaner than their counterparts in smaller firms. Although they may abide fairly strictly by the state's 'three or four times' restriction, they have their own ways of 'getting rich before others'. For instance, they are more inclined to conduct behind-closed-doors dealings among themselves. Commission fees are one common source of extra income. Secret rewards in kind attached to business deals prove to be safer than outright enlargement of one's own salary. Here nothing is too small and no gift too big. Practical benefits received by factory managers range from cigarettes to wine to housing to payment of their children's university tuition fees and soliciting prostitutes at the company's expense. As business autonomy becomes greater, these practices are snowballing, and the value of the 'gift' given and taken is calibrated to the nature and size of business transactions.[19]

What these factory managers do to gain windfalls cannot be entirely hidden from middle-level management and workers. Taking advantage of their newly acquired power in determining remuneration in their units, many workshop managers similarly design for themselves the form of salary that will bring in the highest possible amount of money. Where possible, they also create behind-the-scenes workshop businesses in such a way that they receive commissions and gifts. Workers do not know exactly how much their factory and workshop bosses receive from private channels, but they are conscious of what is going on. Some of them are bold enough to raise collective demands for salary increases and extra compensation through bonuses. Others simply steal products, destroy machinery or adopt go-slows to give vent to their anger at the advantages taken by the managers at different levels.

Monetised industrial relations prove to be very fragile. In 1988 a group of workers at the Shenyang Tractor Factory went on strike. To outsiders the reason may have seemed trivial: their section leader had received 20 *yuan* more in bonuses. However, this illustrates well the sensitive nature of such an issue and the limits of the workers' tolerance of uneven remuneration within a factory. In fact, according to Chinese labour authorities, the majority of industrial disputes occur at middle and lower management levels and involve only moderate amounts of money (Huang Yuan, 1990, p. 140). However, when we link the appalling methods of reaping wealth resorted to by many factory managers, as in examples cited earlier, to the over-reaction from the workers in the Shenyang Tractor Factory, the gravity of industrial wage disputes in China presents itself clearly.

Tension among co-workers

Susan Shirk points out that China's industrial wage reform stresses that pay should be based on objective standards of performance. Compared with the old wage structure, the basic feature of this new tendency has been an attempt to undo the ties that linked pay to specific people based on seniority, and instead to link pay to job, post and work effort (Shirk, 1981, pp. 575–93). In theory, the application of quantitative measures to count and evaluate work results is a process of depersonalising a reward system, thus reducing the potential for tensions among workers which might be caused by subjective allocation of wages by factory cadres. In practice, however, this upset the long-held balance of interests resting on the 'big rice bowl' arrangements. In addition, the technical problems associated with inventing credible and fair mechanisms for spreading benefits, or in other words in establishing a new balance, have so far proved insurmountable.

The profit-oriented wage system is by nature open-ended, as profit is an uncertain variable and fluctuates continuously. In consequence, workers' income floats constantly. This causes difficulty in aligning pay with a certain level of work effort. In the past, group assessments were a main method of determining what a worker had done and how much he or she should be paid in bonuses. Points of contention arose in the assessment but were somewhat contained because the amount of bonus was not significant compared to the fixed salary. More often than not, bonuses were distributed fairly equally in order to preserve group harmony. The current floating wage system has made harmony difficult to maintain. For one thing, a large proportion of the workers' salary is tied to the fluctuating profit. So the setting of a production quota puts workers' livelihood more at stake and thus evokes fiercer contention between co-workers. Group harmony is still regarded as important but in many cases it is adversely affected by strife for material gains. Chinese economists and sociologists call this phenomenon the 'dilution of human sentiments' towards co-workers (Hu Chengfu, 1991, p. 7). This dilution has hurt the normal *guanxi* interactions among workers which are the foundation of the stability of the group. The upsurge of wage-related conflict shows the extent to which the group environment has decayed. (See Table 7.2.)

This statement may seem to contradict an earlier description of the proliferation of collective industrial action. Yet collective action is attempted by one group of workers and often counteracted by another because the irregular reward system gives workers different stakes. And this has been reinforced by a paternalistic clustering of workers with different statuses. The monetisation of labour relations can at once enhance a manager's image as a dispenser of justice when the group becomes fragmented and yet reduce his say in daily management, as discontented workers exert themselves in a more organised manner.

The intensified disputes among workers have been partially due to the fact that the shift to profit as a base for determining wages makes the setting and resetting of quotas and rewards more frequent. This in turn dictates that the group of co-workers should meet regularly to discuss wage issues. Each of these sessions may prove to be a nightmare for some workers. Even if many workers wanted to eschew active participation in the potentially explosive gatherings, as they often did in the past, they can no longer afford to do so: 'The endless group assessments mean that you have to struggle to protect your own interests or otherwise you will always be left in the cold.'[20]

Furthermore, links of mutual support among relatives and friends in the industrial workforce exacerbate these tensions. As wages monetise the relations among co-workers, the immediate result is that the already fragmented workforce becomes even more fragmented. From the

Table 7.2 Assessment of colleague relations, 1991 vs. 1984

	Assessment of managers			Assessment of technical staff			Assessment of workers		
	Worse	Better	No change	Worse	Better	No change	Worse	Better	No change
	%	%	%	%	%	%	%	%	%
Workers vs. workers	42	35	24	45	34	20	33	37	28
Workers vs. technical staff	39	41	18	39	38	23	31	46	23
Workers vs. managers	52	29	19	56	28	16	46	33	21
Managers vs. managers	46	36	18	51	34	15	42	37	20

Source: Feng Tongqing, 'Biange zhongde gongren jieji heibu jieceng guifam jiqi Xiomguam Shehui Wenti' (Changing relations within the working class and social implications), *Guanli shiji*, no. 2, 1996, p. 3.

mid-1970s to the mid-1980s the officially sanctioned practice of recruit-ment of employees' children affected the organisational texture of the workforce. A large proportion of workers now have close relatives in the workforce. And the smaller the factory, the graver this situation becomes. For instance, in the Hongdu Molding Factory 45 per cent of the 765 workers have at least one family member in the same factory. According to a survey of several dozen factories by the labour department in Hunan, the relatives network in the labour force of each factory reached 35 per cent on average, with the highest 72 per cent in one factory. The survey report revealed that the conflict over pay issues became more serious as the rate grew (Lun Yuan, 1991, p. 7). Large factories suffer the same symptoms, although with less visible adverse effects. These are, however, the factories that have been pressed most strenuously to carry out the reform of 'rationalising workers'.[21] Many recent surveys have disclosed that, when the section and group leaders proceeded to place their followers in better posts, this, too, grouped workers into different factions. Consequently, if one worker was not satisfied with what he was paid, he might drag his coterie into the conflict. One worker told me that he was fed up with factory life because the stresses on worker solidarity had mounted to an unbearable degree, brought to a head by the frequent wage disputes among co-workers.[22] In short, the industrial wage reform in the late 1990s will have to tackle disorder in remuneration before it can be institutionalised to the satisfac-tion of workers. Otherwise, the chaos may become a source of tension that will undermine other reform packages in state-owned enterprises: workers will gradually lose confidence in reform. Russia has already shown the world how this can happen.

Part IV

De-statisation: an ownership and organisational analysis

8 Corporatisation and privatisation

The party's consensus at its Fourteenth National Congress in 1992 to transform the Chinese economy into a market model brought the reform from the periphery to the core of the economic system. Specifically, it involves a change in emphasis from price adjustment and redistribution of decision-making power between the centre, locality and enterprise, to a reform of the ownership system. This was manifested in the party's announcement that the key word *guoying qiye*, or state-run enterprises, which connotes the nature of the state/enterprise relationship as one where the former directly runs the latter, would be replaced by *guoyou qiye*, meaning state-owned but not necessarily state-run. In 1993 the Eighth National People's Congress amended the Constitution to legalise this strategic change. Currently *guoyou minying*, or state-owned but privately or corporately run, has become the guideline for China's enterprise reform. Indeed, the market consensus has placed China's economic reform at a crossroads: the government has plans to convert the majority of large and medium-sized state enterprises into shareholding corporations and to lease or privatise most small firms. This is bound to generate far-reaching consequences for China. For instance, privatisation and corporatisation will remove the foundation of the *danwei* system, because a corporatised firm is closer to an economic entity than to a political institution. In such an entity the corporate governance structure will leave a much smaller space for party cells to function; cadre status will be eliminated, and wage and employment policies will be formulated independently (SETC, 1994, p. 49). This chapter analyses the new direction in China's economic reform, which, according to Vice-Minister Cheng Qingtai of the State Commission of Economics and Trade, will be the focus of China's economic reform in the next few years (*New China News*, 3 February 1995) and its impact on the change in China's ownership structure.

DE-STATISATION: CONCEPTUALISING A TRANSITIONAL PHENOMENON

The concept of de-statisation in this chapter embraces the process of changing property relations between the state and state-owned enterprises. It describes a transitional phase of China's reform: while the state's direct control at the micro level is being phased out, it still wields powerful leverage over state firms based on state ownership. This half-way phenomenon is poised to change but the change will take a fairly long time, a feature that distinguishes China's transition from that of other transforming command economies.

The transfer of property control

The conceptualisation of de-statisation rests on a theoretical breakdown of the notion of property rights. In western scholarship property rights are a set of concrete legal relations such as the right to use, to derive income from use, to exclude others, and to exchange goods and services (Putterman, 1995, pp. 1047–64). This breakdown provides us with a guide to evaluate a command economy in transition: with the transfer of specific rights such as income and management from the state to property users, the concept of socialist ownership is gradually becoming an empty shell.[1] More concretely, under the Stalinist model all these four rights were concentrated in the hands of state planners, so there was little need to clarify the specific rights any further. China's reforms have partially separated ownership and property rights as specifically defined. This has occasioned a process of decontrol both in administrative and in ownership terms. In the former the concept of de-statisation reflects relocation of control to property users, concretely embodied in the State Council's fourteen managing powers granted to producers.[2] In the latter it reflects dilution of state ownership in an increasingly hybridised property structure.

In theory, the transfer of rights to use, to possess or dispose, and to allocate income can be seen as moving state firms towards privatisation (*minyinghua*) (Hemming and Mansoor, 1988, p. 1). In this light, scholars of the Russian reforms define the acquisition of residual rights of control over firms as spontaneous privatisation, which highlights the *de facto* ability of a firm to determine how its assets are used in all circumstances other than those specified in implicit or explicit contracts (Johnson *et al.*, 1993, p. 147). In practice, the process of de-statisation reflects the revised goal of state-owned enterprises, responding to the market. Before reform, the goal of a factory was to fulfil the state plan. For most of the 1980s the goal could be characterised as double dependence: the factory depended on the state for cheap materials and subsidies but on the market for profits (Kornai, 1985, p. 10). Marketisation has rendered this double dependence highly dynamic. When the state is hardly able to bail a factory out, the latter is to forced to seek survival through engaging in market competition. The factory thus develops its own goals of production centred on profits and, accordingly, seeks new organisational forms other than being an appendage of bureaucracy. This provides impetus for China's current efforts to construct a 'modern enterprise system' in the state sector, commonly known as corporatisation, as a result of both bottom-up pressure from firms to become economic entities in a market environment and the need of the state to reduce subsidies. The de-statising effect is nonetheless the same: the elimination of the bureaucratic bosses from state firms. As one senior Chinese economic official pointed out, the essence of 'state owned, privately run' is gradual removal of direct state management at the micro level (*Beijing ribao*, 20 December 1992). East European reforms have testified that before a smooth path is paved for privatisation it is crucial to neutralise the commanding heights so as to make firms autonomous entities. So in a way privatisation in Russia and Eastern Europe inevitably parallels the withering of central economic ministries (Amodio, 1993, p. 227).

To dilute state ownership

It is inadequate to regard privatisation as merely a transfer of control. For instance, decentralisation in the form of contracting out state factories may not turn them into private concerns. Yet it may alter their ownership structure, as they acquire new property through the contractors' own investments from bank loans, profit retention or self-raised funds. In China this creates a notion of enterprise assets (*qiye zichan*), which expand when a large number of state firms gradually become the main investment body. This notion differs from the concepts of either state or private ownership. China's economists compare it to the concept of social ownership in Yugoslavia (Liu Wei, 1991, p. 65), where 'behind the permanent sources of funds of enterprises one cannot find any person to whom these funds belong' (Miller, 1989, pp. 430–48). Yet the Chinese notion does identify the factory and its workers as the owner. This originated from the definition of property relations in China's collective firms where fixed assets theoretically belong to all staff. This kind of social ownership is thus called enterprise ownership. As the share of collective property increases *vis-à-vis* the state's, the state's initial design of separating owner-ship and management rights turns to stimulate factories to seek more powers of control with the integration of ownership rights and manage-ment rights on their own terms (Liu Guoguang, 1988, p. 12). To the extent that the previously monolithic state ownership is diluted by such a hybridised ownership structure, privatisation of the state sector *begins* with de-statisation. Indeed, collective ownership has served as a channel to transform the 'big public's assets' (the state's) into the 'small public's assets' (the factory's) and then into private assets (through the factory-based distribution process) (Ma Hong, 1988, p. 236).

The ongoing reform of corporatisation of state factories is a further step in the transformation of the state ownership system. The conversion based on the stock system may be compared to a reversal of the nationalisation movement in China in the 1950s, which eliminated private concerns by continuously injecting state property into their ownership structure. More and more non-state property is now 'grafted' into the state sector as a 'fast track' to modernise the loss-making, technologically obsolete firms which the state is financially unable to save (*Liaowang*, no. 7, 1993, p. 9). State ownership is thus partially denationalised. Joint ventures in the form of 'one factory, two or three systems' have become common among large and medium-sized state-owned enterprises, resulting in a constant decline of the dominance of state ownership.

China's reform has shown that in order to achieve a level of efficiency in capital allocation and management, it is necessary to dilute state ownership by injecting non-state property into it. This highlights the risk of property use in market competition. Moreover, the management of a mixed ownership structure calls for the creation of a legal and institutional framework commensurate with market dictates. The correlation between diluting state ownership and a firm's autonomy can be seen from the different rates of productivity growth in state firms according to whether they have or have not been converted into joint ventures.[3] Compared to other post-socialist economies, China's ownership reform through hybridising state and non-state properties represents a distinctive path.

A covert strategy for privatisation: ideological revisionism

While de-statisation can be seen as the early stages of, and a necessary gateway to, privatisation, the concept spells out a Chinese strategy for ownership reform antithetical to the shock therapy prescribed to the former Soviet bloc, where the political authorities issued public decrees privatising state factories. Supporters of a gradualist approach to economic reform believe that the Big Bang strategy will not achieve the desired goal of changing the behaviour of state-owned enterprises. Without a full-fledged market these state-owned enterprises will only monopolise the sector, even though they are privatised (H. Zhou, 1994). In contrast, the incremental strategy seems to be more logical. It first directs state firms to reduce their dependence on central planning. It then promotes easy entry of non-state concerns into the national economy. Only when state-owned enterprises are aggressively challenged in intensified market competition will their behaviour fundamentally change (W. Hauagan and Zhang Jun, 1996, p. 4).

The concept of de-statisation converges with a gradualist school of thought in an analysis of command economies in transition (Pei Minxin,

1996, pp. 131–45). Ownership reform in China is state-controlled, its depth and pace being conditioned by a number of constraints for reallocation of political and economic interests. For instance, the interests of planners have to be considered in the ongoing government reforms accompanying the corporatisation reform, as a large number of cadres must leave their current positions. Workers, too, have to be protected in one way or another, for the corporatisation reform is sure to shut down many firms.[4] Ideologically, the party's adherence to the 'socialist road' still generates pressure on the practitioners of ownership reform, even though the state-controlled privatisation strategy now stems less from a worry over ideology than from concern over loss of control. With no easy solutions available, these constraints have dictated a Chinese pattern of quasi privatisation by way of moving to the 'core' of state ownership from the peripheries. This is apparent in the shift of emphasis from the contract system in the 1980s to corporatisation in the 1990s. Even in the initial stage of corporatisation, the state will impose limits on stocks owned by the private concerns.

Therefore, at the theoretical level, there has to be a 'middle course' for ownership reform, which should at once retain a superior proportion of state property in the national ownership structure and help to scale down the liability of the state for loss makers. Against this backdrop the corporatisation reform has become the consensus of the day. Yu Guang-yuan has argued that public ownership is not a unique trait of the socialist economy and that joint stock companies are not a form of privatisation. It is basically a change in mode of management from state control to cooperative control (*Jingji ribao*, 5 August 1993). Some officials and scholars attribute the country's economic ills to the fact that privatisation has not gone far enough.[5] But they draw a line of self-defence when translating the ideological question of privatisation into policy proposals. What they do in practice is to press ahead with quasi privatisation while vocally adhering to the idea of predominant state ownership. They insist that the ownership reform should make four distinctions: between key sectors of the economy and others of lesser importance; between large and small state-owned enterprises; between centrally controlled enterprises and local ones; and between different regions (Xiao Liang, 1989, p. 1).

This classification gives ideological justification to the 'graft' of non-state property into state ownership: the dominance of state ownership should not be counted mathematically but rest on state control over the strategic sectors. With such control there is no need for the state to own or run firms in non-strategic sectors (*Guangming ribao*, 6 November 1995). This ideological revisionism is based on the necessity of using capitalism to save Chinese socialism. After all, China's post-Mao reform has been a process of adopting capitalist measures to run the economy (Solinger, 1989, pp. 19–33). Liaoning Province, the most enthusiastic proponent for transforming state-owned enterprises into joint ventures, viewed the 'graft' of foreign investment into its backward industries as a second industrial revolution holding the fate of millions of workers (*Jingji ribao*, 23 April 1994). In fact, the province has done the 'graft' so success-fully that, to duplicate the success, its governor Yue Qifeng was promoted to be the 'number one' leader in the neighbouring province of Hei-longjiang, which is also part of the so-called northeast China phenomenon where a large number of loss-making state firms are concentrated.[6] For Yue, the need is clear: among the province's 976 large and medium-sized state-owned enterprises, only 10 per cent are equipped with the tech-nology of the 1980s. Owing to lack of funds fewer than one-third have been systematically renovated in the last decade (Yue Qifeng, 1992, p. 33). To upgrade the rest would easily cost 100 to 200 billion *yuan*, this being wildly beyond the capacity of not only the provincial but the national government. Not to upgrade them, however, means that over 70 per cent of the plants would continue to make a loss (*Guangming ribao*, 2 May 1994).

What Yue did was simple: he encouraged the factories to offer their land and facilities fairly cheaply to foreign investors and transform them-selves partly or wholly into joint ventures. On the basis of this 'grafting', the joint ventures would be further transformed into joint stock com-panies. In 1992 alone the province approved 'grafting' for 754 state firms including all major enterprises in the area. By now 260 stock companies have emerged from these joint ventures (*Guangming ribao*, 2 May 1994). As the profit rate of the province picked up visibly, the Liaoning experi-ment has been seen as 'the dawn light' for China's state sector and followed by other provinces.[7]

That the CCP has now made it state policy to use foreign investment to save state firms reveals a logic in China's reforms: when the market evolves to a point where it dominates economic activities, one form of the mixed economy or another has to emerge.[8] So the essence of de-statisation is a kind of quasi privatisation. Now many state firms also have hopes of domestic non-state investors for 'grafting', which further promotes a mixed property structure in the state sector.

Yet the Liaoning example also shows that, as far as large state-owned enterprises are concerned, the state can control the process by selecting who should be the partner and what level of funds should be injected into what industries. The fact that its ability to do this is eroding goes hand in hand with the rising need of state firms for non-state investment. Therefore, de-statisation as a strategy for quasi privatisation is both a subjective design and a logical development in a state economy in tran-sition.

The analysis of this logical development emphasises the future pros-pects of the state-controlled ownership reform. This is crucial because many ownership reforms are implemented quietly, a phenomenon that analysts dub 'can do but not talk'.[9] To decipher China's quasi privatisation requires a further study of its state industrial and commercial sector.

According to the SCRES, in the late 1980s the state industrial sector comprised 463,210 factories in public ownership at the township level or above. A breakdown of this revealed that only 11,540, or 2.5 per cent, of these were large or medium-sized and only one-tenth were centrally controlled. Moreover, out of these 463,210 firms, 302,000 were collective concerns. At the local level, the majority of firms were run by the township government, while the county-level factories numbered less than 50,000. If we further divide state-owned enterprises by industrial sector, we find that about half of them belong to light industry. Among the rest in the heavy industrial manufacturing sectors, the bulk were small factories with large and medium-sized state-owned enterprises numbering only 2,321 and 5,590 respectively (SCRES, 1988, p. 157).

These figures become very important in our analysis of China's ownership reform when we bring into the picture the 'four distinctions' mentioned earlier (p. 167). Clearly the majority of China's state and collective factories are politically privatisable. Even for most large and medium-sized state-owned enterprises in strategic sectors, one form of quasi privatisation or another has taken place, as the Liaoning experience proves, and this will accelerate with the progress of corporatisation. In fact, the effects of quasi privatisation have been reflected by two parallel processes of de-statisation in the strategic and non-strategic sectors. Corporatisation based on the stock system is being introduced into the former, breaking down monolithic state ownership. More outright privatisation measures have been implemented in the non-strategic sectors under the formula of 'state owned but privately run'. One SETC report categorically recommends that in due course the majority of small state firms should be privatised in order to generate money to finance the development of the priority sectors, a state social welfare system and relocation of state staff (SETC, 1994, p. 48). This two-track reform strategy has now been officially adopted by the party centre as *zhuada fangxiao*, literally translated as revitalising large state firms through corporatisation (*zhuada*) and letting go small ones through privatisation (*fangxiao*) (Li Chunting, 1996, p. 37). *Fangxiao* is similar to selling state factories in Eastern Europe, according to the Chinese participants at an international conference held in Beijing in late 1995 (*China Business Times*, 6 November 1995). Its purpose was twofold: (1) to reduce the government burden of bailing out those small firms; and (2) to raise money in order to relocate workers in the state sector. Privatising medium-scale and small state-owned enterprises will have a far-reaching impact in both economic and political terms: nationally they make up 99.8 per cent of industrial concerns, employ 75 per cent of the workforce, produce 60 per cent of GNP, and submit 40 per cent of taxes (*China Business Times*, 14 June 1996).

THE CHANGING NATIONAL OWNERSHIP STRUCTURE

The effects of de-statisation can also be seen in the changes in the structure of production.[10] At the abstract level, the structure offers a picture of property relations in an economy, as the dominant mode of production imparts its essential characteristics to the whole system (Milanovic, 1991, p. 7). According to the official classifications of China's firms, nine forms of ownership exist today: state, collective, Sino-foreign joint ventures, private, individual, joint investment, shares and stock, foreign proprietorship, and Hong Kong, Macao and Taiwan concerns (*Zhongguo tongji xinxibao*, 7 December 1992). State ownership is still the major mode in statistical terms. Yet the very fact that non-state ownership forms have proliferated indicates that the predominance of state owner-ship is being reduced. The state sector produced 78 per cent of GNP in 1978 compared with a little over 43 per cent in 1993, a figure below that of 45 per cent in 1952, shortly before China's nationalisation drive (Guo Zhenyi, 1992, p. 1; Chen Xiaohong, 1996, p. 144). In terms of the national capital structure, foreign investment of about US$153 billion (nearly 1.4 trillion *yuan*) has been registered in the top ten receiving provinces in the last decade and compares strongly with state industrial assets of 3 trillion *yuan*, accumulated over forty years.[11] By mid-1996 the number of foreign industrial concerns and joint ventures in the country had reached 120,000, employing 17 million workers, or over one-quarter of workers in the state sector (*China Business Times*, 14 August 1996).

State factories now employ only 18 per cent of the national working population. In cities they employ 40 per cent of urban employees (Chen Xiaohong, 1996, p. 144). Between now and the year 2000 72 million city dwellers will enter the labour force. At the same time 15–20 million surplus workers in state-owned enterprises will have to be made redun-dant and over 200 million rural people will have to be relocated (*Guangmin ribao*, 11 April 1996). In the meantime the state sector will be able to absorb only 22.5 million job seekers. As each new industrial position costs about 15,000 *yuan* in capital investment, the state simply has not the financial strength to take on such a large number of employees.[12] Since 1994 the workforce in state-owned enterprises has actually been shrinking. All this points to one direction for development: promoting faster expansion of the private sector is the only viable way of lessening the pressure. According to the World Bank, by the end of the 1990s, even if China were not to implement any large-scale privatisation programmes, the rapid growth of non-state sectors would still contribute twice as much to GNP as is contributed by state-owned enterprises.

According to the well-known economist Liu Guoguang, the increase in the number of private enterprises in 1993 compared to 1992 was 70.4 per cent; in employment, 60.7 per cent; in registered investment, 207.5 per cent; the corresponding figures for 1994 compared to 1993 were

81.5 per cent, 74 per cent and 113 per cent. Tax remittance in the same period more than doubled. For the first time in 1993 urban private investment exceeded rural, with a proportion of 53 per cent compared with 46.7 per cent in the overall structure, a development of major significance (*Jingji ribao*, 24 April 1994). (See Table 8.1.)

A fast-growing private sector has proved to be an indispensable precondition for China's privatisation process. In addition to playing a major role in creating employment, it has provided valuable dollars from its export-oriented industries and submitted tax revenues with which the state can subsidise loss-making state factories.[13] More importantly, the private sector has prepared the financial ground for the private concerns to penetrate into state-owned enterprises and has fostered the convergence of the two sectors. For instance, in Congqing City alone, the municipal government put 1,000 state and collective factories to tender from private buyers (*China Business Times*, 30 April 1996). The existence of a large number of 'new rich' in China has put the country at a visible advantage compared with Russia in scaling down state ownership (Goodman, 1992, p. 350). In short, de-statising the state economy from the invasion of the non-state sector is a unique feature of China's economic transformation.

CORPORATISING STATE-OWNED ENTERPRISES THROUGH THE STOCK SYSTEM

Although still at an experimental stage, corporatisation has gradually moved to the centre of China's enterprise reform. In March 1991 Premier Li Peng raised the issue of stock reform when addressing a national conference on economic reform: the enterprise conglomerates (*qiye jituan*) could not work unless they were transformed into joint stock companies. Without a clear delineation of property rights, profits generated by an enterprise conglomerate could not be properly distributed among member factories, making it difficult for them to cooperate (Jin Jian, 1992, p. 362). Later that year Li approved the report of the SCRES advocating furthering the shares reform, expanding it to non-enterprise conglomerates. During his south China tour, Deng categorically rejected accusations that the shares system would lead to capitalism. His green light at once caused massive stock-shares 'waves' in the country.

Decision making and contents

The sudden policy change on the stock system by Li Peng raises unanswered questions about the decision-making process.[14] It is, however, an indicator of the CCP leadership's recognition that it is time to tackle the 'core problem' of ownership in the country's economic system (*Renmin ribao*, 15 May 1993).

Table 8.1 The growth of the private sector

	Total number of private industrial firms		Employment (10,000)		Registered capital (billion yuan)	
	Number	Growth rate over the previous year (%)	Number employed	Growth rate over the previous year (%)	Amount	Growth rate over the previous year (%)
1990	9.8	8.3	170.0	3.8	9.52	12.6
1991	10.8	10.0	184.0	8.0	12.30	29.0
1992	14.0	29.0	232.0	26.0	22.12	80.0
1993	24.0	70.0	373.0	61.0	68.10	207.0
1994	43.0	82.0	648.4	74.0	144.80	113.0
1995[a]	56.3	30.0	763.2	18.0	246.00	70.0

Source: Jiang Liu et al. (eds) *Blue Book. China in 1995–1996 Analysis and Forecast of Social Situation* (Zhongginshetui kexue chubanshe, 1996), p. 323.

Note:
[a] To the end of June 1995.

One of the factors triggering the party's decision on corporatisation has been a sharp rise in the corporate losses of state-owned enterprises since the 1990s. In 1990, 27.6 per cent of state-owned enterprises registered a loss. The figure rose to 43 per cent in 1995. In the first quarter of 1996 for the first time in the PRC's history the state sector registered an all-sector loss of 3 billion *yuan* (*Gongren ribao*, 25 June 1996). On the other hand state subsidies to loss makers have also reached an untenable level. For instance, the state spent 51 billion *yuan* in 1991 to help cover the losses but that was far from enough. In that year the state sector made a recorded loss of more than 100 billion *yuan*. There were also over 50 billion *yuan* of unreported losses. At the same time unpaid investment loans which came due in the year reached 104 billion *yuan*. When all these figures are added up, they amount to 12.6 per cent of GNP, 62 per cent of state revenue, 75 per cent of the national wage funds, and 45.3 per cent of the capital investment in 1991 (*Liaowang*, no. 47, 1993, p. 10). State-owned enterprises, once the sole source of revenue to the state, are now milking the state treasury in an unsustainable way. Chen Yun's anxiety about this development was clearly conveyed by his son Chen Yuan, vice-governor of China's Central Bank, who stated that loss making was not just an economic problem but also a political one, with dire consequences for the party (Chen Yuan, 1991, p. 18). Indeed, this openly expressed concern has served as the rationale behind the leadership's relaxed attitudes towards the monopoly of state property. The following case illustrates the difficulties a state factory suffered during this period of painful transition.

The Jiangxi August First Linen Fabrics Factory is the second largest linen factory in China, employing more than 6,000 workers. From 1989 to 1992 the factory registered losses of over 60 million *yuan*. Among the debts, borrowed 'circulation funds' and unsaleable goods have exceeded the factory's fixed assets twofold. Travel reimbursements alone, just one of the items of money owed to workers, reached about 800,000 *yuan*. This used to be a model factory with a 'glorious past': during its thirty-year history until 1988 it submitted profits to the state valued at 200 million *yuan*. This is about twenty times the money the state had invested in the factory.

The factory's predicament can be primarily attributed to the command economy. Between 1958 and 1984, it produced only one product: gunny-bags, as prescribed by the state. In the Seventh Five-Year Plan period (1985–90), a large number of village and township gunny-bag factories emerged almost overnight, the industry being labour-intensive and having low levels of capital investment and technology. Consequently, in contrast to national production of 560 million gunny-bags in 1988, 1.5 billion rolled off production lines in 1989, while the market became saturated once production reached 700 million bags. State factories bore the brunt, with the August First Factory worst hit. Still basking in its special status as the second largest in the country, it was entrapped by its single-product structure.

The factory had stuck to the old ways of production management and labour controls. Of 6,000 workers, only 2,000 worked on production lines. Over 600 management staff manned forty-eight offices and departments but they could not propose any feasible methods for marketing the products in stock. As a result, about 1,000 workers had to wait for relocation and another 1,000 tendered their resignation. Moreover, the factory had to support another 1,000 retired staff. Thus every worker on the production lines had to support three other people. The factory had become a 'living fossil' of the command economy amidst a changing economic order.

However, the workers and managers had their own complaints against the state. They believed that they should not be held responsible for the sorry state of the factory. In the past the state took all the profits and left nothing for the factory to upgrade its facilities. This policy created the vicious circle found in all state factories: when a factory was healthy, the state continuously drained its profits until it became so weak that it had to receive a transfusion of 'blood'. When the factory recovered, it was milked again until again it became feeble. There was no mechanism by which the factory could generate its own 'blood'. Had the command economy not undergone the post-Mao reforms, this situation might have been prolonged but not indefinitely – the state itself would eventually have run out of steam, as happened in the USSR. However, the market in China has rung the death knell for this type of state/enterprise relationship. The state's grants no longer come automatically, as it has aggressively adopted the market and profit-oriented investment policies. More importantly, the state now cannot afford to give out subsidies freely, as it faces enormous financial problems itself. It is against this backdrop that Chinese leaders finally arrived at a consensus that state-owned enterprises should become stock companies so as to reduce the state's stakes. As an official in the SCRES pointed out to me in 1992, if a stock company makes profits, it may help the state increase revenues through increased dividends and taxes. Otherwise, the state is not obliged to maintain the 'paternalistic ties' beyond its share of liability.

More insights can be drawn from further analysis of the August First Factory. From October 1992 when the market for linen fabric products began a new period of boom, the August First Factory designed a number of new products with positive market prospects. Yet the state banks firmly rejected its application for additional loans on the grounds that it was on the brink of bankruptcy. Without even circulating funds, the factory had to witness the market being quickly taken over by the more affluent township industries.[15] The state has not declared the factory bankrupt, just because it fears the political and social backlash which would result from laying off 6,000 workers with no safety net in place. As a result, the provincial government offered a series of 'favourable policies' to the factory, including partial waiver of its debts and exemption from taxes. But the banks still refused to lend additional funds unless the factory mortgaged its land, although they agreed to provide loans for the factory to pay minimum wages, or about 70 per cent of the basic salary.

The significance of this story is that currently over 60 per cent of all large and medium-sized state-owned enterprises nationally are experiencing a similar fate (*Gaige neicang*, no. 5, 1996, p. 4). What can the state do? White uses the term 'riding the tiger' to describe its dilemma: it is dangerous to ride a tiger but equally dangerous to dismount – and let the factories go under (White, 1993). According to former Vice-Minister Gao Shangqun of the SCRES, the state had to choose between bankrupting a number of firms or itself going bankrupt. He summarised the importance of the issue:

> Now the enterprise reform has reached a critical pass: all that can be changed has been changed, and we now must tackle the ownership system. This is the key to the creation of a market economy, but the key to this change is first of all a change in our traditional thinking on ownership issues.
>
> (*Jingji ribao*, 25 May 1993)

On the other hand, the stock reform will be based on shaky ground if it is not contained within a well-defined theoretical framework. Despite the fact that the Chinese authorities have seen the risks involved in such an endeavour, many reformers are idealistic about the stock system as the solution to the problems facing state-owned enterprises. A hasty approach towards the stock reform may sow the seeds of collapse if the factors contributing to loss of control are present. Clearly the stock reform is not a panacea, especially as so many interests are at stake. This fear was well expressed by Li Yining: 'When housewives crowd not into the vegetable market but into the stock exchange, the danger signal flashes.' As the prospect of loss of control is always present, the fate of the stock reform remains unassured.

The new property ties

Corporatisation through the stock system is a step forward from the contract reforms in terms of transferring property rights between the state and factories. The contract reform has failed to develop clearly defined property relations between the owner and user, since it is mainly an administrative transfer of property use, leaving room for bureaucratic interventions. China's economists believe that the transition from the contract system to the stock system is an automatic process because the emergence of various mixed property structures requires new kinds of business organisation with legally sanctioned status. Corporations based on the stock system are the best form (Li Yining, 1992, p. 8).

The ongoing corporatisation reform is an attempt to define and personalise property in legal terms. Property in a factory owned by different parties, such as the state, the factory itself, corporate investors and individuals, should be identified by stock holdings. So the stock system is seen as a mechanism for converting state-owned enterprises into corporations, and for establishing different quasi owners to ensure the business autonomy of producers. Gao Shangqun elaborated the relations between the stock system and corporatisation as follows:

> A stock firm must fulfil three basic requirements inherent in a real corporation. First, it must be a civil entity with legal property ownership; second, shareholders only assume limited liability for the debts; third, shareholders entrust the property management to a board of directors whose managing principle is solely profit.
>
> (Gao Shangqun, 1994, p. 3)

China's stock system has in essence been envisaged as a corporate ownership system where a company possesses and manages properties belonging to the public (Gao Shangqun, 1994, p. 5). This concept is antithetical to that of state ownership, which is both absolute and abstract. It is absolute, in that the economic powers stemming from state ownership give state cadres specified channels and unlimited powers to dictate microeconomic activities. It is abstract, in that public ownership is vested in the hands of bureaucrats, rather than reflected by any clearly defined capital entities. These cadres are not liable when property is lost. The stock reform centred on corporate ownership is designed to dilute the absoluteness of the state's direct control over plants through abolishing most of the commanding heights (Gao Zimin, 1993, p. 10) (more on this in the next chapter). At the same time, as the state and corporations are defined as the ultimate and practical owners of the property, the state's links with its property are mainly governed by the shares it controls in a corporation and by the dividends it extracts from its stockholding. As a result, according to Vice-Minister Hong Hu, the practical property rights must be wholly transferred to the firm, making it a new capital principal with all the rights to determine the management of the property, policy of distribution, form of business organisation and appointment of managers (Yang Songtang, 1993, p. 8). In short, the stock system is to be the main vector of transformed state/enterprise relations, separating ultimate and practical ownership but at the same time integrating the two parties' interests through the accrual and distribution of dividends.

At the macro level, corporatisation can help to reform the system of property management. Under the command economy the concept of state property has been arbitrarily split into two categories in China: incremental capital and stock capital. The former describes the capital invested in an ongoing project and the latter the fixed assets after the project becomes operational. Each is placed under the management of two sets of state bodies, the State Planning Commission (for the former) and the Finance Ministry (for the latter). This gives rise to an abnormal situation: there is no need for the investor to care about the outcome of investment, while the property user has limited access to the investors' initial decision process (*Qiye gaige tongxun*, no. 6, September 1992, p. 12). The reform creating independent investment bodies will unify the artificially separated processes of capital management and will make investment decisions economic rather than bureaucratic.

This gives the state a viable way to lessen its heavy burden of subsidies to loss makers and the heavy interference of bureaucrats in the management of firms. Gao Shangqun has pointed out:

> When the investment companies as main shareholders serve as property caretakers of the state in relations with state firms, they will relieve the unlimited liability of the state, which now invests in a plant and accepts for better or for worse the results of its management. Instead, these companies take only limited liability according to their amount of shares. They lose their investment only to the point where they cannot recover the money when the factory is badly run but are not obliged to grant further subsidies.
>
> (*Jingji ribao*, 20 April 1993)

THE CREATION OF THE STOCK SYSTEM

How many state-owned enterprises are expected to follow this route? Corporatisation mainly covers the large and medium-sized state firms. However, according to a senior State Council official, the state will continue to control directly 15 per cent of its large and medium-sized factories (*guoyou guoying*) in key sectors, such as the military industries, mining of precious materials and large public facilities such as telecommunications, that the state believes are too important to let go. The state will maintain control over a proportion of shareholdings among firms in certain sectors, such as energy and transportation, so as to retain sufficient leverage to regulate the economy. For the remainder, the state would take a policy close to 'hands-off' (*Qiye gaige tongxun*, no. 2, May 1992, pp. 6–10).

Types of stock companies

Generally speaking, the stock reform will create corporations of four major types: (1) corporate stock companies of limited liability; (2) 'internal shares' companies issuing non-transferable shares to staff;[16] (3) joint stock companies which can issue public offerings but cannot trade shares on the stock exchanges; and (4) joint stock companies which can trade shares on the stock exchanges. While the second group is to be dominant in terms of numbers, the first is the most important because it embraces the majority of the large and medium-sized state enterprises in the country. The state has exercised tight control over the final two kinds.[17] Here the state is concerned not only about the economic conditions for the reform (e.g. the operation of the stock exchanges), but also about socio-political consequences, such as the level of popular acceptance of the rules of the shares game or the backlash from the ideologues and some central planners who are always fearful of the effects of privatisation inherent in such an endeavour.

A limited liability company is a corporation with two or more share-holders which are corporate persons, not individuals. The state has imposed several restrictions upon a limited liability firm that distinguish it from a joint stock company: (1) it may issue investment certificates but not stocks to shareholders; (2) the transfer of shareholdings is conditional; and (3) the number of shareholders is restricted.[18] These regulations are designed to ensure that a substantial proportion of shareholdings remains in the hands of state firms participating in the company and, therefore, that the dominance of state ownership continues. But under this principle the firm holds all practical property rights to the shareholding as a full legal and civil body. Because the limited liability companies are to repre-sent the majority of large and medium-sized factories in the state sector, the designers of the reform argue that the shares reform will not change the socialist nature of the country's economic system. On the other hand, the shareholdings in these firms as a whole are to be effec-tively dispersed to allow each party to bear only limited liability in proportion to its investment (*Gaige*, no. 2, 1993, p. 42). This is very important to the state. As each party erects a 'safety valve' between the company (which is liable for its debts to the full extent of its fixed assets) and the state, this reduces the latter's obligation to subsidise it when a loss is incurred.

A company issuing shares to its staff is officially called a 'fixed direction' (*dingxiang*) shares company (private placement in a 'fixed direction'). The purpose of the reform is threefold, according to Vice-Minister Hong Hu: raising capital, redefining property relations (between the state, factory and workers), and arousing workers' concern for the factory's well-being (*Renmin ribao*, 10 April 1993). One State Council economist argued that only by turning employees into shareholders can the contra-diction of a state firm pursuing short-term gains (thirst for higher pay) and long-term development (dividends from stocks) be reconciled (Wu Jiaxiang, 1989, p. 32).

Only limited numbers of state-owned enterprises are to be converted into stock companies of the third and fourth types, which can issue shares to the public. Liu Guoguang compared this policy with the practice in the USA, where only 1 per cent of all firms list their shares on the stock exchanges (*Gaige*, no. 1, 1994, p. 8). The third kind of stock companies are to be created mainly through promotions and are permitted to sell shares on the stock exchange. Usually their creation requires a minimum of three institutional promoters, whose subscriptions to shares must exceed 35 per cent of the total to be listed. To ensure state control over the conversion process, private and foreign concerns are not allowed to be promoters. The foreign capital in a joint-venture firm should not exceed one-third when it is being corporatised. And the holdings of any single person must be below 0.5 per cent of the total shares issued (Wang Jian *et al.*, 1992, p. 125). Clearly these discriminatory regulations reflect the concern of the state over the holdings of the state sector. The fourth type of stock company is to be created through a prospectus (specific and public offerings). The firms as such are permitted to issue stocks to the public but their shares are not to be listed on the stock exchanges.

Types of shares

In the three stock company regulations, the SCRES established four categories of shares: state shares, corporate shares, private shares and foreign shares. Every type of share is to confer the same rights and obligations. Practically speaking, the nature of the economy in transition will hinge upon the uneven growth of these types of shares.

State shares are shares held by state agencies and are, in general, common shares. There is no restriction with regard to state shareholdings. *Corporate (legal person) shares* are shares owned by various institutional owners. There are some restrictions on this type of share. For instance, if one corporation owns 10 per cent of the shares of another company, the latter is not allowed to hold any shares in the former. *Private shares (natural person shares)* can be further divided into two categories: management and employee buy-outs and shares purchased by individuals on the stock exchanges or through the companies' public offerings. Both kinds of shares are treated as ordinary shares and subscribers to both kinds need to enter their names on the certificates. The difference is that the employees receive preference in subscribing to the shares when their company lists public offerings. *Foreign shares* are shares held by foreign investors. They do not include the Chinese 'B' shares offered on overseas stock exchanges. According to the Chinese explanation, the 'B' shares offered by state firms on the overseas stock exchanges are small in volume, as compared to the overall subscription.

During the stock reform an increasing number of stock companies set up a new category of shares, in spite of opposition from the government. These are called *collective shares*. With a hybrid ownership structure emerging in contracted factories, most of their managers strongly resist the state's requirement that the company's own fixed assets be incorporated into state shares, when factories are being converted into joint stock companies (Wang Jian *et al.*, 1992, p. 77). They argue that the collective shares originated from the property a factory accumulated during the transition when direct state control had given way to a degree of independence in the operations. A large part of the factory's assets had been created from its own social welfare funds. This is important because this part of factory ownership has a function of compensating underpaid workers through a series of social welfare schemes, such as housing and medical care. It is not only part of the production goal of the factory but also an outcome of its distribution principle. To scrap the collective shares amounts to denial of a basic right of the workers.[19] During my fieldwork in China in 1992, I found that most of the converted firms in Beijing had actually instituted collective shares from which employees extracted additional income in dividends.

While the proportion of shares owned by different parties varies, the first two kinds predominate, as the state prefers to engineer a controlled reform of corporatisation.[20] Generally, the number of people who can afford large quantities of shares remains small. This gives the state and companies a lot of advantages, especially given the long capital accumulation of large and medium-sized state-owned enterprises. Moreover, the state prescribes the proportion between collective shares and state shares through its control over investment companies or banks. According to a survey of stock firms by the Shenzhen government, corporate holdings now exceed the state's (Jin Jian, 1992, p. 356). It is likely that in inland provinces the percentage of state shares is much higher; however, the percentage of corporate shares is growing the fastest.[21]

The state's conversion programme

The SCRES has worked out a comprehensive programme for the corporatisation reform, which deals practically with the means of conversion and prescribes a time-frame for it. Generally speaking, there are fourteen mechanisms for the conversion:

1 a new firm created by multiple investors may be made a limited liability company and each investor may hold stock certificates to express his/her limited liabilities;
2 existing joint ventures may be converted to limited liability companies;
3 a joint stock company may be established through promotion;
4 a factory may be converted to a joint stock company through public offerings, with its registered fixed assets turned into share subscriptions.
5 a factory may be converted into a joint limited stock company through specific offerings, with its existing stock capital turned into share subscriptions;

6 a factory may be converted into a limited joint stock company through private placement, with its stock capital turned into share subscriptions;

7 a number of factories may merge to form a limited liability company with each party's assets evaluated to determine the allocation of investment certificates;

8 a factory may establish a joint stock company in its subsidiaries through specific or public offerings;

9 a number of factories may merge to form a joint stock company with their fixed assets, patents and marketing networks, etc. serving as shares;

10 a factory may be converted into a limited liability company with its creditors (the banks or investment companies) using their loans or their creditors' rights as share subscriptions, while its fixed assets are transformed into shares;

11 a factory may be converted into a limited liability company with the investment from various philanthropic foundations or insurance firms turned into stockholdings, while its fixed assets are transformed into shares;

12 a factory may be converted into a limited liability company by absorbing foreign capital;

13 a factory may be converted into a limited liability company by absorbing capital from the domestic non-state sectors;

14 a factory may be converted into a joint stock company by issuing 'B-shares' abroad (SCRES, 1993, p. 42).

As far as the timetable is concerned, according to the SCRES's report to the State Council, large and medium-sized state-owned enterprises whose production and sales have already been directed largely by the market could be corporatised at an earlier date, mainly in the form of limited liability companies. These include: (1) all the large and medium-sized state-owned enterprises in the special economic and development zones and in the sectors of commerce, services, construction and light industry; (2) most large and medium-sized state-owned enterprises in the sectors of building, manufacturing, metal processing, transportation, electronics and petrochemicals; and (3) some large and medium-sized state-owned enterprises in the telecommunications, electricity and defence industries. Such state-owned enterprises comprise nearly 80 per cent of the 13,000 large and medium-sized factories under the state budget. The transformation of category (1) state-owned enterprises should start during the period of the Eighth Five-Year Plan (1991–5). The remaining factories in categories (2) and (3) should be converted by the year 1998, raising the total to 90 per cent.[22]

A number of measures have been taken to prepare for the transition.

As far as large and medium-sized state-owned enterprises are concerned, the most important are the following.

1 A large number of enterprise groups have been formed and granted full property management responsibilities. By the end of 1991 more than 2,500 enterprise groups of various sizes had been created.

2 A large number of large and medium-sized state-owned enterprises have been transformed into joint ventures, particularly through the injection of foreign capital. Subsequently these will be converted into corporations (Qiu Jinji, 1992, p. 45). Shanghai, for instance, has converted one-fifth of its 1,600 large and medium-sized factories into joint ventures, including 143 projects with foreign investment averaging over US$5 million each and involving nearly 100 transnationals (*Guangming ribao*, 24 March 1993).

3 Laws and regulations regarding the corporatisation reform have been promulgated to regularise the conversion process. The most significant is the Corporation Law promulgated in 1993.

4 The improvement of the existing two stock exchanges in Shenzhen and Shanghai has been given priority in order to accelerate the shares reform. This improvement is both technological, as computerised networks are introduced, and institutional, with the establishment of legal and administrative surveillance.

5 In 1993, the State Council launched a national project to have all state-owned fixed assets re-evaluated.

6 Since 1 July 1993, the state sector has been implementing a new accounting system, which is said to be designed according to international practices.

7 Intermediate organisations such as accounting and law firms and independent investment bodies are being developed.

If things go as planned by the SCRES, by the year 2000 most of China's state-owned enterprises should be operating within a new hybridised ownership structure and have a new relationship with the state. There have been doubts about the ability of the government to carry through this huge reform project as smoothly as planned (*Jingji ribao*, 1 December 1995). The prescribed timetable is astonishing, when compared with even capitalist economies which have privatised a much smaller state sector over a fairly long period of time. In fact, some reform-minded economists advocate revising a standard practice of the past: i.e. first experimentation, then points distillation, then universalisation. They argue that the traditional method of reform is unworkable with the stock reform:

> A stock company under this experiment and the stock system possess a qualitative difference. The former is aimed at changing property structures at the individual factories. The dominant economic concern is fund-raising. The latter is aimed at changing the ownership system

country-wide. The economic purpose is to realise the rational allocation of resources. There is a close connection between the scope and the efficiency of the reform. So the success of the stock reform is reflected not by the fact that a few firms have listed their shares in the stock exchanges but by the conversion into shareholdings of the state's predominant position in the ownership structure.

(CASS, 1992, p. 6)

The 10 August 1992 incident at the Shenzhen Stock Exchange testified to the danger of allowing only a limited number of companies to mount public offerings. The small amount of shares available at the exchange caused a serious imbalance of demand and supply. As a result, the price of the shares rocketed so high as to lose touch with the intrinsic value of the shares. This fanned a mood of speculation and widespread corruption. Unlike the contract reform, over which the state could exercise fairly effective control, the stock reform contracts the government with a cruel reality: if the reform is to be carried out at all, it must be implemented in an effective way to meet the pressing public demand.

The implementation process

As regards implementation, strides have been taken since 1992. In a report to the State Council in early 1992, the SCRES proposed that the rate of conversion for the first and second categories of stock companies (the limited liability companies and the firms issuing shares only to their employees) should accelerate, while the number of companies in the third and fourth categories should be restricted; that is, the third type should be treated on an experimental basis only in Guangdong, Fujian and Hainan, and the fourth type only in Shenzhen and Shanghai (*Qiye gaige tongxun*, no. 3, 1992, p. 6). In late 1991 Li Peng approved a plan by the SCRES, entitled *On Quickening the Development of the Large Enterprise Conglomerates*, which designated fifty-five national conglomerates to be converted into stock companies, starting from those established around 1985. Those remaining to be converted would be entrusted with full property rights and delinked from their bureaucratic chains as a transitional measure (*Qiye gaige tongxun*, no. 3, 1992, p. 6). In 1996 the second wave of conversion of national conglomerates, numbering nearly 100, was initiated. Given that these groups are the backbone of China's key industrial sectors, the reform marked a turning point in the ownership reform. As for the remaining 2,000 smaller enterprise conglomerates, the State Council approved the SCRES's proposal that any which had made profits for three years running should be considered for conversion (*Qiye gaige tongxun*, no. 3, 1992, p. 6).

After the 10 August incident, the State Council quickly expanded the experiment in third category firms and increased the number of companies allowed to enter the fourth category. In early 1993, the State Council ordered most provinces to convert a number of well-run state enterprises into stock companies with public offerings (type three) and chose two or more large firms to list their stocks on the Shenzhen and Shanghai Stock Exchanges (*Guangming ribao*, 5 July 1993). At the end of 1991 there were 3,220 share companies in China's state sector after seven years of industrial reform. In 1992 alone an additional 1,060 companies (excluding those located in Shanghai and Shenzhen) became operational. A change also occurred in company size, as many of the new stock companies were converted from large and medium-sized factories (*Liaowang*, no. 4, 1993, p. 5). Of these companies, the majority – about 86 per cent – fall into the category of 'fixed direction' stock companies (employee buy-outs); 2.5 per cent are companies with public offerings; and 12 per cent are joint limited liability companies (*Jingji ribao*, 17 April 1993). Among the four groups of stock companies, group three has been growing fastest. For instance, in 1992 there were only fifty-three such companies listed on China's two stock exchanges. By the end of 1996, the number had jumped to 501, a nearly tenfold increase (*Jingji ribao*, 16 December 1996). The last group has a variety of forms. Some are dominated by one principal shareholder and others may have an equal distribution of shares owned by a group of partners.

The following two case studies show how stock firms are being created in state-owned enterprises.[23]

Case one

The Shandong Electric Pump Factory illustrates how a medium-scale state factory was transformed into a joint stock company through public offerings. A key producer of maritime pumps and one of the first fifty large or medium-sized state-owned enterprises in the province to seek stock reform in 1992, the factory was a second-grade state factory with over 1,100 workers.[24] The factory was chosen for the reform because it had registered an increase of over 1 million *yuan* in after-tax profits for three years in a row, a precondition for state approval and public confidence in its shares.

In order to provide an accurate valuation of the factory's property, the first step in the conversion to a joint stock company is to assess the fixed assets that both the state and the factory had invested as stock capital in the past. Under the auspices of the the ABSP of Zibo City, where the factory is located, the city's Office of Audit Affairs undertook a thorough evaluation of the factory's fixed assets, which stood at a value of 40.87 million *yuan*. Of this amount, the state's invested capital was 28.1 million *yuan*, and the factory's own investment 12.77 million, including a welfare fund of 5.13 million. The welfare fund was then excluded because it could neither bring profits nor be used as collateral in case of liquidation. So the overall value of offerings based on the factory's net assets was 35.73 million *yuan*. After this assessment the factory formally changed its name to the Shandong Electric Pump Company Limited.

The company could now issue shares to the public. It decided to sell one million share certificates, each valued at 10 *yuan*, but sold at 12 *yuan*. According to the principle of equal rights for all shareholders, the factory's net assets of 35.73 million *yuan* were valued at 29.77 million. The offerings were divided into two parts, corporate and private (the percentages unknown). The minimum sum to qualify a shareholder to become a representative for shareholders was 100,000 *yuan*. The company also encouraged its workers to buy shares in order to forge a bond of interest making them more committed to the well-being of the company. One shop party secretary called for his workers to buy as many as 2,000 *yuan* worth of shares apiece.

According to the company's brochure explaining its offering, the capital newly acquired through issues of shares would be used mainly for upgrading technology in order to increase exports and the scale of production. It was planned that by 1995 its sales income would have reached 120 million *yuan* with net profits of 13.6 million *yuan*. This bright prospect for the company's development attracted a warm reception from the public. On the first day shares worth 1.5 million *yuan* were sold.[25]

Case two

The Shanghai Jiabao Industrial Company Limited represents the type of conversion based on an enterprise group. Its predecessor was the Shanghai Jiabao Electric Lighting Company, a loose enterprise group comprising four individual factories. This enterprise group was created in 1990, but under the 'three-no-change' principle (which disallows any change in ownership forms – whether state or collective – administrative ties and channels of profit distribution) not only were the four factories unable to coordinate their production and sales to meet pressure from the market, but they themselves were involved in constant internal competition. Each had to answer to its own bureaucratic bosses, each produced similar products, and each fought for investment funds from limited sources.

In October 1990 the four factories agreed to turn this loose enterprise group into a limited joint stock company. The company issued initial shares in a public offering valued at 106.26 million *yuan*. This figure includes the net assets of the four factories, valued at 81.26 million, and offerings to legal persons of 15 million *yuan* and to individuals of 10 million *yuan* (the value of each share was 10 *yuan* sold on the basis of a stock premium for 50 *yuan*). The four factories merged into one, and the company removed all previous administrative overloads. The highest control body is the general meeting of shareholders at which the board of directors is elected. And for daily management the company practises the responsibility system where the general manager is answerable to the board of directors. All the members of the board of directors, general and deputy general managers had to buy 200 shares. They could transfer a maximum 50 per cent of shares during their terms of office and only after two years in service, a policy designed to peg their career commitment to the well-being of the firm (Lu Wanxin, 1992, p. 27).

TOWARDS QUASI PRIVATISATION

As pointed out by Bowles and White in an article written before the CCP had reached a consensus on the corporatisation reform, share issues had been economically unimportant but politically important in that they challenged the ideological and institutional underpinnings of a socialist economy (Bowles and White, 1992, p. 575). Following this line of argument, this section will analyse the implications of corporatisation, such as those leading towards quasi privatisation, which are inherent in such social engineering.

Stock issues have been an effective means of privatising state concerns worldwide since the 1970s. When the post-socialist economies embarked on the road of privatisation, they all adopted stock reforms. Even though China's stock reform is not intended to privatise the state sector, the outcome of the reform has created mechanisms reducing state ownership. The resulting effects of *de facto* denationalisation have become increasingly apparent. A 1991 survey of shares traded on the Shenzhen Stock Exchange disclosed that shareholders had aggressively taken hold of large sums of state shares controlled by the firms offering shares to the public. The proportion of state and corporate shares in these firms had been in constant decline, as a rapidly growing number of private investors entered the 'share frenzy' (Lu Ren, 1992, p. 53). In another sample survey of twenty joint stock companies in 1991, the average proportion of shares was as follows: state shares, 22.6 per cent; corporate shares, 14 per cent; collective shares, 13 per cent; private shares, 37 per cent; and foreign shares, 14 per cent (Jin Jian, 1992, p. 356). These results may well reveal a trend: private and foreign shares will become increasingly important; the precise legal definition of the collective shares remains to be clarified. In non-listed stock firms, the erosion of state assets has been similarly dramatic, often with the backing of local officials. Generally speaking, this is reflected in what is effectively quasi privatisation in the state sector: an erosion of state property due to flawed implementation of corporatisation; and the logical effect of privatisation inherent in such a reform.[26] This is shown in the following.

1 Deliberate under-capitalisation in order to reduce the proportion of state shares. There are many methods by which this can be done. For

instance, a large number of factories calculate only the net assets on their books, ignoring the cost of land, non-productive buildings and facilities. The most popular method is the exclusion of 'invisible' assets such as patents and intellectual property. According to Finance Minister Liu Zhongli, 8,500 state firms had been injected with foreign capital in 1992. Over 5,000 of them did not conduct capital assessments at the time this was done, causing serious erosion of state assets. Indeed under-capitalisation occurred in virtually all stock companies in the process of conversion (*Jingji ribao*, 21 July 1993).

2 Different rates of dividends for different kinds of shares. Usually, the rate of dividends for private shares is made higher than that for corporate shares, which is higher in turn than the state's.[27] One Hunan firm that I visited had stipulated that the dividend rate for private shares was to be 3–5 per cent higher than for the firm's collective and state shares. The holding agency (in this case the Municipal Machine Bureau) deliberately turned a blind eye to this because, I was told, the firm paid dividends and taxes at a level higher than its remittances on profit under the contract reform. It thus became a showcase, and cadres in the bureau hold the private shares of the company. Because of this leniency, instead of submitting them to the state, the firm could keep a portion of the dividends from the state shares at its own disposal.

3 The free handout of collective shares as gifts to members of the 'fixed direction' companies. As mentioned earlier, one component of the collective shares is a factory's welfare fund accumulated from its retained profits. Once this fund is calculated as part of the factory's net assets for offerings under the category of collective shares, factories openly hand these out to workers as 'social security shares' or 'incentive shares'. The state's previous control over the social welfare fund is thus circumvented. In practice, firms deliberately confuse the lines between the social welfare fund and funds under other categories: the corporate and collective property (*Jingji ribao*, 17 April 1993). Thus the collective stock becomes a grey area in terms of property definition, a so-called 'no head' ownership.

4 The privatisation of the corporate shares. The corporate shares are regarded as the public component of the stock system, as they originated from either the firm's own investment or investment from other state concerns. Generally, however, these comprise another grey area in the stock system. Quasi privatisation can take place on two fronts. The first concerns shares subscribed through the firm's own investment, which are treated in a similar way to collective shares, with the same handout process. The second involves corporate shares subscribed by state bodies in joint stock firms, only to be freely distributed to their staff later or sold as private shares on the stock exchanges. According to Yu Guogang, deputy president of the Shenzhen Stock Exchange, when the Wanke Company first instituted corporate shares in 1989,

these amounted to 5.298 million share certificates, or 13 per cent of the total shares subscribed. By mid-1992, 2.93 million of these share certificates had been sold to private buyers. The company thus earned 50 million *yuan*, of which 30 per cent was allocated to build staff housing. Another 10 per cent was used to purchase shares of other companies for speculative purposes. The remaining 60 per cent were considered social welfare premiums earmarked for free distribution to staff later (Wang Jian *et al.*, 1992, p. 76).

5 The transfer to outsiders of the non-transferable private placement (*neibugu*) of shares to employees. In theory, the internal shares are created more as a measurement of property than as real shares. The state stipulated that although stock bought by members of a work unit carries a value based on which staff are to receive dividends, they are still the property of the firm and indirectly of the state. Workers could transfer their internal shares only to people within the unit. Yet there have been gross breaches of the rules. A survey of several provinces revealed that of 20 billion *yuan* of internal shares issued in 1991–2, only 10–20 per cent were still held internally. The rest had secretly found their way to the public at large (*Renmin ribao*, 10 April 1993).

6 In order to achieve a demonstrable effect in the experimental firms, many local governments have temporarily suspended the extraction of dividends for state shares and only stick to the levy of taxes. In other cases they reduce the rate of dividends from the state shares. The objective is reasonable enough: not to increase the burden on these firms by extracting both taxes and dividends and thereby surpassing the prior level of their remittances to the state. Yet this has caused an unbalanced growth of different types of shares, with the proportion of state shares shrinking rapidly (*Liaowang*, no. 40, 1993, p. 4).

There is, in short, an increasingly serious drainage of state property into private hands channelled through the malpractices mentioned above. This rapid erosion of state assets in state-owned enterprises has averaged 100 million *yuan* a day, with half a trillion ending up in private pockets in the last decade (*Jingji ribao*, 4 December 1995). At the moment, owing to the experimental nature of the stock reform, it may have not reached unbearable proportions. On the other hand, the available information has indicated that the mechanisms inherent in the corporatisation reform have unleashed a trend towards state property being diversified. The following features further encourage this development.

First, even though state shares ostensibly are not allowed to be traded on the stock exchange owing to the fears of central planners concerning privatisation, the experience of both Shanghai and Shenzhen has proved that it is nearly impossible to adhere to this in the stock market. When the price of a share becomes too high, the company is forced to release more shares to ease further rises in price. Often the released shares are state shares. Although this practice has been fairly successful in maintaining a rough equilibrium, more and more state shares have landed in private pockets in this way. Over 40 per cent of the shares circulating on the Shenzhen Stock Exchange are state shares, and they change hands every day. As a result, the genuine proportion of other kinds of shares in firms with public offerings has been on the decline (Wang Jian *et al.*, 1992, p. 92). This decline will accelerate when the state approves the open trading of state and corporate shares in the future (*China Central Television*, 2 July 1993).

Second, most of the limited liability and non-listed joint stock companies are to be created through joint investments. A review of the fourteen ways of converting state-owned enterprises reveals that seven are related to the injection of capital from collective, private and foreign concerns. Although the state has stipulated a minimum proportion for state shares, once the firms become operational it is again difficult for them to adhere to the prescribed proportion. There are ample examples where state-owned enterprises seek more and more investment in the form of shares from private and foreign concerns. In fact, this has been strongly encouraged by local governments as a major mechanism for revitalising the state sector. For instance, Tianjing approved 630 joint venture projects with foreign investors from 1984 to 1994 (projects at the municipal level). Among these, foreigners controlled the majority shares in 235. In terms of overall investment, they owned 75 per cent, and thus hold the power of veto over the management of these joint ventures (*Guangming ribao*, 29 November 1995).

Thirst for investment has pushed local governments to go beyond the general guidelines of the SCRES that foreign capital should be restricted in the key areas of the national economy. For instance, the fast-expanding economies of Shanghai and Shandong are handicapped by insufficient electric power. The two governments have decided to convert their entire power industry to a stock system based on joint ventures. Shandong allowed Gordon Wu, a Hong Kong capitalist, to control 50 per cent of the shares (*China Central Television*, 2 July 1993). Guangdong has gone further in soliciting foreign shares. The majority of its large public works have been funded by large blocs of private and foreign shares (*Jingjin ribao*, 27 July 1993).

As a third factor, the growing financial strength of individuals to get rich quick by buying into state ownership through stocks heralds a further long-term dilution of state ownership. Today China boasts one million millionaires ready to grab state firms in order to enlarge their capital. Currently, on paper the gross asset value of the state sector is evaluated at about 3 trillion *yuan*, compared with an equal amount in private bank deposits (*Guangming ribao*, 8 November 1955). Indeed, the non-state sector is increasingly aggressive in penetrating state ownership. By the end of 1991, 22.5 billion *yuan* worth of shares had been issued and 137.3

billion *yuan* of state bonds and debentures put into private hands; the year 1991 also saw huge demand for the securities. This foreshadowed a change in China's structure of financial capital, which generated huge pressure both on expansion of non-state concerns and speedy divestment of the state sector (Xie Ping, 1992, p. 36). This trend accelerated, given the fast circulation of shares in 1992 and 1993. According to Liu Hongru, former Vice-Minister for the SCRES, stock transactions worth 69.28 billion *yuan* were made in 1992, 13.4 times the 1991 figure of 5.15 billion *yuan* (*Beijing Review*, 17–23 May 1993, p. 13). By May 1993 the market value of the shares on the Shenzhen and Shanghai Stock Exchanges had reached 317.7 billion *yuan* – despite tight state restrictions on issuing shares (*Jingji ribao*, 25 June 1993). In 1996 alone, shares worth 10 billion *yuan* were offered on the Shengzhen and Shanghai Exchanges. Now 22 million people in China have become shareholders (*Renmin ribao*, 16 December 1996). The evolving stock system has created a force which increasingly weakens administrative control.

THE FAR-REACHING IMPLICATIONS

The essence of China's economic reform is that while the state tries to control the pace and depth of change, this acquires a life of its own leading to the weakening of state control. What begins as a transfer of management power gives birth to a new diversity in organisational forms and a plurality of property rights (Nee, 1992, pp. 1–27). This intermediate property structure has been driven further and further by new pressure for efficiency and flexibility, resulting in a major ownership reform with corporatisation as a natural outcome.

Predictably, de-statisation based on ownership reform has exerted strong effects on both state/enterprise relations and state/society relations. In the political realm, the ownership reform will hasten the decomposition of the state's hierarchical dictatorship rooted in industrial bureau/enterprise relations (Xie Qiuhan, 1992, p. 67). Long-leased firms and, to a lesser extent, share companies are the first to get rid of 'bureaucratic bosses' and lose their bureaucratic ranking. This removes a key feature of the *danwei* system which reduces a firm to an appendage. Central planning is increasingly irrelevant to their production concerns. They will thus take fewer political orders from the party/state. Stock firms in Shenzhen and elsewhere have shown that they are interested mainly in the accrual of capital and are largely free from the concern of other state-owned enterprises to engage in political activities. The political function of state ownership will diminish gradually, as it becomes more and more meaningless to property users. It may then become possible for the slogan 'small government, big society' to bear fruit.

As far as social change is concerned, the trend to privatisation will alter social stratification by concentrating wealth in certain directions. The gap between the 'new rich' and ordinary people will become more visible. Moreover, the reform will cause a large number of state-owned enterprises to go under, as the state starts to assume only limited liability for loss makers and unemployment is ideologically legitimised. The current efforts to do away with the 'big rice bowl' system will be stepped up with unpredictable social consequences.[28]

Equally important is the stimulating effect that the corporatisation-based ownership reform exerts on the development of the legal system *vis-à-vis* the regulation of share issues and company activities. This has facilitated promulgation of a set of laws such as the Company Law, Antitrust Law, and Law against Improper Competition. In the last two years a body of over 300 related laws and regulations either have been enacted or are being drafted, this representing a major step towards a full-fledged market economy (*China Business Times*, 26 August 1996). A leading official in the SCRES made it clear: any failure in the stock reform could more probably be attributed to enthusiastic supporters of the reform who nevertheless do not understand the workings of the system than to those who oppose it for rigid ideological reasons.[29]

Economically, the big drive towards corporatising state-owned enterprises offers new opportunities for foreign investment. In order to save its loss-making firms, the state has granted preferential conditions to those foreign corporations which are willing to play the 'graft' game. There is reason to believe that this practice will continue for some time to come. As a result, the national ownership structure will undergo further transition and move away from state domination.

In summary, although the drive to state-controlled *de facto* privatisation advances fairly slowly, it heralds a new direction in China's economic reform, which may exert more lasting effects on the country's economic system than all previous reform measures in the last decade. Time is needed for a more comprehensive evaluation of these effects. However, this government-imposed revolution deserves attention in both theoretical and practical terms, as it opens a new page in China's social and economic transformation from socialism (You Ji, 1995, p. 61).

9 The construction of a new economic model[1]

This chapter deals with a gradual process of separating state-owned enterprises from the command bureaucratic chains. To this end it describes a new set of institutional arrangements that is emerging, sketching an embryonic model of state/enterprise relations for China's market economy. Based on the restructuring of the ownership system and relying on the commercial operation of state assets rather than administrative allocation, this round of administrative reform distinguishes itself from the previous rounds by two clear objectives: redefining the government's economic functions and reshaping the government's operational mechanisms. Both will be made to service the market-led micro-economic activities. One outcome of this far-reaching reform will be a major overhaul of the administrative network linking state-owned enterprises to the party/state. State-owned enterprises will thus lose their hierarchical ranking which is a key feature of the *danwei* phenomenon. Indeed, without this administrative status, it will become difficult for state firms to exercise many political and state control missions. De-statisation in this organisational sense represents a crucial component of *de-danweiisation* of state-owned enterprises. Therefore, the ongoing administrative reform constitutes a profound political reform. This is why Chinese commentators call it an administrative revolution. In so far as the reform affects both the economic base and the state superstructure at the same time, it may eventually amount to a quiet revolution from above.

THE EMERGING NEW MODEL FOR CHINA'S MARKET ECONOMY

According to Luo Gan, Secretary General of the State Council, this reform of removing the commanding heights is aimed at establishing a new system of macro-economic regulation, whereby state economic bureaucracies will be relieved of supervising micro-economic activities and state-owned enterprises will be relieved of their administrative bosses (*Renmin ribao*, 22 July 1993). This new system is to be achieved through a thorough restructuring of the state administration, currently under way at all five levels of government from the centre to the province, prefecture, county and township.² The goal of the reform is to demarcate anew the government's three levels of power over state firms, those of: *popo* or the administrative superior; *laoban*, or the asset owner; and *zhongjieren*, or linkage between the market and producers. To this end, a large number of specialised industrial bureaux will be removed and nationally over two million state cadres, or 25 per cent of a total of 9.2 million working in government, will be streamlined by the end of the 1990s and more in the next decade (*Banyuetan*, no. 7, 1993, p. 28). This centrally imposed reform is now recognised as holding the key to the success or failure of China's social transformation. As pointed out by Jiang Zemin, altering state functions has become the biggest issue. Without breakthroughs in this area, reform cannot be brought to the core of the old system and a market economy cannot be established.³

Property management and operation

The new economic administrative model is guided by western agency theory (Di Linyu, 1995, p. 23). Under an agency relationship the principal owns and the agent manages resources covered by the contract between them. The agent's ability to exercise temporary property rights over these resources (by convention, use rights, income rights and transfer rights) depends fundamentally on the delegation of those rights from the principal (Solnick, 1996, p. 214). In China's case, the contract is more in the form of user's asset accrual to the principal. More concretely, the new model is supposed to meet the following assumptions: (1) if the state still possesses residual claimancy, separation of state asset administration and operation is possible; (2) the owner of the assets is interested mainly in asset accrual rather than detailed micro management; (3) property users have only one goal in asset operations, namely maximising profits; (4) the state as the asset owner may create the best incentive mechanisms to protect its property without compromising the autonomy of property users; and (5) the running of this multi-level principal/agent system is cost-effective (Yang Rueilong, 1995, p. 13).

In implementing this theoretical design, the reform is pursued on the following fronts. First, following the previous efforts to separate government administration and business management in the state/state-owned enterprise relations, the current reform will further separate the state's unified functions of government administration and property management. Chinese economists (who describe the reform as *zhengzi fenkai*) agree that that without the separation of the latter functions, it is impossible to separate the former effectively (Jiang Yiwei, 1990, p. 51). Second, the reform will create conditions for the government to guide state-owned enterprises' market activities through sectoral industrial policies rather than bureaucratic decrees. These policies are largely indirect economic levers employed to allow a level of business autonomy at the micro level. Chapter 8 discussed the nature of property relations between the state and corporatised state firms. Here the analysis is focused on the administrative side of property ties in the new model.

In China over the past four decades, each industrial ministry, each level of local government and each industrial agency within that level have invested in state-owned enterprises. This has created a multi-level sectoral/local property control system, which has divided the national economy along central *tiaotiao* and regional *kuaikuai* lines. In this system, as noted earlier, the industrial bureaux are at once administrative superiors to their factories and the owners of their property. The relative failure of the contract reform lies in the fact that even though the new contractual boundaries have imposed barriers against bureaucratic interference in the daily affairs of firms, bureaucrats are still required by the central and local governments to exercise property control over their subordinates. They are supposed to evaluate new investment projects proposed by producers and conduct annual asset investigations. Often property control is reinforced by or confused with administrative control. Acting as the representative of the owner (the state), bureaucrats see intervention in micro-economic activities as their natural right, which not only makes business autonomy a myth for producers but also provides managers with excuses to evade responsibility for business failures.

At the same time, this multi-level administrative system along the lines of *tiaotiao* and *kuaikuai* has been further complicated by a 'multi-headed property monitoring system', which comprises the government's general economic offices such as planning, commerce administration, environment protection, taxation, audit, etc. Again each of these bureaux exercises general and specific economic controls over factories in the capacity of caretaker of state ownership. They can cause real problems for state-owned enterprises, as any one of them can shut down a factory's production lines because of some easily found fault. In addition, the *tiaotiao* and *kuaikuai* administrations over factories can overlap. The vertical agencies are entrusted with state sectoral policy supervision and so they tend to interfere with the production of local factories. At the same time, because the ministerial factories have to recruit workers locally and contribute to community development, they are also to some extent under the control of local government. Consequently, state-owned enterprises have had to respond positively to at least two masters in order to stay out of trouble (Granick, 1992, p. 20).

The ongoing administrative reform aims to construct a new property management system in order to break down both sectoral and branch boundaries in the national economy (Tong Zongkun, 1993, p. 61) As a result, the traditional *tiaotiao* and *kuaikuai* bureaucratic systems will be superseded in the new situation. The key features of the new system are as follows:

1 A new property management agency is to be created under each level of government. It will recentralise the powers over state property operations that are currently vested in central and local industrial bureaux. Its mission will be to take care of the interests of the state as the ultimate owner of all state property;

2 The new system will be multi-layered, reflecting the reality of multi-level investment mechanisms rooted in China's national economy. It will specify and quantify centrally, provincially and locally owned property and thus draw a clear line between property rights. This multi-layered system differs from the former multi-level bureaucratic system in that it is not segregated along sectoral lines and it is a unitary system with each lower level answerable to the higher one and the highest one answerable to either the NPC or the State Council.

3 The new multi-level ownership authority will not be directly involved in property operations, as it will entrust property management rights to subsidiary holding companies.

4 Parties in the 'multi-headed monitoring system' will continue to exercise state social and economic administrative functions. Yet they will not assume control over the property operations of a firm. Their mission is restricted to ensuring that the firm abides by the rules of competition in the market and by state regulations (Liu Guoguang, 1988, p. 32).

Functionally, the separation of state economic administration from ownership management means that the current property control system must be split into two tiers: state monitoring and business operation (Liu Guoguang, 1988, p. 128). The existing national and local ABSPs will assume the first task. As administrative authorities, they will ensure that state property is not being eroded by malpractices. They have two powers at their disposal. First, as the representative of the property owner, they retain the authority to oversee the operation of state assets, including the power to appoint the chair of the board of directors of major state property corporations. Second, although in future the main body of investment will be shareholding corporations, the ABSPs may intervene in their decision-making processes for the sake of state macro regulation and asset regrouping. Their power to relocate stock capital under special circumstances is seen as the major lever by which the state implements its sectoral industrial policies (*Guangming ribao*, 4 October 1995). Yet their administrative functions are mainly carried out within a legal framework. So their major task is to formulate the rules of the game for property users. The business operations, on the other hand, are to be directed by the market in accordance with international practice.

Organisationally, according to Pan Yue, deputy director of the national ABSP, property operations can be conducted mainly through three forms: (1) shareholding companies created locally or through industrial sectors, which enjoy the special legal person status of a corporation; they should retain a significant proportion of the shares of subsidiary state firms; (2) state industrial agencies that are entrusted by the state to run state property operations in special sectors such as the defence industry; and (3) state-owned and state-run corporations. Pan further elaborated the rationale for the reform: state property can be classified into two conceptual categories, namely a competitive type for profits and a servicing type for social benefits. State shareholding companies will chiefly come under the former category. For the latter, the running of state property can further be divided into two forms: state monopolies – these will be the special agencies and companies identified in (2) above; and non-monopolies, principally state utilities – the state-owned and run companies identified in (3) above (*Guangming ribao*, 4 October 1995).

Other key economic institutions are to be established to assist the framework mentioned above. For instance, the creation of independent investment bodies (state investment companies, banks, foundations and insurance companies) is crucial to the success of the new model (*Qiye gaige tungxun*, no. 6, 1992, p. 10). According to a special research report, these investment companies will be entrusted by the state with operating its new investment projects. The companies under the central government will run central projects and the local ones will run local projects (*Dangdai chanqun jizhi ketizu*, 1995, p. 49). The importance of these new investment bodies is that they serve as intermediaries between the ABSPs at various levels and the producers, thus acting as a buffer against the likely administrative pressures exerted by the former on the latter. The links between the ABSPs, investment bodies and producers are basically to be expressed in monetary terms.[4] That is, the ABSP will see that it receives sufficient dividends from the fixed assets entrusted to the investment bodies and holding companies, which in turn will ensure that firms under them submit adequate dividends from profits.

At the national level, it is proposed that the national ABSP will become an independent agency entrusted by the NPC or the State Council to administer property belonging to the central government. It will also be empowered to safeguard state property run by local ABSPs. Under it will be the six national investment companies currently under the SPC. The Construction Bank should be transformed into a specialised national investment bank.[5] Except for a number of large conglomerates which have already been granted full property rights by the State Council, these investment bodies will oversee the property of large and medium-sized state-owned enterprises attached to the central ministries. As holding companies, they will extensively offer shares to other organisations, e.g. banks, foundations and insurance companies. In the relationship between them and the centrally run state-owned enterprises, the former will act as the major shareholders but possess no direct administrative powers (Gao Zimin, 1993, p. 10).

At the provincial and municipal levels, this model is being tested enthusiastically by a number of cities. Hainan is the first province and Shanghai the first municipality to transform their entire industrial administrative system on this model. According to Xu Zhiyi, director of Shanghai's Economic and Trade Commission, all the city's industrial bureaux except the Bureau of the Pharmaceutical Industry have been transformed into either holding corporations or sectoral associations and are being removed from the municipal government structure (more on this later, p. 202) (*China Business Times*, 12 June 1996). The design for the local operation of the new model comprises a three-level state assets management system. At the top is a provincial or municipal commission, the legal representative of all state assets in the locality, which oversees the running of state property. At the second level are a number of general corporations (*Guozhi yunying gongsi*) which assume the role of ownership principals and are in charge of state assets. These corporations further delegate to the third-level companies authority for operating state property. Companies at this third level are to be composed of three types: subsidiary holding companies; solely state-owned and run subsidiaries; and subsidiary joint companies. In this new system the provincial/municipal commission is the administrative authority which makes strategic policies regarding the management of state property. The state asset-running companies are economic entities composed of key investment bodies. The third-level companies will actually operate the assets (*Renmin ribao*, 18 July 1993). Although the second level will mainly be created from the specialised economic bureaux, they will no longer be within the government structure, and therefore will no longer hold political and administrative functions on behalf of the party/state. The third-level companies are to be converted mainly from the second-grade administrative corporations (*xingzheng gongsi*) under a particular industrial bureau. They usually have a number of factories under them. In the new system they will become holding companies or conglomerates. In this transformation the vast bureaucratic hierarchy will be gradually digested into a corporatised hierarchy with each level linked through property ties. This signals the beginning of the end of the four-decade dictatorship of *tiaotiao* and *kuaikuai*. For a description of the model at the central and provincial levels, Figures 1 and 2 offer some crude sketches of the new model.

Sectoral guidance

The other major component of the new model is sectoral guidance. According to Gu Jiaqi, deputy director of the Central Staffing Commission, this is an inevitable replacement of *tiaotiao* or branch dictatorship (*bumen guanli*) as market reform takes hold. While branch control is an administrative method with which the central and local governments dictate micro-economic activities, sectoral guidance comprises a body of macro mechanisms such as industrial policies, coordinations and services,

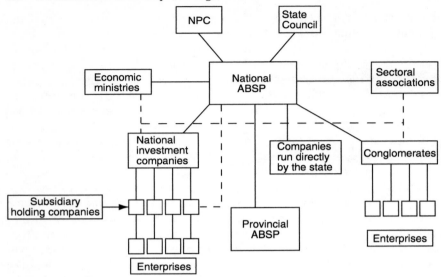

Figure 9.1 Bureaucratic hierarchy of ownership relations at the central level

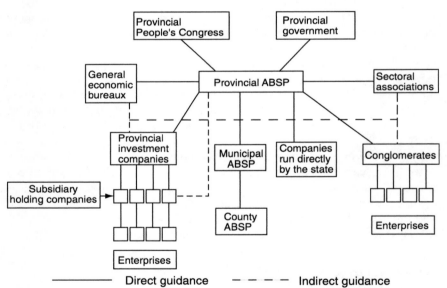

Figure 9.2 Bureaucratic hierarchy of ownership relations at the provincial level

e.g. providing relevant information to producers (Gu Jiaqi, 1995, p. 4). Branch control is conducted through allocation of investment, products and human resources according to quotas. So it has not covered factories in the fast-expanding non-state sector. As a result the *tiaotiao* dictatorship has severed the national economy into various disconnected parts.

Furthermore, with the progress of industrialisation, more and more new industrial sectors will emerge. For instance, by the Chinese definition, the country had seventy-five large industrial sectors in 1993. One year later the number went up to ninety-seven. Within each large industrial sector, there are an increasing number of sub-sectors: the number rose from 310 to 368 from 1993 to 1994 (Lu Guotai, 1996, p. 17). Under the model of branch control, this would mean setting up new government offices constantly to run each new sector and sub-sector. This is impossible. Sectoral guidance, however, is built upon market regulation, although it may mean strong government influence. Chinese leadership is still exploring the nature, scope, contents and mechanisms of sectoral guidance (Gu Jiaqi, 1995, p. 4).

One difficulty encountered in the endeavour is redefining the relations between the state, sectoral organisations and companies. Two new concepts have emerged from the new model. The first is that government will play a role in sectoral guidance. This role is defined as assuming meso-economic management functions. The state projects the long-term development of a particular sector, formulates preferential policies to achieve certain objectives, and monitors the market situation for the sector in order to avoid over-production. Sectoral associations need to be created to coordinate state sectoral management and state-owned enterprises. Ultimately they will be run collectively by state and non-state firms in the sector, just as their counterparts in the market economies are. For instance, they should fulfil the task of servicing the whole sector in terms of coordinating prices, especially for export, providing market information, informing the government of the demands of association members. However, they are not yet ready to fulfil their projected functions and are more like an extension of state sectoral agencies. This can be clearly seen from the administrative functions that the National Textile Industrial Society (NTIS) still assumes after having been converted from the Ministry of the Textile Industry in 1993. Yet in the process of transition, according to Deputy Minister Hong Hu of the SCRES, the bureaucratic ties between the state, state-owned enterprises and those sectoral associations will be phased out. In particular, the relationship between a sectoral association and a member firm will not be that between an administrative boss and a subordinate (*Renmin ribao*, 25 July 1993).

However, at the beginning of the transition, these associations will remain the channels through which the state monitors state-owned enterprises. There are now over 250 registered national sectoral associations and over 1,000 regional sectoral associations (*Renmin ribao*, 18 July 1995). Most of them have kept some of their former administrative functions. For instance, the NTIS still allocates export quotas to different regions (more on this later). Even in the future it is proposed that the core members of these associations will be key state firms in each sector. Normally the heads of the associations will, on behalf of the state, assign various tasks to these key firms in order to 'influence' the entire sector, similar to what the MITI does in Japan.[6] In this imitation of Japan Inc., there may emerge an organic corporatism in China's socialist market economy. This post-Deng Chinese state corporatism, as some scholars argue, entails a process in which the state determines which organisations will be recognised as legitimate and forms an unequal partnership of sorts with them. The associations are sometimes even channelled into the policy-making forums and often help implement state policy on the government's behalf (Unger and Chan, 1995, pp. 29–54).

THE REFORM OF THE CENTRAL BUREAUCRACIES

In the previous rounds of government reform since 1949, a number of ministries were axed and functionaries laid off, but soon afterwards new ministries sprang up and more staff were recruited. For instance, the administrative reform in 1988 reduced the number of offices at the ministerial level from over ninety to forty-four. Four years later the number had risen back to ninety. Meanwhile, over 42,000 staff employed by more than 900 agencies at the bureau level were on the payroll of the State Council. And the numbers of institutions and staff directly attached to the central bureaucracy reached 3,000 and two million respectively (Ni Di, 1992, p. 14).

The ongoing administrative reform was launched in July 1991 when the State Council froze the number of staff at the centre. The Eighth NPC in March 1993 advanced the process when it approved the State Council's three-year reform programme as the first step. This focused on removing certain government functions that seriously impeded the activities of state-owned enterprises in the market (Yin Guohua, 1993, p. 18). Subsequently, a fifteen-year two-phased long-term programme has been drafted as the guideline for the overhaul of the state structure. By the year 2000 the first phase is projected to create a government administrative system that is centred on servicing the evolving market economy. From then, the reform will move on to constructing a 'modern administrative system' by the year 2010. 'Modern administrative system' refers to the features of government commonly found in advanced market economies, such as indirect government, checks and balances, and 'small government and large society' (Ye Wen, 1996, p. 24).

In practice the central thrust of the first-phase reform at the national level is characterised by the streamlining of industrial ministries, which is regarded as the key to the overall economic reform (Ke Meicheng, 1995, p. 7). China's central economic administrative system is composed of two parts. The first comprises agencies in charge of making general policies and trans-ministry policy coordination. These include the SPC, the Finance Ministry, the Central Bank and so on. The second part comprises the specialised industrial ministries and a similar number of general corporations directly attached to the State Council. The two parts combined employ about 70 per cent of central government staff (Zhang Chenglian, 1991, p. 89). According to the rationale for reform of the second part, as summarised by Professor Li Yining, bodies which are allowed to survive will have to carry out new tasks at the grassroots level, paid for by manufacturers.[7]

The strategic importance of cutting back the central industrial ministries lies in the fact that they still control a large number of products in both mandatory and directory plans. One figure often quoted by both Chinese and western analysts indicates the reduced coverage of the state plan. That is, the number of producer goods of different kinds in the central mandatory plan (controlled by the SPC) was reduced from 256 in 1979 to nineteen in 1992. But few scholars point out that the number of products in the mandatory plan controlled by the central industrial ministries was still as large as 400 in 1991, compared to 2,000 in 1979 (Li Peilin, 1992, p. 112). These 400 products consisted of strategic materials, the control of which gives the central planners enormous power in the national economy, particularly over large state-owned enterprises. The reform of bureaucracies at the central level is aimed simultaneously at streamlining the industrial ministries and at further reducing the coverage of ministerial mandatory plans. It is this aspect that distinguishes the current government reform from previous efforts.

The first-phase streamlining of the industrial ministries has been directed along two fronts. The first is the immediate abolition of three specialised ministries. The second concerns the internal restructuring of the industrial ministries which are to remain during the period of transition. The abolition has affected the Light Industry Ministry and the Textile Industry Ministry which were converted into sectoral associations in 1992. Although they are still within the structure of the State Council, they have been downgraded into non-administrative bodies (*shiye jigou*). The Aeronautics and Aerospace Industry Ministry was turned into two separate commercial corporations (*jingji shiti*), which fall into the category of the 10–20 per cent of conglomerates directly run by the state, mentioned in Chapter 8. The elimination of three ministries represented only an initial step in the reform of central economic bodies. There are plans to reduce the number by a further three or four before the year 2000 (Zhongyang bianwei, 1995, p. 8). Some central ministries will be transformed into sectoral associations (Tang Jin, 1993, p. 7). Others will become economic entities. Preparations are now being pursued for transforming ministries including Railways, Transportation, Telecommunications, Energy and Civil Aviation (*China Business Times*, 22 May 1995). In 1995 the functions of the Electrical Power Ministry were taken over by a number of national electrical power companies (*Guangming ribao*, 27 December 1995).

Lou Gan stated the key reason why the three ministries were abolished:

the market has played the dominant role in directing economic activities in light industry and the textile industry (Zhongyang bianwei, 1995, p. 8). For instance, by 1993 almost all business transactions of the factories under the Textile Industry Ministry were taking place in the market. The ministry was left with few meaningful responsibilities in administering the sector. After it was turned into the NTIS, it would no longer formulate annual plans of production, material allocation and technological inno- vation for state-owned enterprises in the sector. It would delegate most authorities of finance, investment and asset operations to producers. And it would cut administrative ties with a very small number of large enter- prise groups formally under the ministry, although still exercising the narrowed function of *nomenklatura* over them. For instance, the NTIS appoints only the general manager and the party secretary rather than their deputies as well, as it did before. In the transitional period the NTIS will retain some administrative functions, e.g. distribution of textile export quotas to different regions and to some of its immediate affiliates, allo- cation of a few key products such as silk and wool that still appear in the mandatory plans owing to chronic short supply, and appropriation of investment funds made available to the textile industry by the SPC. The last mission inevitably involves the assessment and approval of investment in national projects, a key component for using sectoral industrial policy to influence the direction of the market. As a result, the NTIS let go a large number of specialised bureaux and cut back staff posts by 44 per cent to 280 (Han Hai, 1995, p. 6).

Internal restructuring is mainly pursued through abolishing the special- ised bureaux in those ministries still in operation. The central theme is again to reorient the ministries from administering micro-economic activi- ties to sectoral guidance. Organisationally, an industrial ministry has two major components in administering economic activities in its sector. Among its two dozen bureaux, about half are what are called general policy bureaux. They assume the functions of both short- and long-term planning, statistics, audits, foreign affairs, coordination and so on. The other half are run on functional lines, that is they control specific products, normally placed under central mandatory planning. For instance, the Ministry of the Machine Industry used to have a number of bureaux for machine building, e.g. bureaux for industrial machinery, agricultural machinery and military machinery. Within the bureau of industrial engin- eering, there are departments of light machinery, heavy machinery and so on. These specialised bureaux and departments have enormous power over the factories that produce these products. Each of them (sometimes each of the departments under the bureaux) has a number of 'fixed spot' factories under its control (*dingdian chang*, or factories specified for certain products) that it monitors *vis-à-vis* fulfilment of the plan and supply of raw materials; it even makes recommendations on the appoint- ment of managers to the relevant department in the ministry or local government. Usually, when the factories encountered any difficulties they could not resolve by themselves, they would seek ministerial help. For this, they would first go to the bureaux. Administratively, only through them would they gain access to higher authorities. In other words, the bureaux are the key joints in the command economy linking state plan and manufacturers. Paternalistic ties are most clearly reflected between these bureaux and the 'fixed spot' factories, causing other factories in the sector to complain that they are only 'stepsons'.[8]

The abolition of these specialised bureaux is a precondition for the relationship of the state and state-owned enterprises to change from one based on administrative decrees to one based on sectoral macro guidance. With the removal of the mandatory plans, the functions of the 'general policy bureaux' can be fairly easily changed to those of sectoral guidance, executing the government's industrial policies. As a further step, the remaining ministries can then be converted into business associations like the Ministry of the Textile Industry. The following two cases reveal the extent to which the reform of the administrative system affects the economic bureaucracy.

The Ministry of the Chemical Industry is one of the ministries retained for the time being in the State Council structure. According to its Minister, CC member Wu Wenying, the direction of change is away from the current mode of control over state-owned enterprises in terms of administrative allocation and towards sectoral guidance for all factories in the industry, regardless of the nature of their ownership. This change in function was reflected in the reduction of numbers of products in the ministry's mandatory plan (from twenty-seven to three), thus paving the way for the ministry gradually to streamline most of its specialised bureaux. But the minister went on to say that a few bureaux still remained because they were still required to monitor production of items allocated by the plans. At the same time the ministry could not get rid of all its micro-economic controls at this stage because it needed to take care of the production of about 250 items in fifteen categories currently prescribed by directory plans; although the number had fallen from over 500 a year before (Wu Wenying, 1993, p. 4).

The elimination of specialised bureaux is also the principle under which other industrial ministries were restructured in 1992. Again, the purpose is to remove the functions of these central bodies in managing micro-economic activities. The merger of the Ministry of Commerce and the Ministry of Raw Materials into the Ministry of Domestic Trade serves as a good case for analysis.

The Ministry of Commerce was an important body of central control. Under the command economy, manufactured goods were not at the disposal of the producers but had to be assigned through a state network of allocation in which the Ministry of Commerce played a crucial role. At the top of the system lay specialised bureaux such as the Bureau of

Hardware and Electrical Goods, the Bureau of Mechanical Products, and the Bureau of Industrial Goods for Daily Use. Each of the bureaux had specialised departments such as home electrical goods, chemical hardware and so on. Under these bureaux and departments were allocation stations of four grades. Grade one comprised ministerial centres in the form of national companies responsible for allocating goods across provincial borders. The next level comprised the provincial stations under the control of the provincial bureaux responsible for allocating goods within the province. This network went down to the municipal and county levels. One complicated aspect of the network was the specialised nature of each allocation station: a hardware and electrical goods station could not supply chemical goods. And each station had a list of clients pertaining to its rank in the hierarchy. Thus a centrally run factory very often had to order its materials through grade one stations. It needed a document from the relevant bureau in the ministry to go to these stations. The structure made many anomalies possible.

For instance, a ministerial steel factory in Shandong needed a boiler. It had to apply to the Ministry of Metallurgy, which then made an order to the SPC. If the order was approved, it then went to the relevant ministry. The ministry's grade one station that specialised in such goods would arrange for the factory to obtain a boiler, probably made in Shanghai. Then the factory would wait for months for the boiler to be delivered. However, the factory's next-door neighbour might be a boiler producer making the very boiler the factory needed. But the neighbour could not offer the boiler because it was listed with the grade two station under a provincial bureau of supply. It was because of this command structure that Chinese economists called the economy an administrative or allocative economy.

The market reform has partially changed the situation. The booming market increasingly provides producers with alternative sources of supply and sales. The steel factory may now go directly to its neighbour to buy a boiler. However, the supply system is still to some extent related to the specialised ministerial bureaux which administered the state mandatory planning. For instance, the quota system for certain products is still operational, requiring central and local allocation through the network described above. The current reform removing the specialised bureaux is meant in essence to eliminate the allocative chain in the remaining part of the administrative economy, thus making room for smoother market transactions.

As far as actual steps are concerned, the Ministry of Commerce abolished the Bureaux of Daily Industrial Goods Administration, Non-staple Food Administration, Native Produce Administration and others before 11 October 1992, as prescribed by the State Council. Meanwhile, the ministry divided the roles of these bureaux into different blocs to be taken over by various functional bodies. Many of their allocating functions have been delegated to the trading companies immediately attached to the ministry. These companies turn the administrative allocation into commercial deals. The sectoral functions of the abolished bureaux (mainly the formulation of general macro policies and sectoral development plans) have been transferred to various general policy bureaux in the new ministry. Some of their administrative functions (e.g. powers to approve the business scope of ministerial factories and provincial bureaux) have been eliminated. Although there is a period of transition in which the economic functions are run by administrative means, such as approving investment projects proposed by enterprises and maintaining a list of industrial goods in the centre's mandatory plans, detailed control over micro-economic activities will increasingly be phased out (Shi Xin, 1993, p. 42). And this restructuring in the Ministry of Commerce has provided a foundation for the new Ministry of Domestic Trade to change its previous functions associated with being a central watch-dog.

THE REFORM OF PROVINCIAL AND LOCAL BUREAUCRACIES

The industrial ministries serve as the hubs of the command economy in that they are the 'dragon head' of the *tiaotiao* systems, in which industrial bureaux were established at all levels beyond Beijing. Therefore the removal or restructuring of central ministries paves the way for the administrative reform in the regions.

The significance of the reform streamlining the specialised industrial agencies can be seen more clearly at the provincial and local levels. The central ministries run only a tiny proportion of state-owned enterprises, although they are the most important ones. Moreover, the ministerial enterprises are among the largest, and many of them have already been converted into corporations with fairly independent operations. In contrast, the majority of state-owned enterprises are under the tight control of local bureaux. Statistics published in 1988 revealed that among 93,658 state firms, 39,689 were run directly by the provincial bureaux, and 49,136 by the county bureaux. Almost all the 367,842 collective factories were run by local bureaux (SCRES, 1988, p. 157).

Another important aspect of the reform lies in the number of these bureaux to be removed. A central industrial ministry may have several bureaux at the provincial level. For instance, the Light Industry Ministry has at least two bureaux in each province (although these are mainly run by the provincial government): the First Light Industry Bureau, which runs state-owned enterprises; and the Second Light Industry Bureau, which runs collective mills. The Machine Building Ministry may have many more bureaux in its local bureaucratic chain. As an example, Liaoning has a heavy machinery bureau, an automobile bureau, a mining machinery bureau, a military industry bureau and so on. What is worse, as stated earlier, is that at the provincial and municipal level these bureaux have also set up a number of administrative companies of the first and second grade, which add to the list of bureaucratic superiors to factories. It is this 'Parkinsonian fission' of industrial bureaux that not only has inflated the size of the government structure but also has put numerous shackles on producers. Very often a factory manager is ordered to do something by the head of the superior company one day, and the next day this instruction is countermanded by a bureau head who happens to visit the factory.

The reform of the administrative system at the provincial and municipal level is being carried out along similar lines to the reforms of the centre. It starts with reducing the scope of administrative functions of state economic agencies and then moves to phasing out the specialised sectoral bureaux from the government structure. The name of the game is *gradualism*, which reflects the harsh reform environment. In fact, the practicability of the reform hinges on three preconditions.

1 Satisfactory outlets must be found for a large proportion of the nine million economic cadres whose positions are to be abolished.
2 Steps between the centre and localities must be coordinated. If a central ministry is first streamlined, it is fairly easy for its local departments to be removed. Otherwise the locality is under pressure from the ministry to maintain its local presence, for without corresponding agencies the locality may lose access to centrally sponsored cheap materials, projects and free overseas trips. For the centre, the remaining bureaux can also serve as a brake on the economy because when the need to cool down chronic overheating arises, the local bureaux are the mechanisms to do it.
3 Pilot schemes must be carried out successfully. This is necessary if upheavals in policy implementation are to be avoided when the reform is carried out nationwide.

In short, gradualism means the art of control over massive social engineering where the factors of timing, content, compensation and compromise are crucial to success (Zhang Zhijian, 1992, p. 12).

Administrative reform at the provincial and municipal levels is characterised, furthermore, by its uneven development. In general, the coastal provinces have gone much further than the inland regions. This is logical, as the market has played a more important role in the coastal areas. The Guangdong provincial government, for instance, had detached six economic bureaux from the government by the end of 1992, when many inland provinces did not even have a plan for the reform (Xiao Mei, 1993, p. 10). Since 1993 the reform has gradually advanced in all localities. Nationally, 170 such bureaux had been removed by the end of 1995, of which 110, or 65 per cent, have been turned into economic entities (e.g. holding corporations) and have thus lost their administrative status over factories. Many others were transformed into property management companies. Hainan, Shenzhen and Shanghai went the furthest. In Hainan there are no specialised industrial bureaux left. Some non-experimental areas have also implemented the reform quickly. Tianjing, for instance, has halved the number of bureaux in its government structure. The national average number of provincial industrial bureaux is 13.7, or 30 per cent of all bureaux in a provincial government, a visible decline from 1993. Yet this is still regarded as far too many. The next round of administrative reform will deal with them (Xu Yue, 1996, p. 15).

The streamlining has been conducted along three patterns. The first is to transform a given industrial bureau into a general shareholding corporation with a few enterprise groups attached to it. Its main task is to oversee the running of the property of these groups in its capacity as the representative of the ultimate owner (the state). In the process of transformation, its previous powers of planning and investment approval should be transferred to the provincial/municipal planning commission; the powers of managing and coordinating everyday production of the groups should go to the commission of economics and trade; and the powers of remuneration and social welfare to the labour and personnel bureaux (Chen Yongjie, 1995, p. 16). The second is to convert some of the industrial bureaux into large conglomerates, composed of large state-owned enterprises. The third is to create sectoral business associations out of the abolished bureaux whose large numbers of medium and small-sized firms are more easily directed by the 'invisible hand'.

Shanghai is said to have progressed quite far with the reform, owing partly to its status as the national experimental site and partly to the determination of its municipal leaders (Yin Guohua, 1995, p. 16). According to former *Renmin ribao* chief editor Hu Jiwei, the municipal government decided in 1992 that most of the specialised economic bureaux would be abolished in three years (*Jingji ribao*, 12 October 1992). The mayor of Shanghai, Huang Ju (now party secretary), announced in July 1993 that a three-level state asset management system had been established under a municipal management commission for state property headed by Politburo member Wu Bangguo. Shanghai's strong leadership commitment to the reform has created favourable conditions for a fairly quick overhaul of the economic bureaucratic chain. Once state-owned enterprises are registered in the Municipal Commission, and the increment in the value of their property is overseen by state investment bodies (e.g. holding companies), they will gradually be detached administratively from their bureaucratic superiors. This undercuts the very existence of the specialised economic bureaux.

Beijing's case is interesting in that the city has formed sectoral business associations yet for some time still kept the sectoral bureaux. This is the phenomenon called 'one organisation with two nameplates'. One leading researcher in the municipal government asserts that this coexistence is only transitional. Ultimately, bureaux will be supplanted by associations or other economic entities. For the time being, these bureaux still have a role to play in coordinating macro- and micro-economic activities. In addition, there is a serious problem of relocating the personnel: the bureaux employ about 50,000 cadres. This number is augmented by the staff in the two grades of administrative companies below the bureau level. Most of them will have to go as well once the streamlining is finished.[9]

At the county and township levels the reform of the administrative system has been implemented with greater force. In fact, the reform at the county level pre-dated that at the centre by three years. Because most factories at this level were extra-budget ones, their production and sales were subject to the market at an earlier date and more thoroughly. Accordingly, the existence of the specialised bureaux has caused more conflict *vis-à-vis* the dual-track allocation system, as their administrative control was pursued but with less compensation in allocated cheap goods. This has been reflected, moreover, in the incessant trade wars between regions. The local protectionism adopted by these bureaucratic authorities severed the national market.

On the other hand, many state-owned enterprises at these two levels may be kept under tighter control by the county and township governments because of their proximity to the administrative powers. This proximity has become a burden to the factories, as they are subject to endless demands from local cadres for 'donations'. What makes relations worse is obscure property ties. Sometimes ownership control is more direct, at other times bureaucratic power is exercised with naked force.[10]

The main thrust of the reform at the county and township levels is to eject all state economic and technological agencies from the government structure. About 350 counties have experimented with these reforms since 1990 (*Renmin ribao*, 26 May 1992). The current central policy is to allow each county to decide on the basis of its own conditions whether to introduce the reform, although its provincial government has to approve its reform plans. Put another way, the counties are not forced to implement the reform before they are ready. However, many counties outside the pilot schemes are encouraged to carry out the administrative reform on their own initiative (Tang Ji, 1992, p. 4).

The official account states that most of China's 1,898 counties welcome the reform. Over half of them generate revenue smaller than their budget and are heavily dependent on state subsidies. The chief reason for this has been a proliferation of government agencies and overstaffing. According to the vice-governor of Shanxi Province, 50 per cent of its counties are unable even to deliver salaries to their staff on time. The county leaders think the reform presents the best way out of this predicament (Wang Shuanxi, 1992, p. 12). In fact, administrative reform at the county level is much broader than simply detaching the specialised economic bureaux from the government. It also affects party and government institutions. The principle of 'small government, big service' requires party cells to be trimmed to a minimum of staff. Other non-governmental institutions will also be removed from the state structure gradually (over three to five years) and will become responsible for their own revenue.[11] Because this book focuses on state/enterprise relations, it concentrates on the reform of government economic agencies.

Addressing a national conference on county reform in September 1992, Li Peng outlined the State Council's position on the issue of relations between the county economic agencies and their affiliated concerns. He said that the former should not assume any administrative functions over the latter. To this end, firms' ties with the county government should amount to no more than that of submitting taxation (*Renmin ribao*, 11 February 1993). Two months later when touring Shishi City, Fujian Province, Li Peng expressed his vision of the county's handling of government/enterprise relations: 'you invest, we welcome it; you make profits, we levy taxes; you violate the regulations, we apply penalties; and you go bankrupt, we are sympathetic but no more than that' (*Shenzhuo xueren*, no. 1, 1993, p. 32). Certainly, there is a long way to go before this statement becomes reality. The general direction of the county reform, however, signals that the state/enterprise relationship at this level is poised for a fundamental change.

A case study: the reform in a poor county

It is difficult to generalise about the effects of county reform. There are different models under which the reform is carried out in different places. In general, coastal provinces have tended to take a 'Big Bang' approach, 'dismantling the temple first and then letting the monks go'. This means that the sectoral economic bureaux are removed from the government at a stroke and a large portion of the staff are reallocated elsewhere.

Researchers in the SCRES gave the following three reasons why this model was possible in these places. First, the market is more mature, as indicated by the fast growth of the tertiary sector, the village and township industries, and foreign investment. So more employment outlets are available for government staff made redundant in the reform. Second, the economic conditions in these areas are favourable for compensating cadres dismissed from office. In late 1992 I saw at the entrance of the county government headquarters of Panyu, Guangdong, a public notice stating that anybody employed by the government office and institutions directly affiliated with it could receive a 50,000 *yuan* settlement if he/she tendered his/her resignation. In addition, he/she would obtain a lump sum payment according to years of service (the minimum was one and half years). Third, in these places the cadres' sense of career success has largely changed from a focus on official rank to a market self-valuation.

This allays resistance to 'dismantling the temple'. As a result of the thorough retrenchment, state-owned enterprises have gained unprecedented autonomy to conduct business.

In contrast to the 'dismantling the temple first' model, in inland counties like Yuanping, Shanxi Province, the model is to build a separate 'temple' before the conditions for removing the previous one are ripe. So a period of transition (normally up to three years) is allowed for county economic bureaux to be delinked from the government budget, although organisationally they are supposed to be stripped of their power to administer firms.

Yuanping County has a population of 445,000. In 1991 its GDP stood at 600 million *yuan* with revenue of about 52 million *yuan*, less than the income generated by most townships in Panyu. In the process of reform, the government has reduced the number of its offices at the county level from forty-six to twenty-one, and its staff from 912 to 478, exceeding the centre's prescription of a 25 per cent reduction at the initial stage. Cadres at the department level (*keji*) dropped from 232 to 132, by 43.2 per cent.

The axed bureaux included those of manufacturing industry, first and second light industries, grain, commerce, materials, economic coordination, agriculture and animal husbandry, agricultural machinery, village and township industry, and water conservancy. These bureaux have been mainly transformed into corporations as the first-grade legal person and the factories formerly under them became the second-grade legal person, for the transitional period.[12] Their relations with both the government and the factories are based on profit contracts. As economic entities, some of them became service centres offering clients paid technological assistance and professional consultation, such as for crop protection and the maintenance of agricultural equipment. Their formal administrative functions are assumed by a new economic and trade commission. However, the commission has no direct leadership ties with factories. Therefore it does not have authority over their management appointments, investment plans and wage matters. The welfare functions formerly assumed by these industrial bureaux have now been handed over to government offices responsible for the welfare of the local community as a whole. These offices include the labour bureau, the public health bureau, state-run insurance agencies and so on.

So far, most of Yuanping County's industrial bureaux have been decoupled from the state administrative budget. For instance, the Agricultural and Animal Husbandry Bureau and Agricultural Machinery Bureau were turned into service centres. With the redefined functions, the county government gave up ten core economic missions which have been taken over by factories. The two most important ones are final decision making on factories' investment of funds they have raised themselves, and the authority to lease, transfer and mortgage their fixed assets. In addition, factories were told to exercise 'three open' powers: 'open employment' (hiring and firing), 'open operation' (business autonomy) and 'open distribution' (remunerative autonomy).[13] The conflicts between factories and the bureaux turned companies have continued, owing largely to unclarified relations of property rights. However, to a large degree, factories have more decision-making power than before.

THE FIGHT FOR CONTROL OF STATE-OWNED ENTERPRISES

Soon after the industrial reforms were launched in 1984, local economic cadres took on the decision-making powers which the centre had meant to delegate to state-owned enterprises. This constituted a major reason why Deng proposed in 1986 that political reforms should focus narrowly on the curtailment of the powers of middle-level economic cadres (Deng Xiaoping, 1987, p. 132). However, this limited effort failed to deliver real results. This has cast a heavy shadow on the current round of reforms of the administrative system.

An organisational analysis of the changes in state/enterprise relations of the last decade may be summarised by the words a 'fight for control of state-owned enterprises'. The future of China's industrial reform hinges upon the outcome of this war, which reflects a wide range of crucial issues. For example, the provision of business opportunities to the cadres to lure them away from their current positions is closely connected with worsening corruption. For another, the centre has been working hard to transfer to state-owned enterprises the fourteen enumerated powers now vested in the hands of middle-level bureaucrats. However, since this central policy mainly takes the form of administrative orders without adequate backing from an established legal framework, its progress so far has been far short of government expectations. Although the deepening reform of the administrative system apparently disadvantages the economic bureaucrats, the fight has intensified.

In general, two patterns of changing state and enterprise ties have emerged. First, administrative control has been replaced by emerging corporate control as factories that have got rid of their superior bureaux now have to face various general corporations. Originating from the industrial bureaux, these corporations function as the new boss or 'mother-in-law'. Second, the property of factories that are still under specialised bureaux is regrouped. Arrangements vary, and include direct property accrual contracts with the bureau's boss, membership of a cross-sector, cross-locality enterprise group, or a merger with a factory which has already got rid of its bureaucratic boss. Such measures have enabled enterprises to circumvent direct control by the bureaux.

For second-category factories, transitional measures have been worked out to guarantee a degree of autonomy for factory management. One key reform in this direction has been the introduction of a series of redefined responsibility systems signed directly between large and medium-sized firms and the provincial and municipal authorities. In Beijing, for instance, the municipal government has signed contracts with 444 large and medium-sized state-owned enterprises (*Renmin ribao*, 19 April 1992). The main purpose is to make the remaining industrial bureaux superfluous and to place state-owned enterprises in a stronger position to resist the intervention of other immediate superiors.[14] Business autonomy for the enterprises has been enhanced, as they are subject to fewer detailed controls by a provincial government.

Along these lines, the Beijing municipality stipulated that all state-owned enterprises practising the new reforms have authority to change the state's remaining mandatory plans if they feel there is not enough market demand. Except for a few commodities whose prices are controlled by the State Council, state-owned enterprises have the power to price their products. They can freely recruit workers according to their needs and formulate their wage policies and institutional arrangements. And they can make decisions on any new production projects within an investment limit of 10 million *yuan* and technological renovation projects within an investment limit of 30 million *yuan* without approval from their bureaucratic agencies. Clearly these reforms have been meant to curtail effectively the authority of middle-level economic bureaucrats and pave the way for their eventual elimination.

Corporate control and commercialisation

Focusing on the first-category factories, it is still too early to draw any definite conclusions about the nature of the new relationship between an enterprise and its new superior corporation.[15] However, there have been a number of changes in this bilateral relationship, the most visible being the effort to replace the former bureaucratic controls with corporate controls, as mentioned earlier (p. 197). Corporate control means a kind of principal/agency relationship based on the former's owner status over the latter. Theoretically, corporate control acts as a buffer between the ABSPs and producers. A corporation's control over its subsidiaries is realised through influencing the decision-making process of their boards of directors. Since both the holding corporations and the subsidiaries are economic entities and legal persons, their relations are basically economic rather than administrative.

The most significant impact has come from efforts to commercialise the economic commanding heights. Intended to buy off the bureaucrats who will lose their cadre status within the party/state, this policy is as old as the reform itself. It accompanied the original rural reform, where commune cadres were released from office but granted opportunities to make big money. The industrial reform has entailed the same need to buy cadres off, and similar ways of doing so, as its progress turns many government offices into obstacles to the development of the market. In response to interventions by middle-level bureaucrats, in 1987 Zhao Ziyang initiated an administrative reform in industrial ministries, according to which most of their specialised bureaux were to be removed.

Soon Zhao and his followers found themselves challenged by two difficulties: (1) how to reassign the large number of cadres affected by the streamlining; and (2) how to keep the national economy running smoothly when the functional bodies in central ministries were dismantled but the market had not become mature enough to drive micro-economic activities. The State Council introduced a transitional programme that turned the specialised bureaux in central ministries into semi-administrative and semi-business companies. These companies still had access to state capital and materials. But instead of allocating these directly to their affiliates, they sold them to them at intermediate prices, and acted as salesmen for the factories rather than as state agencies transmitting the goods according to the central plan. It was argued that when the market became mature, the semi-administrative nature of these firms would diminish, and they would then be generally guided by market signals. As the reform would prevent a vacuum from forming during the transition, it represented a rational compromise acceptable to central planners. In fact, in having access to both state goods and the power to do business, the former economic cadres could reap enormous benefits through their connections with government offices. While this might reduce their hostility to the reform, at the same time it constituted a serious source of corruption. The social cost to the government and reformers was staggering. It was no coincidence that in step with the institutional reform in central ministries, the number of bureaucratic firms grew at breathtaking speed. In Beijing alone, 703 were registered between January and May 1988. Most of them were affiliates of central ministries (*Jingji ribao*, 27 July 1988).

The new round of administrative reform is evolving along a similar path. Being an important channel for relocating economic cadres, corporatisation of government agencies has become a key mechanism to ensure stability in central and local administration. This is actually a key component of a convergence strategy pursued by the post-Deng leadership: the Jiang/Li coalition, or Jiang/Li *tizhi*. The strategy in a sense recognises the key interests of the state administrative system and central planners in the reform and aims to transform them only gradually. Therefore, the party leadership was able not only to campaign for the reforms itself but also to absorb the inertia of state bureaucracies and central planners. Yet the general direction of convergence should also be clear, as set out by Deng during his south China tour in 1992: reform must prevail over inertia. The task is a tough one: Zhao Ziyang and Li Peng failed the test. They both regarded their interactions not in terms of convergence but as efforts to obtain supremacy. Jiang has so far succeeded in achieving a level of cooperation with Li, which is why there have been no major factional eruptions. But the price has been inhibition of the pace of change in China's political and economic systems, a phenomenon that can be described as pro-immobilist (You Ji, 1996).

According to the SCRES, the transformation of specialised bureaux into corporations is an inevitable outcome of the transformation of the command economy into a market economy. So the reform should be encouraged as long as the newly created corporations are delinked from the state structure (*Jingji ribao*, 22 April 1993). With this 'green light' given by the Jiang/Li coalition to protect the vested interests of the bureaucrats, history is repeating itself, as is apparent in the current rush to establish corporations. By the end of 1992, there were 486,700 state-run corporations in the country. Of these, 226,000 were registered in 1992 alone, and one in every ten was established by party and government offices (*Jingji ribao*, 2 March 1993). Compared with 1988, the party's consensus on the market spelt a clearer theoretical objective and time-table for the new round of reforms; these had been missing in the previous attempts. While this consensus may make implementation of government reform easier, more importantly, it serves as a prerequisite for any system-atic political reform. The reform effort is now being carried out at all levels of government rather than just at the centre; it is accompanied by a reform in the ownership system that undercuts the foundation of the existing bureaucratic structure; and it is driven by the growth of the market and a reduction of planning.

To a degree, this trend to commercialise bureaucratic economic control has been instrumental in broadening market activities, for the new cor-porations not only coordinate the business transactions of state-owned enterprises under them but are engaged in market exchanges themselves. Indeed, although they also try to take advantage of their former status in the command economy, as the market grows there is a built-in trend in these bureaucratic firms to move towards further marketisation. This has promoted commercialisation of the relationship between government and producers. According to state regulations, after an initial period of up to three years, the corporations are to be dislodged from the state budget. In other words, while they are treated as extensions of the organs of political power, they must create their own sources of revenue.

Another feature of the commercialised state/enterprise relationship is reflected in intensified bargaining between state-owned enterprises and their corporate superiors. However, in the evolution of corporate ties, the intensification of bargaining may not indicate tighter control of the corporations over the firms below. On the contrary, commercialisation has reduced control precisely through the bargaining process. The command economy was characterised by bargaining, as different interests existed. Yet strict planning had never left sufficient room for real bargaining. Both the Soviet and the Chinese experiences have shown that freelance bar-gaining often caused disciplinary reactions from the party/state. Now commercialisation has enlarged the scope for bargaining, and this is an indicator of weakened state administrative control. State-owned enterprises have consequently gained increased strength to bargain for more autonomy. Although the fight continues, the balance of power is shifting in favour of state-owned enterprises, which are aware of the degree of difference in the power embodied in an administrative boss and in a business boss. This gives state-owned enterprises the courage to fight back against the controls placed on them by the corporations. The following case study is a good example.

A study of bureaux turned corporations (*fanpai gongsi*)[16]

The Beijing Liulihe Cement Factory is the largest cement factory in the Beijing area, employing 5,000 workers and with annual sales of more than 200 million *yuan*. In 1992 the factory was forced to join the Beijing Building Material Corporation, newly converted from a government bureau. For the corporation it was of vital importance to have the factory incorporated into it. There were several reasons for this: (1) it had to have a few core factories to claim the status of a large enterprise group, and the factory was the largest among over eighty in the group; (2) as the factory earned 70–80 per cent of all the revenue in the sector concerned, without it the corporation was not only unable to fulfil its tax commitments to the municipal government, but was also unable to cover its loss-making factories; and (3) the factory was the only one in the sector that could provide not only the bulk of operating fees for the corporation which had just been cut off from the state budget, but also the bulk of the wages and bonuses for its 200 or so staff.

Accordingly, the manager of the factory was called to attend a meeting at the corporation, where, like all the other participants, he was asked to fill in a form. The forms all had the same format and wording: 'I, of xxx, will join the corporation voluntarily and abide by the charter of the corporation. . . .' The manager voiced strong opposition to joining the corporation, but the head of the corporation mustered all the power he could to coerce him, including the party's 'organisational principle'. The manager finally gave in.

Soon the manager found what was in store for him. He was notified that since the corporation had become the first-grade legal person, the full legal person status (first-grade) of the factory was withdrawn and it would become a second-grade legal person; that the factory had to submit a proportion of its profits as the corporation's management fees; that it had to surrender all its R & D funds for new products to the corporation on a monthly basis and the funds would be returned quarterly after 30 per cent had been retained within the corporation; that the factory's retained funds from depreciation had to be handed over to the corporation for 'unified usage'; and so on. What the corporation demanded was to take the factory's financial power into its own hands. The last two items alone affected 30 per cent of the factory's operating funds of 20 million *yuan*. At a time of cash flow shortage in China, this was a quite large sum of money, even for such a large firm.

Other factories in the corporation would probably have to accept these demands because they were not in a strong bargaining position. Some even saw advantages in relying on the corporation, which could subsidise their losses through a transfer of profits from factories with good market performance. This was not the case with the Beijing Liulihe Cement Factory. According to Yao Bowen, the factory's chief accountant, when the corporation was delinked from the government structure, it could not help the factory in any way. The factory had to cope by itself in the search for investment funds, raw materials and transport. Its technological innovations would require several hundred million *yuan*, which the corporation was in no position to obtain for it. In short, the corporation was a shell.

The manager launched a counter-offensive. He ordered the accountant not to surrender any of the money demanded from above. He told the head of the corporation that the factory accepted that the corporation was its superior, and because of this the factory was willing to take all financial responsibility for the corporation's staff, that is, the factory could pay 4,000 *yuan* each to its staff on the condition that it 'be left alone'. When this proposal was rejected, the manager issued an ultimatum to the head of the corporation that if he insisted on his demands, the factory would openly announce in the newspapers that it was withdrawing from the corporation. And if the corporation dismissed him, he would bring a lawsuit against it. In his own words, this conflict would 'cause either the death of the fish or damage to the fishing net'.

There is no doubt that the pivotal role of the factory allowed it to challenge the corporation in a way that other factories could not. And because of this role, the factory received the total support of the mayor of Beijing, who told the general manager and party secretary of the corporation in the presence of the factory manager: 'The factory was nearly suffocated under your "ties"; if you want to ruin the factory, I will suffocate you first.' The manager admitted later that in spite of the mayor's harsh words, he could do little in reality.

This was not so much a personal fight as a structural conflict, a matter concerning the strategy for deepening the reform. From the government's point of view, when specialised economic bureaux become corporations, direct ties between them are severed as the bureaux become delinked from the bureaucratic rankings, state budget and pool of government personnel. The new principal/agency relations between a corporation and its subsidiaries are built upon property ties rather than administrative controls stemming from official ranking and planning quotas. In our case study, the corporation did not interfere with the factory's daily management in terms of what to produce and what to sell. It had a general contract with the factory, largely based on a quota of dividends the factory had to submit each year. In a sense the corporation tried to function as the caretaker of state property, although it had not learned how to do it without resorting to administrative pressure. It is fairly understandable that it demanded some financial authority over the factory. The most important motivation for this was the contradiction between the corporation's need to increase the income of its staff and its lack of other resources. The downgrading of the factory's legal person status did not affect its operations under the current situation in China.

The producers, however, have a completely different point of view. It is difficult for them to distinguish corporate controls from administrative controls. Any controls hinder their search for autonomy. Moreover, the so-called corporate governance can be detailed and may involve administrative coercion, particularly over personnel appointments and financial arrangements. Producers' reactions to these corporate ties are generally negative, underlining the changed nature of bargains: whereas these used to involve cheap materials and production quotas, more fundamental rights vested in an independent producer are now at stake, including personnel and financial responsibilities, which were non-negotiable only a few years ago. This indicates a qualitative change in state/enterprise relations: anything short of basic business autonomy will not satisfy the profitable factories.

The struggle for the control of factories is predictable when a command economy is in transition but still under the party/state. The state envisages the bureau turned corporation (*fanpai gongsi*) as a transitional phenomenon, as the quantitative change of the reduction of administrative functions becomes a qualitative change to an independent business entity in the form of a shareholding company. According to He Yang, an influential official/scholar in the SCRES, the difference between a *fanpai gongsi* and a holding corporation is threefold: the latter has its own assets and business to operate in the market; it aims to make profits and accrue capital; and it has administrative links with neither the state nor its subsidiaries (*Jingji ribao*, 24 July 1995). This definition shows why the Beijing Building Material Corporation forced the cement factory to join it. For without subsidiaries these bureaux turned corporations cannot have their own assets, business or profits. Nor can they become economic entities. Yet when they make a factory formally under them their subsidiary, its business autonomy will definitely be affected. For example, to meet the state's requirement that they be financially self-reliant (*vis-à-vis* the state budget), they have to make their subsidiaries 'contribute'. This inevitably damages the interests of the factories under them. Again, to establish its authority and image, the corporation is tempted to interfere with the marketing and sales of its subsidiaries, and this is felt to be worse than administrative control.

Clearly, the 'subsidiaries' believe that these non-substantial corporate 'shells' should not have been set up in the first place. Recent strong resistance from factories nationwide has shown the level of their determination not to accept a corporate *popo*. More fundamentally, this growing conflict poses a huge threat to the ongoing mainstream reform of corporatisation in China's state sector. In the design of the reform, the bureau turned corporation represents a key component in the evolution of new state/enterprise relations: as holding companies or investment corporations they link the state and producers through property (rather than administrative) ties. Our case study shows the acute contradictions which arise. As mentioned earlier, these corporations are supposed to create a 'buffer zone' between the state (the ultimate owner) and producers (actual users of state property). The problem is that they cannot stand on their own feet. They have to be dependent either on the state or on their subsidiaries. For instance, if they are holding companies, do they invest in their own interests or those of the state? If the former, their shareholdings are corporate shares (*farengu*), different from state shares, and so they are not 'buffers' any more. If the latter, they simply act as an extension of the government. Again, they are not 'buffers' any more. Therefore, the blueprint for the new corporate model may contribute to the progress of marketisation but it contains many flaws and becomes distorted in practice. To some extent the idea has turned out to be simplistic. In some cases it works, as our case study reveals. More often, it does not. In fact, it is very difficult for the holding companies built on state agencies to cut their intimate ties with the state; it then becomes difficult for the reform to achieve real separation between government and state-owned enterprises or real separation between state administration and state property operation (Chen Wentong, 1995, p. 5).

This intensified struggle for control of state-owned enterprises has also alarmed the leaders at the apex of power. In a media report of the case mentioned above, Zhu Rongji categorically branded the struggle as obstructive to market reforms and proposed stringent measures to rectify the situation. He pointed out that the corporations would give rise to sectoral and regional monopolies, although he also acknowledged the need to set up these corporations in the course of the reform of the administrative system (*Jingji ribao*, 2 March 1993). Zhu's ambiguity here reflects a serious dilemma for the designers of the reform: they want state-owned enterprises to be directed by the market; however, in dealing with bureaucrats, they do not have a better alternative to the policy buying them off. As one prominent Chinese economist points out, the government is not only the leader of reform but also an object of reform. It is not only the driving force for reform but sometimes the obstacle to reform. Some government officials may be conscious supporters of reforms but may sometimes unconsciously oppose them (Tang Fengyi, 1995, p. 7). Does Zhu Rongji's comment reflect this tendency? Worse still, intentionally or otherwise, this paternalistic supervision by economic bureaucrats may have been creating a new system of vested interests similar to the *nomenklatura* capitalism seen elsewhere in socialist economies in transition.

10 Concluding remarks

This book demonstrates the effects of the post-Mao industrial reforms on state/enterprise relations and on shopfloor politics. These effects are characterised by the dismantling of party/state controls at the grassroots, as embodied in the process of *de-danweiising* industrial work units. However, as the transformation of the state sector is still ongoing, with visible changes observed from month to month, any conclusions drawn about this dynamic process are necessarily intricate and tentative.

It has become increasingly clear that China's state-owned enterprises have become depoliticised since the reforms were launched in 1978, and that the key to this depoliticisation is the change in the functions of the party in the state sector, from an all-embracing authority to an organisation that has progressively narrowed its activities in many crucial areas of enterprise control. This development is both a deliberate design by the party leadership and a logical outcome of China's industrial reforms, as the incompatibility of a political organisation supervising factory management has become ever clearer in the transition of the economy towards the market.

Although party cells in state-owned enterprises are still powerful, particularly in large and medium-sized factories, their power base has been gravely eroded by a set of institutional reforms within both their leadership structure and their party cells. As shown in Chapter 3, the introduction of the director responsibility system gravely affected the party's monistic leadership and has given rise to a 'two centres' dispute between party secretaries and factory managers. At the national level, this reflects a deep-rooted concern of the party over whether it can continue to hold firmly on to its monopoly of power, which depends heavily on whether it holds effective control at the grassroots. Within a state firm, not only have the inertia and habits associated with monistic party domination continued to find a constituency among political staff, but party vested interests are entrenched in the remaining institutional framework of control. The current top party leadership wants to maintain this framework in case it is needed for reimposing controls, as in the aftermath of June 1989. The dilemma for the CCP leadership is that tight control over the grassroots through party cells may inhibit economic growth, stimulate abuse of power by party cadres and alienate the majority of workers, thereby threatening the party's legitimacy and monopoly of power. The 'two centres' rivalry reflects soul-searching in the party during a period of massive socio-economic change.

Nevertheless, a trend is becoming clear. As documented in Chapters 4 and 5, the reforms of the party's industrial apparatus will continue to weaken party cells in state-owned enterprises. For instance, the new cadre contract reform will undercut the party's industrial *nomenklatura* system. A large number of managers will lose their permanent and hierarchical cadre status and rank, and, as a result, the political authority attached to that status. The demarcation line separating cadres and ordinary employees is thus being blurred. With this reform, the criteria for selection and evaluation of managers have also become basically non-political. This change has reduced political consequences for workers who complain about their immediate managers, these no longer so directly representing the party/state. Moreover, the reform has paved the way for introducing a large contingent of professional managers and stimulating their entrepreneurialism. This in turn may help to nurture a new middle class with distinctive economic and political interests in China.

The bankruptcy of the official ideology has helped to stifle the vitality of party industrial cells. Organisational entropy has set in as a result. Many dysfunctional symptoms, such as the collapse of large numbers of party basic cells and a drying up of party reserves, have become evident. Of particular significance is the emergence of many 'fault lines' in the party's 'transmission belt', as revealed in the discussion in Chapter 5 of the aborted attempt to purge 1989 Tiananmen activists. This indicates that somewhere in the process of transition from socialism, the decay of the CCP's industrial body will reach a point beyond repair.

The trend towards 'de-statisation' has similarly picked up momentum. Among other things, the new ownership structure and hybridised property system within the monolithic state ownership system have had a far-reaching impact on state/enterprise relations. The separation of property rights and management rights in the contract reform has enhanced the managers' autonomy in production, remuneration, investment and sales. So, too, has the creation of enterprise property through investment of retained profits and bank loans. Although this form of property has never been clearly defined in legal terms, it has generated a more pronounced sense of self-interest on the part of state-owned enterprises, which increasingly see a need to strengthen their management rights *vis-à-vis* their newly acquired property. Hybridised ownership has also brought political pressure on the state, as not only managers but workers fight to protect their interests embodied in contracts. Worker protest against authorities at various levels has become a way of life on shop floors.

Current efforts to corporatise state-owned enterprises will promote further ownership reform. For most small state firms, the reform will be carried out through spontaneous privatisation; that is, the state will allow non-state sectors to buy or take a long-term lease on small and medium-sized state concerns. This has been happening on a massive scale since 1990. This book is more focused on corporatisation of large and medium-sized state-owned enterprises, mainly through conversion into limited liability companies or joint stock companies. The rationale for this dramatic change can be approached from different angles. At the theoretical level, if China really goes in for a market economy, the current organisation of state-owned enterprises has to change fundamentally because it is essentially a product of the command economy, in that they are an 'appendage of state bureaucracies'. The Chinese leadership has realised that state-owned enterprises have to become economic entities in order to compete effectively in the market. Most state-owned enterprises have already learned this lesson from the 'squeeze' on them by the non-state sectors. Corporatisation is really a matter of life or death for many state-owned enterprises in a more aggressive, tougher competitive environment.

In practical terms, two factors have affected this transformation: the explosion in subsidies by the state to loss-making factories, and the need to raise funds to rescue technologically obsolete state-owned enterprises. There is a strong link between the two. It is increasingly clear that the state cannot afford to subsidise large numbers of loss makers. Mechanisms have to be found to let state-owned enterprises shoulder the burden by themselves, or at least a substantial proportion of it. This factor has underscored Chinese attempts at corporatisation. It is increasingly clear, too, that the state cannot afford technological upgrading of those large state factories created before the post-Mao reform. Therefore, many of them will continue to make losses. The state has made a strategic decision to save these factories by injecting into them foreign capital and funds from society at large. To this end, however, the first condition is to transform the current formula of factory organisation and ownership structure.

Industrial reform at the micro level necessitates a reform of government bureaucracy, which, too, is a product of the command economy. The logic of this administrative reform is apparent: when state firms are corporatised, why should there still exist a vast and costly economic bureaucracy? The new model of government/enterprise relations, presented in Chapter 9, provides a basic line of thinking among Chinese officials and theorists on the construction of a new economic model for the country. At present the blueprint is not crystal-clear, either within or outside China. However, the central consensus on the market economy may help the practitioners to muddle through. There is no doubt that establishing the basic principles of the new model will be a fairly long and painful process involving sectoral guidance through industrial policies, macro regulation through macro-economic levers, and commercial operation of state property by investment bodies. Some Chinese optimistically claim to have seen the light at the end of the tunnel: with political hurdles for marketisation removed, a *direction* for China's reform at both the macro and micro levels has now been fixed after fourteen years of 'crossing a river by probing for stones'.

Will China privatise its state sector? One of the factors contributing to the failure of market socialism in Eastern Europe was the fact that the communist leadership wanted to have some market-oriented reforms but to maintain state ownership at the same time. The double dependence of state firms caused economic confusion. On the other hand, many economic difficulties in these countries can be partially attributed to comprehensive privatisation of state factories without enough marketisation. There is a strong connection between market reform and privatisation. The point is that if China wants to have a market economy and if it wants to corporatise its state sector, privatisation is bound to take place in one form or another. This book has introduced the concept of de-statisation to describe a state-controlled course of quasi privatisation in China's state sector, mainly through diluting the dominant position of state property to improve market efficiency. As more and more foreign and non-state capital is injected into the structure of state ownership, the effect of privatisation will be more clearly felt.

The dogmatic concept that socialism is built upon the domination of state ownership still holds some ground. Voices against the erosion of state property are heard continuously. Moreover, the industrial bureaucrats have a big stake in the control of the bulk of ownership in the national economy. This has been behind many discriminatory rules against private stock making up more than a certain proportion of share subscriptions offered by state companies. However, it seems that the loss of control over the corporatisation process has presented a more serious threat to the development of the stock system in China, despite a consensus on a fairly quick expansion of the reform to more state-owned enterprises. The path of reform will not be easy or smooth. Most crucially, whether the reform of corporatisation can qualitatively improve China's state sector remains to be seen.

In the area of remuneration, the state's tight control over income distribution has been broken. To a large extent, this has been by the state's own design, as manifested in the principle of making a factory 'an independent body of distribution'. The leading Chinese economist Liu Guoguang has clarified the logic behind this design: that it is inconceivable to allow a state factory to engage independently in market activities but not allow it to have autonomy to decide on its own wage policies (Liu Guoguang, 1988, p. 301). Here the post-Mao industrial wage reform has achieved a breakthrough by abolishing the centrally controlled and nationally unified eight-grade wage system – with a profound impact on de-statisation. On the other hand, the structure of workers' payments largely retains the characteristics of the old wage system: low time-rate pay (the normal wage), high irregular pay and high subsidies. This is the chief cause of the *ad hoc* nature of the post-Mao industrial wage system.

The industrial wage reform has greatly affected the tripartite relationship between the state, enterprise management and workers. Between the state and enterprises, the new mechanisms of wage allocation (with the 'linkage system' as the mainstay) have enhanced the status of a state enterprise as a community of interests. While the state hopes that an enterprise will increase tax and profit remittances through generating more profits in the market, the enterprise is strongly influenced by a desire to keep more profits for itself so as to increase wages to workers and staff, a phenomenon also directed by the market. This desire has in turn fundamentally altered the goal of state-owned enterprises' production: from fulfilment of the state's plan to an effort to extract more income from its market activities. Consequently, a struggle has intensified in which the state tries to control the floating part of an enterprise's wage bill, while the enterprise tries to reduce the fixed proportion within the overall income distribution. The result is the rapid growth of 'semi-secret and irregular' distributions over which the state has only weak control.

Meanwhile, workers' perceptions of the state have also changed. Their dependence on the state for their entire income has been reduced to dependence only for a base income, guaranteed as the fixed part of their wages. As pointed out in Chapter 6, now that the fixed proportion of wages for a large number of workers has dropped below 50 per cent, their factory and workshop management have become the key sources of wage rises. This leads workers to enter into an alliance with managers to fight against state intervention. The new system of wage distribution constitutes the rallying point for an enterprise to be transformed into a 'community of common interests', often in opposition to the state.

Within an enterprise, the devolution of the contract responsibility system to sub-factories, workshops and sections required delegation of authority for remuneration to smaller units. This has changed the locus of the factory's distribution of power, paving the way for a new type of labour/management relations to emerge. The delegation of power over incomes to lower-level managers has enhanced mid-level managers' say in a key aspect of management. Yet at the same time, the reduced distance has brought pressure from workers to bear on the managers at lower levels. As a result, labour relations have become increasingly intense.

One factor leading to this change is that, owing to the weakened political and ideological controls over shopfloor politics, more and more informal groups have emerged, usually centred on a few influential figures who are not always in agreement with management. Another factor is workers' feeling of insecurity about their income due to the *ad hoc* nature of wage distribution in the wake of the market reform. They need to come together for collective action. Disputes over remuneration have strengthened the cohesion of these groups. At the same time, wage disputes have also brought to the surface strife among workers, often rooted in the mechanism of uneven distribution of welfare provisions. Allocation of factory housing, for instance, has always been a source of conflict among employees. Each time a wage increase is made available for competition, past wounds may be reopened. Consequently, a fragmented workforce has rendered the workshop atmosphere difficult to manage.

The changed remuneration system has also produced a lasting political impact on state/society relations. Distribution at the lower levels has created settings for informal collective bargaining for wage promotion. Although this is often a kind of spontaneous reaction to what workers believe to be unfair wage policies, its significance lies in the fact that workers have become more conscious of their interests and rights in wage matters. Consequently an upsurge of struggle between managers and workers has forced the government to adopt collective bargaining as a mechanism to ease mounting tensions. In doing so, the state believes that it has assumed a role of power broker. However, the fact that the state has had to grant the initiative of collective bargaining to workers reveals how far its authority has been eroded. In contrast, workers have obtained more space for manoeuvring. It is too early to predict whether these formal and informal efforts at collective bargaining will have major political ramifications, comparable to those achieved by Solidarity. But the creation of the Autonomous Workers Associations in 1989 demonstrated that given the right political situation, an organised workers' voice can speak out loudly against the state.

As mentioned earlier, the *danwei* system constitutes the infrastructure of the party/state, and any change in this regard involves a significant redefinition of the boundaries between the state and society. Therefore, the process of *de-danweiisation* has been and will remain a zig-zag course whose results will determine the shape of China's future. For instance, as shown in Chapter 3, it has taken more than a decade of battle for the CCP to experiment with a new enterprise leadership structure, in which the management, rather than the party committee, is in command of the firm. A final decision has yet to be made. Chevrier has pointed out that the greatest obstacle to the director responsibility system does not lie in the remnants of the high-level command structure but in the lingering power of party organs (Chevrier, 1991, pp. 109–31). That the successive administrative reforms in China did not produce desirable results was largely due to the intransigence of the state bureaucrats responsible for carrying them out. As many of them had a high stake in the status quo, their strong resistance could well be anticipated, a fact which casts a heavy cloud over the current round of administrative reform. In short, the basic structure of the party/state in the form of *danwei* has not been as damaged as it may appear, although the trend of *de-danweiisation* may have acquired a life of its own.

The development of depoliticisation and de-statisation may not lead to democratisation for some time to come. At the grassroots, depoliticisation and de-statisation have largely taken the form of selective decommissioning of multiple *danwei* controls far short of a fundamental political reform that gives workers such basic rights as organisation of autonomous unions. With politics retreating from shop floors, workers have gained more room for non-political activities. However, many of the institutional reforms are not yet firmly enough rooted to allow a 'free and knowledgeable public' to emerge. Workers remain indifferent and cynical towards 'politics'. So far, workers' actions have been characterised by passive and sporadic agitation against managers, often in the form of enlisting support from the state.

China's transformation proceeds along the lines of its own authoritarian tradition. Dialectically this raises the questions of how to control and how to control better. The cruel truth for the CCP is that while tight control may not guarantee any lasting monopoly of power, relaxation is also fraught with crisis for an authoritarian regime. The Romanian experience proves the first point, and the reform of the USSR testifies to the second. Although China's situation differs vastly from both, its own history convinces party leaders that when change is inevitable, the questions of who takes the initiative and how it is timed are crucial for the regime's survival. One leading cadre in the Central Party School argued:

> If we first inaugurate the changes while we are still relatively strong, we can manage the direction and pace of change. What Deng Xiaoping has contributed to the party is his two timely initiatives to push the country towards change in 1978 and 1992.[1]

So the revolution from below has been regarded as serving the purposes of the party. Dismantling totalitarian institutions within the *danwei* system is meant, from the party's point of view, to help ease tension between workers and the state, especially when the majority of workers remain politically indifferent. My interviews with workers revealed that by and large they welcomed these reforms because they could enjoy more choice. For instance, job transfer has become easier, and they can now travel without the approval of their work units. They certainly have a lot to be angry about, especially about overt submission to their immediate bosses, which points to the need to dismantle the *danwei* controls further. The CCP's design of easing controls at the grassroots but keeping a tight grip on national politics distinguishes China's path of transition from that of the European socialist states, but does not fall outside the pattern of East Asian scenarios of political and social change.

In the process of social change the state in East Asian countries endeavours to remain powerful in order to: (1) coordinate economic development; and (2) ensure a reasonably even distribution of income during the process of modernisation. Both requirements may argue for the preservation of an authoritarian superstructure. But at the same time, the state can precipitate a loosening of controls over the economic and social pursuits of the population (Vogel, 1991). Whether this can work for China depends, among other things, on whether Chinese work units achieve greater autonomy from the party/state, and most importantly, on the depth of the ownership reform currently under way in China's state sector.

To sum up, the development of depoliticisation and de-statisation has brought about major changes in the core functions of the industrial *danwei* system. While the systemic innovations are clearly intertwined with systemic continuities, the former may represent the life of the future, with the latter becoming increasingly moribund. In light of this evolution, what hypotheses can we derive from the changes discussed in this book?

The first hypothesis is closely related to the idea of work unit socialism and enterprise corporatism. As is argued throughout the book, two major functions of the industrial *danwei* system – as a political institution and as an appendage of a bureaucratic agency – have been largely eroded. On the other hand, one key role of the *danwei* system, namely its function as a welfare provider, will remain crucial for workers, probably more so than before, owing to tremors caused by the transition currently being felt by workers. This parallel evolution will continue for quite a long time until the welfare function of a work unit is gradually taken over by the state or other social organisations outside the factory.[2]

So looking forward in time, a state factory that is depoliticised, de-ideologised and generally freed from bureaucratic whims would come fairly close to the model of work unit socialism. In their relations with workers, managers can less easily wield state power to suppress workers' demands. On the contrary, they may need to ally with workers in resisting unwanted interference from state agencies. Workers' pressure is also bound to increase. The state's encouragement of collective bargaining on shop floors may drive a wedge into the so-called community of interests of managers and workers. The remuneration reform has removed the shield of the state in wage matters and thus has exposed managers directly to workers. To meet this challenge, managers may have to play the game of 'divide and rule' more effectively. A fragmented workforce will only worsen tension in the workplace, increasing the difficulties caused by informal politics (Dittmer and Lu, 1996, p. 256). As a result, community of interests is meaningful only in terms of a state firm's relations with state bureaucrats. Tension is particularly marked in the area of social welfare provisions. As the state tries to shake off its socialist responsibilities, work units have to feed redundant employees, distribute housing and increase workers' income on their own. Very often the state is behind workers in their ever rising demands: the most effective way to meet its goal of social stability. In a way the model of work unit socialism is a very expansive one.

On the other hand, an enterprise catering to a variety of workers' needs but maintaining links with the state may stand as a buffer between the state and workers. Through the filter of an enterprise many state authoritarian controls will be diluted in intensity. At the same time, however, the enterprises under such a model also serve the state's purposes. They constitute a stabilising factor in the course of social transition: they generate taxes, increase employment and provide welfare benefits to a large number of workers, thus alleviating the burdens on the state. More generally, severing the intimate ties between politics and economics represented by the *danwei* system may make the transformed enterprise less vulnerable to the changing political environment. Firms no longer need to care much about ideological 'shocks' or events such as the anti-spiritual pollution movement. This will actually contribute to economic stability, which may in turn help to lessen the likelihood of social instability.

A transformed firm may also fit the East Asian development model, which emphasises collectivism in a social organisation and an effective role for the state. This model entails institutional mechanisms in a firm whereby workers are granted as many welfare services as their work units can manage but at the same time they are denied basic political rights. The firm takes on collectivist and mutual obligations between workers and management. This paternalistic feature of enterprise corporatism can be found in many employment arrangements sustained by enterprises, not only in China but also in other East Asian industrial communities, although varying to considerable degrees.

A second hypothesis, again looking forward in time, is that the development of depoliticisation and de-statisation in state-owned enterprises will fundamentally change the mode of state control over society. Unlike in the former USSR and the East European socialist countries, which had strong elements of a police state, China's state/society relations have been more organisation-oriented, that is less reliant on the formal machinery of the state and more on the organisational networks rooted in people's workplaces (Lu Feng, 1993, p. 81).

As stated earlier, workplace control has been enforced in large part through the party system. However, party industrial cells are gradually losing their organisational vitality and are decaying. This, together with the removal of a number of state control functions from the workplace, such as those related to state and public security and political monitoring, has led the population to gain more confidence in pursuing their own activities. Although work units still exercise effective control over workers' welfare, factories' compartmentalism has nurtured a rebellious attitude towards the party and the state. The alliance formed by managers and workers to extract more income from the state is especially damaging to the political hierarchy. To some degree, we have observed that this is already changing the nature of control inherent in state/society relations. Many state firms still assume government administrative control functions, including family planning, arranging documents for marriage, household registration and so on. But as these functions are generally stripped of political content, they have had a less deterrent effect on workers than before. Many control mechanisms formerly exercised by the *danwei* system have either been removed altogether or lost effectiveness, such as the need for permission to travel, and restrictions on job transfer and moonlighting.

As these developments continue, the giant party/state will eventually be seen to have feet of clay, as its foundations lose cohesiveness. To enforce unpopular measures, it will more often have to rely on the hardware of the state machinery. As the reform under way alters the existing political order without any visible replacement, this will have further transformative and destabilising implications. People gain more freedom as their organisational bondage falls apart, but at the same time they ignore laws and regulations. One can perceive enormous uncertainties ahead for the country's development. In dealing with the dynamics of change and a more sophisticated population, the longer the CCP maintains and institutionalises the current policy line, the more difficulty it will have in retreating from reforms in the future, and the more likely it is that disaffection may lead to other political solutions (Goodman, 1991, p. 18).

The positive side of this development is the gradual phasing out of political and personal controls rooted in the *danwei* system: the authoritarian infrastructure of the party/state withers and a new social base for political change comes into being. When the ordinary Chinese enjoy more choices in their daily pursuits, this may indirectly reduce the tension between the state and people. The best the party can hope for from this is that loss of control in the workplace may help to slow down its internal decay, as its corrupt rank-and-file members are deprived of their power in the process. In the meantime economic growth must be sustained to improve the standard of living of workers. However, against this optimistic thinking a worst-case scenario of the country becoming ungovernable looms large (Harding, 1992, pp. 36–48). If this becomes reality, the state will lose cohesiveness, and the corruption of those in power, alongside banditry and violence by those with nothing to lose, will lead China's journey 'back to the future'. China will confront both tremendous opportunities and the possibility of crisis in the twenty-first century.

Notes

1 INTRODUCTION

1 The word 'state' is used here in the broad sense defined by Gordon White, as denoting 'a complex organisational system comprising three sets of basic institutions at central level and below: political (notably the party), administrative (governments at each level and their subordinate bureaucratic agencies) and coercive (the PLA)'. See Gordon White (ed.) *The Chinese State in the Era of Economic Reform*, London: Macmillan, 1991, p. 2.

2 The word 'appendage' is popularly used by Chinese economists to describe the highly dependent status of a state factory on the state. See Zhou Shuliang, 'Reform of the Planned Economy and Planning System', in George Totten and Zhou Shuliang (eds) *China's Economic Reform: Administering the Introduction of Market Mechanism*, Boulder, Colo.: Westview Press, 1992, p. 25.

3 Many western scholars of the former Soviet Union and Eastern Europe hold such a view. The extent to which the attempts to reform by the Communist Parties in the Soviet bloc failed has proved them correct. See, for instance, the articles written by Robert Miller, in Robert Miller (ed.) *The Developments of Civil Society in Communist Systems*, Sydney: Allen & Unwin, 1992, and Enrique Baloya and James Morris, *Conflict and Change in Cuba*, Albuquerque: University of New Mexico Press, 1993, p. 41. Whether change means collapse in the socialist countries in Asia, only time can tell. But there is a possibility that convergence can occur there, as the current market reforms dictate greater change with greater force.

2 A QUIET REVOLUTION FROM BELOW

1 The term is from John Wilson Lewis, *Leadership in Communist China*, Ithaca, NY: Cornell University Press, 1963, p. 4.

2 Interviewees of Perry Link told him that they felt that they were owned by their *danwei*. This word 'owned' was also repeated many times during my interviews with workers in China. See Perry Link, *Evening Chats in Beijing*, New York: Norton, 1992, p. 68.

3 In fact, Walder was among the first to point out the changes in his recent writings. For instance, 'Wage Reform and the Web of Factory Interests', *China Quarterly*, no. 109, 1987, pp. 21–41.

4 The words 'active consent' are from Christine Buci-Glucksmann, *Gramsci and the State*, London: Lawrence & Wishart, 1980, p. 93, quoted in Peter N. S. Lee (1991a, p. 156).

5 A number of workers in their sixties told me that at the beginning of their

careers as workers, they still called their factories *womenchang*, or 'our factory', but gradually they changed the vocabulary to *women danwei*, or 'our *danwei*', which they said meant they unconsciously followed the social vogue.

6 However, tensions in other areas may have worsened. For instance, monetised labour relations have given rise to increased conflicts between workers and managers and among workers themselves.

7 See, for instance, Deng Xiaoping's speech to People's Liberation Army ranking officers on 19 June 1989.

8 For a detailed analysis of *tiaotiao* and *kuaikuai*, see Jonathan Unger, 'The Struggle to Dictate China's Administration: The Conflict of Branches vs Areas vs Reform', *The Australian Journal of Chinese Affairs*, no. 18, July 1978, pp. 15–45.

9 The linkage wage system is a profit-oriented, institutionally based wage arrangement. By the beginning of 1990, 70 per cent of Chinese state-owned enterprises had carried out this wage reform. See Wage Research Task Force of the State Planning Commission, 'Qiye gongzi tong jingji xiaoyi guagoude yanjiu' (Research on the mechanism of linking aggregate wage and economic efficiency), *Zhongguo gongye jingji yanjiu* (Studies on the Chinese industrial economy), no. 3, 1991, pp. 49–54.

10 By western standards, indirect control is basically monetary control, which clearly is not the case in China's linkage reform. However, compared with the state's unified wage system, the factory's power in deciding remuneration matters has made state control much less direct.

11 For a quantitative analysis of this transition, see William Byrd, *The Market Mechanism and Economic Reform in China*, Armonk, NY: M. E. Sharpe, 1991, particularly Chapters Three and Four. According to Gao Shangqun, Vice-Minister of SCRES, the number of state-allocated raw materials has shrunk from 256 to nineteen. While effectively limiting the state's ability to meet the demands of the majority of state-owned enterprises for cheap goods, the reduction has forced them to rely more on the market for supply (Gao Shangqun, 'Guanyu shichang jingji de jige wenti' (On some issues of the market economy), *Qiye gaige tongxun*, no. 6, September 1992, p. 5).

12 Pearson has convincingly analysed the diminishing functions of party cells in the non-state sector. The same is happening in state-owned enterprises that either have been privatised or are on long-term lease (Margaret Pearson, 'Breaking the Bonds of "Organised Dependence": Managers in China's Foreign Sector', *Studies in Comparative Communism*, vol. 25, no. 1, March 1993, pp. 62–5).

3 THE REFORM OF THE ENTERPRISE LEADERSHIP STRUCTURE

1 Because of the limits of space this section will be confined to a review of policy processes at the apex of power that consciously transformed the industrial units into settings of political control.

2 These figures included mainly workers in manufacturing industries, mining and railway transportation, which the Chinese call *chanye gongren*, or the industrial workforce. The total number in the industrial workforce (including the private sector) was about three million and the total urban workforce (including the tertiary and commercial sectors) was about eight million. See Xiao Liang, 'Zhongguo suoyouzhi jiegou yanjiu' (A study on China's ownership structure), *Shanxi jingji chubanshe*, 1988, p. 57. In addition, in the next two years over

10,000 foreign-owned firms with about 100,000 employees were nationalised and became state enterprises (*Zhibu shenhuo* (Beijing), no. 7, 1991, p. 45).

3 For an analysis of the gang-boss networks and the industrial takeover by the CCP in 1949, see Part 1 and Part 2 of Bill Brugger, *Democracy and Organization in the Chinese Industrial Enterprises: 1948–1953*, Cambridge: Cambridge University Press, 1976.

4 The 'three-antis' (*Sanfan*) and 'five-antis' (*Wufan*) were political movements initiated in 1951 and 1952. The three antis were embezzlement, squandering and bureaucratism; the five antis were bribery, tax evasion, stealing state property, doing shoddy work and using inferior materials, and economic espionage. The Suppressing Reactionaries Movement was launched in October 1950 and continued to autumn 1953, aiming to eliminate elements hostile to the new regime.

5 When I interviewed a number of retired managers and workers in China in 1991 and 1992, on the question of when they felt they could no longer confine themselves to their private lives but had to join in numerous political activities sponsored by party cadres, they all indicated the three years of economic restoration (1950–2).

6 The clampdown on the ACTFU in 1951 did not altogether stop workers from striving to articulate their interests. Over the next two decades there were three more workers' movements, organised or otherwise, that expressed their discontent. See Anita Chan, 'Revolution or Corporatism? Workers and Trade Unions in Post-Mao China', *The Australian Journal of Chinese Affairs*, no. 29, January 1993, pp. 32–5.

7 In the period about 163,000 cadres were transferred to industry, among whom 103,000 went to the state sector and the rest to the private sector. Most of them assumed positions as party secretaries and political personnel (Zhang Shenhui, 1991, p. 269).

8 By the end of 1953 most of the retained personnel had been replaced by state cadres. This was regarded as the precondition for the one-man management system.

9 Mao Zedong's talks with Zhou Enlai, Chen Boda, Tian Jiaying and others on reading the Soviet textbook of political economy between the end of 1959 and the beginning of 1960 (Zhang Zhanbin, 1988, p. 78).

10 Mao Zedong's famous instructions of 7 May 1966.

11 'Mass line' is a special term created by the party to describe a process in which the masses are mobilised by the party to achieve a specific objective.

12 This can be seen in the party's organisational arrangements in state functional agencies where only a *dangzu* or party fraction was established. A *dangzu* and a *dangwei* (party committee) are different in that the latter is a leadership organ established in the government administration of various levels. The former is a body in charge of party internal affairs. They are both established in government functional agencies but do not lead the functional work of these offices.

13 This was revealed by the deputy director of the Party Central Propaganda Department, Gong Yuzhi. According to Gong, Deng remarked: 'It is certainly not correct to say the market economy is only applicable to capitalist societies. Why should socialist countries not practise a market economy as well?' See *Gaige* (Reform), no. 6, 1992. Also see Gao Lu's article in *Jingji ribao*, 9 November 1995.

14 See 'The Enterprise Law' in Hua Gong (ed.), *Zenyang gaohuo qiye* (How to enliven enterprises), Beijing: Xinhua chubanshe, 1988, pp. 1–13.

15 See, for instance, Jiang Zemin's speech on 1 July 1989, in which he gave priority to the principle of 'common prosperity' (*Renmin ribao*, 1 July 1989).

When this was practised in state firms many party secretaries insisted that emphasis on differentiated income among workers jeopardised the party's efforts to uphold socialism (*Zhibu shenghuo* (Beijing), no. 8, 1989, p. 4).

16 The party's industrial lobby consists of party functionaries in state factories, industrial departments of local party committees at various levels, sections in charge of industries in the organisation and propaganda departments of these committees and in the 'transmission belt' organisations. At the centre, the Central Organisation and Propaganda Departments both have bureaux specialising in industrial work and they are responsible to those in the Politburo in charge of political and ideological work. Nationwide the lobby comprises several million full-time personnel.

17 Deng certainly had support from Hu Yaobang and Zhao Ziyang. But at the beginning of the 1980s when Deng raised the issue, their authority had not yet been well established.

18 In a summary of the experimental work, *Renmin ribao* carried complaints from managers who believed that they were tied by six 'ropes', including: (1) the fact that the power to appoint middle-level managers was restricted by the party committee's 'discussion'; (2) the fact that the decision-making process was interfered with by a 'multi-headed system', with party cells and trade unions having veto powers (*Renmin ribao*, 18 May 1987).

19 'Deng Xiaoping tan zhengzhi tizhi gaige' (Deng Xiaoping on political reform), *Zhongguo xingzheng guanli*, no. 1, 1987, p. 1.

20 See Zhao Ziyang's political report to the party's Thirteenth National Congress.

21 Excerpted from a 1986 report of the Shandong Party Organisation Department, *Zhibu shenghuo* (Shandong), no. 1, 1989, p. 35.

22 However, this cadre's perception has been shared by the interviewees of John Child whose field surveys in six Chinese cities revealed the widespread phenomenon of the party industrial cells being transformed into a 'production party' (John Child, *Management in China during the Age of Reform*, Cambridge, 1994, Chapter 4).

23 There is a large body of literature in the Chinese media about managers making major decisions without involving party cells. See the book *Shidai xuanzele tamen* (The era has chosen them), Shanghai: Zhishi chubanshe, 1988, which collects more than twenty case studies of how managers make strategic decisions. Very seldom is the party mentioned.

24 This was the general impression of my interviews with several dozen workers, managers and party functionaries in China in 1991 and 1992.

25 Interview with the party secretary of Beijing No. 2 Leather Products Factory in 1991.

26 There are many accounts describing the above-mentioned phenomenon. See for some vivid examples Yuan Yong (1991). Most of my informants also confirmed this point.

27 This was the opinion of a number of informants in 1991 and 1992. What is worth mentioning is that in 1992 most of them believed that the power centre had moved further towards the manager system owing to the changed environment after Deng's south China visit. Media coverage of this phenomenon is also widespread.

28 For these regulations, see Wu Zhiqing (1991, pp. 178–84). My analysis is based mainly on my fieldwork findings of 1991 and 1992. Since the promulgation of the State Council's Regulation on Changing the Operational Mechanisms of state-owned enterprises in July 1992, many of these requirements have been revoked, according to my interviews in China in late 1992. However, I have not come across an official document that specifies the changes.

29 This account was published in *Zhibu shenghuo* (Beijing), no. 10, 1992, pp. 27–8.
30 Zhou Guanwu was forced to retire in 1995 owing to his close connection with Chen Xitong, former mayor of Beijing, and to his son's implication in a number of scandals.
31 This information was gathered from a series of visits to the corporation in both 1991 and 1992.
32 This account is summarised from a survey by Li Yongming, 'Zenyang chuli T cheng de dangzheng guanxi' (How to handle party/management relations in Factory T), *Xinzheng yu renshi*, no. 3, 1990, pp. 18–20.
33 For instance, many industrial bureaux and party bodies are required to choose people with complementary temperaments to head the two systems, e.g. aggressive managers are provided with less aggressive party secretaries. Punishments are meted out to warn the heads of the two centres of the consequences of rivalry. A rotation programme has been put in place in big factories to have the heads of the two systems shift jobs. But none of these strategies has achieved satisfying results (information gathered from interviews, 1992).

4 THE PARTY'S ORGANISATIONAL REFORM

1 This definition is based on the state wage system which classifies the urban population into two large groups, the worker wage and the cadre wage, although the latter can be further sub-divided into different occupation rate systems. Another indication involves passport categories: anybody holding a government passport is labelled by the customs bureau as a cadre regardless of his/her occupation. See Wu Guoguang, 'The Dilemmas of Participation in the Political Reform of China, 1986–1988', in Roger Des Forges (ed.) *Chinese Democracy and Crisis of 1989*, New York: State University of New York Press, 1993, p. 136.
2 Lin Bin, 'Woguo qiye ganbu suzhi yanjiu' (The quality of enterprise cadres in our country), MA thesis, Sociology Department, Beijing University, 1988. Lin's analysis was based on a field survey of 900 factories in 1986–7. My fieldwork findings generally confirmed his description. However, in many large key factories (still producing goods within the state plan) deputy factory managers and the three chiefs (chief engineer, accountant and economist) are in the party's *nomenklatura*. Some factories have followed this practice only since June 1989. Generally speaking, managers at the workshop level and heads of administrative and technical offices are under the management list.
3 Here the 'state cadres' refers to managers of the middle level or above who are called senior administrative cadres. There is a confusion in the terminology because while we use the word 'manager', the Chinese often use the terms 'manager' and 'cadre' interchangeably to express the same thing. This is partly because a proportion of these managers are still on the payroll designated to state cadres; it is partly continuation of a habit.
4 Information gathered from interviews with a number of senior factory technical staff. They are often invited to attend such political meetings as a sign of the party's intellectual policy.
5 This has been especially true since Deng made his south China tour in 1992. Not only do factory managers see themselves more as businessmen, but more and more cadres in government agencies have given up their positions and jumped into the 'business seas'. See the series of discussions on 'jumping into the business seas' carried in *Jingji ribao*, January and February 1993.
6 The State Council's Personnel Ministry announced that from 1993 on, the

Ministry would no longer issue compulsory cadre quotas to state firms. This meant that each factory could now appoint its own managers according to its needs. The implementation of the reform will cut the industrial cadre system's ties with party and state *nomenklatura* (*China Central Television*, 5 March 1993).

7 Although the reform started in 1988, it progressed slowly. It has gathered speed since 1992. According to my interview with one leading figure in the SCRES in 1992, the goal should be achieved by 1996. Former Minister Ma Hong deemed this reform one of the preconditions for China's market economy (*Zhongguo jingying bao*, 16 October 1992). At the moment it is difficult to gauge how deeply this reform has affected state firms. Increased media coverage indicates that many provinces have pushed the reform hard. For instance, Shenzhen, Hangzhou, Shanghai, Suzhou and a number of other large cities have abolished the state cadre system in state firms (*Guangming ribao*, 28 January 1993). Liaoning is the first province which has officially discarded the state administrative ranking system for all its factories and the state cadre statutes for its factory managerial and technical staff. Among 655,000 industrial cadres, this reform has affected over 410,000 (the rest had already lost their state cadre status as a result of the fixed-term contract reform since the mid-1980s) (*Jingji ribao*, 21 November 1993).

8 The survey was conducted by the National Industrial Managers Association. *Guangmin ribao*, 22 April 1995.

9 The State Council has, however, announced that by the end of this decade all industrial cadres and workers will have been placed on a contractual basis, thus completing the process of decoupling them from the state payroll (*Zhuzhi renshibao*, 10 October 1991).

10 This is the summary of information gathered in more than a dozen state factories during my fieldwork trips in 1991 and 1992.

11 The information was obtained from my visits to a number of factories in Beijing and Hunan in 1991 and 1992.

12 Interview with a number of contracted managers in Beijing in 1991, 1992 and 1995.

13 These conditions are normal requirements set by any employers but when coupled with the control of dossiers, household registration and party organisation relations, they may be effective means of political control. The Personnel Ministry announced that from 3 March 1993 it would not allocate any cadre quotas. This will make the regulation less forceful, although more time is needed to assess the real results.

14 For instance, an increasing number of state-owned enterprises have adopted the setting of an annual salary for the top managers which is closely linked to the firm's profits.

15 The regulation stipulates that contract cadres may raise the question of cancelling the contract two months prior to leaving their posts.

16 *Jingji ribao* carried a sensational debate in February 1993 on what has gone wrong with China's economic system. The debate followed a story that the three 'chiefs' (chief engineer, chief accountant and chief economist) of the Daliang Mechanical Plant, the biggest in the country, had 'fled' to work at a nearby township factory without permission or dossiers, and had taken fifty major technical staff with them. Surprisingly, most of the contributors to the debate, including the Governor of Liaoning, approved of the action.

17 The Ministry of Public Security issued a decree in May 1995 ordering the removal of public security organs in state-owned enterprises by the end of September the same year (*Guangming ribao*, 6 May 1995).

18 The office of mass correspondence and contact holds the mission of handling

people's letters of complaint and suggestions, makes personal visits on certain issues and very often drafts *xiaobaogao*, or 'big brother's' reports.

19 Most ministerial factories are large or medium-sized. The small factories are usually important specialised factories servicing the large ones. So party work has traditionally been stronger in the ministerial factories. In addition, there are not very many small ministerial factories, thus making them easier to control from above, while under the *kuaikuai* system the number of factories is far larger and the levels of control are multiple.

20 These factories contain between seventy and 300 workers. Only one of these factories is under the Electronics Industry Ministry. All the others are local.

21 For instance, more than 60 per cent of the 7,000 small factories in Beijing had been contracted or leased out by the end of 1992 (*Jingji ribao*, 4 March 1993).

22 During my fieldwork I made enquiries on a dozen occasions about the situation of the security apparatus. Except in a few large factories, the department of political security under the party system was merged into the public security department within the management system.

23 Information gathered from my fieldwork. However, the factory security department remains the first contact of the local government's public security bureaux.

24 It is interesting to note that in a few dozen factories I visited in the 1990s, when I asked cadres about how they had handled political dissidents, they all answered that there were none in their factories. They said there were workers with backward attitudes, but when dealing with them, cadres reportedly never linked the cases of violation of work discipline to political crimes. One party cadre told me that everybody complained about some party policies and leaders, even in party meetings. By the standards of the Cultural Revolution, everyone could be counted as an anti-party element. But now, who cared? However, most party cadres I interviewed agreed that the demarcation line was whether people took organised action. Even a non-political organised action, such as a strike for higher wages, would be interpreted as very serious, and would be immediately reported to party and government superiors. It is in this sense that workers' political rights were constantly violated.

25 As I discovered in the interviews, most of these security people were close followers of managers, acting as the latters' bodyguards. So they became the target of attack by workers whenever labour relations turned sour.

26 Impression from visits to these enterprises in 1992 and again in 1995.

27 Information gathered from interviews with a cadre in the Beijing Municipal Party Committee's Industry Department in 1992.

28 This is the summary of media coverage of the concurrent reform, which is quite abundant. My interviewees also confirmed this.

29 Interview with the manager of the Beijing Heavy Machine Plant in 1991.

30 An internal document drafted by the Central Political Reform Office and circulated by the CC in 1987. For instance, in Shandong, the Zibo Prefecture was in the experiment, and in Shanghai, Minhang District.

31 See two party documents, 'Guanyuzhai dongchengqu jinxing qiye shiye danwei dangzuzhi shudi liangdao shidian de yijian' (The decision regarding *shudi guanli* in the East City District); and 'Guanyuzhai Beijingshi dianzi gongye qishiye danwei jinxing dangzuzhi shudi liangdao shidian de yijian' (The decision regarding the localisation reform in the municipal electronics industry), *Beijing shi gaige shinian* (The ten years of reform in Beijing), Beijing: Renmin chubanshe, 1988, pp. 873–6.

32 Information gathered from interviews with a number of party cadres under the reform. However, my impression was that there was no real threat to them at the time, since their ranks remained the same, but their successors

would find it difficult to climb the industrial sectoral ladders if the reform indeed were to phase out the sectoral party hierarchy.

33 Several characteristics in the party work in these factories are: (1) all party cadres do their party work part time; (2) party committees often have to work under the name of the trade unions; (3) party activities exist at a minimum level. There is a good amount of media coverage of this, for instance Lei Lixin, 'Zenyang danghao waizi qiye dangzuzhi de shuji' (How to do a good job as a party secretary in a foreign-owned factory), *Zhibu shenghuo* (Beijing), no. 5, 1992, pp. 8–11. I also visited a number of these factories in Beijing and Guangdong and obtained the same impression.

34 Information gathered during a few visits to the CPS in 1991.

5 WITHERING OF THE PARTY'S INDUSTRIAL APPARATUS

1 There have been numerous media reports on such cases, as expressed by a demand for 'better understanding' of the party's work in state-owned enterprises.

2 Quoted from a party secretary whom I interviewed in Beijing in 1992.

3 *Renmin ribao*, 18 December 1983. Zhao Ziyang reiterated this in his Spring Festival Speech on 21 February 1987 and Jiang Zemin made the same pledge at the party's national conference on ideology in June 1994.

4 Interview with a party cadre in the Beijing New China Printing Factory in 1992.

5 The party's propaganda boss Li Ruihan even told a large group of ideologues that the word 'revolution' should not be used too often and applied to everything (Li Ruihan, 'On Ideological Education', *Zhengzhi sixiang zhanxian* (Political and ideological front), no. 6, 1992, pp. 1–3).

6 This is from a cadre in the Industrial Department of the Beijing Party Committee whom I interviewed in late 1992.

7 *Zhongguo gongchandang fazhan dangyuan gongzuo xize* (The CCP's regulations on recruiting new party members). The same document also required party cells to recruit more young people so as to lower the average age of the membership.

8 This is the general impression most workers and cadres conveyed to me during my field studies in China in 1991, 1992 and 1994.

9 A number of interviewees told me they took to the streets because they were fed up with unfair treatment by their immediate bosses. But they said that in a closed and permanent community, 'you could not break with them so you had to bury the feeling in your heart in order to avoid "little class shoes"'. To join the demonstrations was one way of venting grievances, since the centre represented all of their immediate bosses.

10 Walder and Gong (1993, pp. 4–15). Many of my worker informants told identical stories of how they took to the streets. At the beginning, they pretended to be onlookers. When they saw no action taken by their workshop party branches, 'not even a meeting called by the party secretary, which had been usual in similar situations in the past', said one interviewee, they increased their 'inputs' and proceeded further and further.

11 According to a report by the director of the COD in 1991, more rather than fewer party branches had become inactive since 4 June. See Lu Feng, 'Zai dang de jianshe lilun yantaoban shang de jianghua' (Speech at the conference on the theory of party building), Editors group (eds) *Dang de jianshe lilun yanjiu* (The study of party building), Beijing: Beijing University Press, 1991, pp. 1–10.

12 This re-registration was a mini party rectification campaign. Although the purge of dissidents in the party was the primary objective, it had other tasks such as getting rid of party members who had committed economic crimes, seriously violated party discipline and were popularly regarded as not up to standard (*Chongfa wenjian* (Central Document), no. 10, 1989, pp. 1–2; *Jingfa wenjian* (Beijing Party Committee Document), no. 24, 1989, p. 1).

13 My conversation with the director.

14 Andrew Nathan reported a similar impression after his 1992 trip to China. See 'China's Path from Communism', *Journal of Democracy*, vol. 4, no. 2, 1992, p. 33.

15 It is difficult to obtain any reliable figure on how many party members revoked their membership in 1989. In my former work unit, four out of about seventy party members gave it up.

16 A number of my informants expressed such a view.

6 THE DYNAMICS OF THE INDUSTRIAL WAGE REFORM

1 A broader discussion of a *danwei*'s remunerative functions should include analysis of the *danwei*-based welfare provisions such as housing, medical care, free education for the offspring of employees, and a whole range of social security arrangements. Owing to the limited space, these are not dealt with here.

2 From 1956 to 1984 the state initiated eight wage increases, covering 90 per cent of all workers. This means that, in about three decades, not every worker had a chance to be promoted. See Liu Qingtang, *Qiye gongzi gaige fangan de sheji yu fanli* (The good designs of the wage reform), Beijing: Beijing Institute of Economics Press, 1989, p. 39.

3 In a dual-track system that combines both soft budget constraints and market incentives, the ability of a factory to grant bonuses also depends on its ability to obtain bank borrowings and negotiate with the state for a lower tax rate. These matters will be discussed later.

4 The starting point for the bonus tax was bonuses per year worth 2.5 months' standard wages. The rate for less than four months was 30 per cent of bonus income; four to six months, 100 per cent; and above six months 300 per cent. In 1987 the state lowered the rate, the starting point becoming four months. The rate for five to six months was 50 per cent; six to seven months, 100 per cent; and above seven months, 200 per cent (State Council, 'Gong zi jijin zhanxing guanli banfa' (Provisional regulations on the management of the wage funds), September 1985). Of course not all state-owned enterprises felt pressured by the tax regulations.

5 The reform was meant to create a new remuneration mechanism that pegged the annual payroll of a firm to the fulfilment of a group of pre-determined indicators. This mechanism is supposed to be performance and output oriented.

6 Income entries such as state food subsidies are counted as part of the wage bill but these are excluded when the floating wages are ascertained.

7 The State Council issued a decree on 1 July 1993 that state-owned enterprises would implement a new accounting system, which was designed according to 'international practice'. However, it was announced that it would take at least three years for the system to become operational (*Renmin ribao*, 1 July 1993).

8 'Policy losses' mean that the state imposes on factories the planned prices which are below the cost of their products and raw materials, e.g. coal, electric power and steel. Then the state writes off their losses. As of 1996 there are still a number of these under central control.

9 In 1987 the State Council lowered the industrial regulatory taxes. The rate for 7–12 per cent of the wage increase is 20 per cent; 13–20 per cent, 50 per cent; 20–27 per cent, 100 per cent; and above 27 per cent, 200 per cent (Ministry of Labour, *Laodong zhengce huibian: 1984–1987* (The selected labour policy documents: 1984–1987), Beijing: The Ministry of Labour, 1989, p. 156).

10 For those enterprises already making a loss, the state set a progressive target rate for reducing the deficit, on which the increase of wages for their workers is assessed.

11 'Efficiency income' is the term used to describe all the floating income workers receive because of the increase in a firm's economic efficiency largely based on market sales. In China's case, however, good sales may or may not help improve economic efficiency.

12 Information from an interview in 1991 with a researcher of the Research Institute of Industrial Wages of the Ministry of Labour.

13 Interview with a researcher in the Research Institute of Labour Science, the Ministry of Labour, during my 1991 fieldwork in Beijing.

14 Currently the indicators commonly used in assessment include a factory's tax rate per head, wage/tax rate, capital rate and the gross output value and so on.

15 A number of managers told me in 1991 that their factories' performance in the two-track system was highly dynamic. Much depended on factors beyond their control.

16 Document no. 9, the Ministry of Labour, 1988, *Laodong zhengce zhuankan* (Special journal of labour policies), no. 1, 1989, p. 22.

17 This means that the workers working in the factories under the central ministries in Beijing had not received the increase.

18 This shows the centre's recognition of the extent to which the proportion of the base wage has shrunk in the overall income of workers. Before the reform, the increase of one grade for all workers in a large city like Beijing would certainly have affected the wage level of the city.

19 Document Concerning Labour and Wages, no. 66, 1990, the Ministry of Labour, *Laodong zhengce zhuankan* (Special journal of labour policies), no. 9, 1990, p. 5.

20 Irregular income refers to payments either in cash or in kind which are not formally reported to the government.

21 The first may be calculated on the basis of a factory's report on its wage aggregate, wage increases and income tax. The second is usually counted on a per capita basis according to the state 'red head documents' (official documents), and thus is discernible. For instance, the state subsidy for transportation was 5.43 billion *yuan* in 1987, and for an only child, it was 6.61 billion *yuan* in 1988 (*Zhongguo tongji nianjian* (The Chinese Statistical Year Book), 1989, 1990).

22 The welfare fund included a retirement fund of about 13 billion *yuan*. Excluding this, the overall amount was still quite large because it was only one of the sources from which workers received income outside the standard income. Moreover, this figure only applies to state-owned enterprises under the state budget. If calculated nationally the figure can be as high as 60 billion *yuan*. See Research Group on the Industrial Wage Distribution, the Ministry of Labour, 'Yusuannei guoying qiye shouru fenpai yanjiu' (Research on the wage distribution in the state enterprises under the state budget), *Zhongguo laodong kexue*, no. 1, 1992, p. 6.

23 Interview with a cadre in the Labour Bureau of Beijing Municipality in 1991.

24 A conversation with an officer from the 8341 unit.

7 THE POLITICS OF THE INDUSTRIAL WAGE REFORM

1 Under such circumstances, the reference grade wage is meaningful only when a worker seeks transfer, is on sick leave or retires, as it then serves as the base for reward in his new situation. Information gathered from interviews in the Ministry of Labour in 1991 and 1992.

2 According to the Chinese definition, the first line of production means workers working on machinery; the second line, the supply and logistics sections; and the third line, management.

3 See Liu Qingtang's book, *Qiye gongzi gaige fanan de sheji yu fanli* (Design and paradigms of the enterprise), Beijing Institute of Economics, 1989. It contains the wage reform plans of several dozen factories. Most of these stipulate that rewards to and assessment of workers should be formulated by the lower production units and then reported to factory management for reference only.

4 This statement only describes a general trend. It does not deny the fact that many factory and workshop managers mistreat their workers. Many shop managers do handle industrial relations heavy-handedly.

5 Interview with a workshop director in the factory in 1992.

6 My interview with officials in the Ministry of Labour revealed that about half of all workshops have engaged in their own business in one form or another. In my visits to state-owned enterprises in Beijing, Hunan and Shanghai, most factory managers confirmed that sub-account business activities existed at their plants.

7 For an analysis of China's second economy, see Wojtek Zafanolli, 'A Brief Outline of China's Second Economy', *Asian Survey*, vol. 25, no. 7, 1985, pp. 715–36.

8 Certainly complaints are heard from workers. But the general direction of the wage reform was believed to be in the interests of workers. The small number of workers who are still in favour of the eight-grade wage system are mainly old and retired workers.

9 There are numerous examples to show this. For instance, the housing reform has been experimented with for years but proved unpopular because the citizens do not want to pay high rents.

10 This is my impression based on a number of interviews in factories in Beijing in the 1990s.

11 Most of my interviewees expressed this feeling, although to different degrees.

12 Some of these interviewees did such outside jobs only occasionally. For instance, Mr Li sold 1,000 toothbrushes in 1990. He purchased these brushes at the wholesale price of 30 *fen* each and sold them at 60 *fen* after work, in railway stations to travellers. He earned a little over 300 *yuan* from this second job, which lasted only for a few weeks. But he told me that this was only the second job he had done in the year: 'It takes too much time and there is a question of "face" involved. But if it is convenient, I will do so a few more times each year to help towards the family expenses.'

13 A large number of state-owned enterprises do allow moonlighting. Out of the necessity to relocate 'hidden unemployment', most state-owned enterprises have actually encouraged workers to leave their posts. The second job is regarded as a stepping-stone to this because if successful, it may convince the worker that it is not worth staying with the low-paid first job.

14 From a few interviewees who had 'jumped into the sea', I discovered that many were still young and tired of the *danwei* environment which they said was too restrictive. The usual reason for some older workers leaving state

jobs was that they had business connections. Even so, leaving the state job was a difficult decision.

15 In May 1996 the SETC issued a decree, co-signed by eleven other central agencies, that proposed a number of measures to help workers in grave difficulties. However, the best the central document could do was to require state banks to provide loans to these industries in order to let workers receive minimum wages guaranteed by the Labour Law (*Xinxi shichangbao*, 14 June 1996).

16 A number of my interviewees expressed this opinion.

17 There have been heated discussions in China about the phenomenon of factory managers being murdered since 1987. The discontent of workers over the wage gap between themselves and management is listed as a key factor behind the killings, especially when this discontent is constantly suppressed.

18 According to one of my informants in the SCRES, after 4 June 1989 a check on factory managers' personal income was added to the investigation list of the state's industrial work groups sent to state-owned enterprises at the end of each year.

19 A number of workers expressed this complaint to me in 1994 and 1995.

20 Interview with a worker in Beijing in 1992.

21 The reform was attempted in the late 1980s to reduce the 'hidden surplus workers in employment'. It is still going on, and it has become a routine practice in state-owned enterprises.

22 Interview with a worker in the Beijing 768 Factory in 1991.

8 CORPORATISATION AND PRIVATISATION

1 For instance, Yu-Shan Wu defined the transfer of business power to enterprises as marketisation, and the transfer of income power as privatisation ('Reforming the Revolution: Industrial Policy in China', *Pacific Review*, vol. 3, no. 3, 1990, p. 243).

2 The fourteen decision-making powers include major decisions regarding production, pricing, marketing and sales, purchasing, export and import, investment, autonomous use of retained profits, running the fixed assets, joint operation and merger, employment, personnel, remuneration, the institutional set-up, and resistance to the demands of state agencies for 'donations' (*Renmin ribao*, 1 July 1992). The implementation of the regulations, however, is uneven among state firms. But on the whole the trend is for producers to gain more autonomy at the expense of state agencies.

3 In Shanghai, for instance, among the top 200 large and medium-sized firms that registered good productivity growth in 1993 one-quarter were joint ventures, far exceeding the general ratio of joint ventures to non-joint ventures in the city. Furthermore, the top five best enterprises were all joint ventures (*Renmin ribao*, 29 August 1994).

4 In the 1980s, China's economists had already begun media preparation for the bankruptcy of as many as 300,000 state-owned enterprises. See *Jingji ribao*, 17 August 1988. Now they believe that when these can be sold to non-state concerns, it is not necessary to shut down all of them. Yet there is no doubt that many workers will have to be dismissed. For instance, in the last four years 7.5 million workers in state-owned enterprises have been released from work and have received only part of their wages (CASS and SSBC, 'Zhongguo jingji fengxi yu yuce' (Analysis and forecast on the economic trend in China), *Jingji yanjiu*, no. 6, 1996, p. 18).

5 Information gathered from a number of interviewees in the SCRES in 1992.

See also Yu Jingfu, 'Shenhua guoyou qiye gaige bujing jianchi guojia zhudao' (Deepening enterprise reform should not take the direction of state domination), *Jingji yanjui*, no. 5, 1996, pp. 17–21.

6 According to Deputy Premier Zhu Jiahua, the northeast China phenomenon was due to the region's late withdrawal from the planned track of the economy. In this area as much as 80 per cent of economic activity was covered by central and local planning (*China Business Times*, 23 January 1995).

7 For instance, all state factories at the municipal level of Quanzhou City, Fujian Province, were merged with a Hong Kong firm (*Jingji ribao*, 2 August 1992). One-third of the centrally run electronics industry, or 5,000 factories, have been turned into joint ventures, which produce one-third of gross output value and represent 55.6 per cent of the sector's export (*Jingji ribao*, 16 March 1994). The Chinese media carry numerous reports of such endeavours.

8 According to Wang Guangying, vice-president of the NPC, the policy of creating joint ventures so as to promote exports is outdated. The domestic function of joint ventures such as upgrading technology and altering management mechanisms has become more important (*Renmin ribao*, 18 March 1994).

9 Deng Xiaoping summarised the phenomenon in vivid words during his southern China tour in 1992: 'Don't debate, just try.'

10 In the literature on East European reforms, privatisation can refer to the expansion of the indigenous private sector (Ben Slay and John Tedstrom, 'Privatisation in the Post-communist Economies: An Overview', *RFE/RL Research Report*, vol. 1, no. 17, 24 April 1992, p. 1).

11 Here the figure of 3 trillion *yuan* of state assets should be subject to some qualification, as it includes a large number of state-owned enterprises that have already been contracted or leased to private concerns. The sequence of the ten is Guangdong, Jiangsu, Shandong, Fujian, Zhejiang, Shanghai, Hainan, Liaoning, Beijing and Tianjing (*Renmin ribao*, 26 April 1994). See also Zhou Xiaochun, vice-president of the Bank of China, 'Privatisation versus a Minimum Reform Package', *China Economic Review*, vol. 4, no. 1, 1993, pp. 65–74. The gross value of state assets was 4.15 trillion in 1995, but the debt ratio of these reached as high as 70 per cent (*China Business Times*, 13 August 1996).

12 For instance, excluding the collective sector, state-owned enterprises employ about 67 million workers, compared with 19 million employed by collective factories, and 26.78 million self-employed and workers in private plants (*Cheng Shuxun, Jiushi niandai Zhongguo gongye* (The Chinese industries in the 1990s), Beijing: Jingji Guangli chubanshe, 1993, pp. 138–42).

13 For instance, Wu Yi, Minister for Foreign Trade, revealed that Sino-foreign joint ventures in 1993 achieved 64.7 billion *yuan*, or 34.4 per cent of the value of all China's export and import trade. The private sector submitted over 30 billion *yuan* in taxes to the state, over two-thirds of state subsidies to the loss makers (*Renmin ribao* (overseas edition), 19 March 1994).

14 My interview with some officials in the SCRES revealed some points on the personal side of the decision-making process. Some major reform designers, particularly Gao Shangqun and Jiang Yiwei, had used their close relations with Chen Jinghua, the former Minister of the SCRES, to get separate access to Li Peng, who is the long-time mentor of Chen. In early 1991, they finally convinced Li that the corporate system was the only way to save China's large state-owned enterprises and, as a corollary, Chinese socialism. They believed the joint limited liability companies based on the enterprise conglomerates would preserve the dominant position of the state sector in the economy. It is also interesting to point out that the change of mind started from Chen Yun, the 'commissar' of central planning, who reportedly sent a note to Deng

in 1991 before Deng's south China tour. This stated that if the Soviet experience had shown that this road would lead to a dead end, why should China not try another road, which might also lead to a dead end but could lead out of the situation. This unconfirmed message was obtained from an interview with a member of the SCRES in November 1992. Chen's words best catch the spirit of using capitalism to save socialism (i.e. the party's hold on power).

15 This story was carried in *Jingji ribao*, 24 May 1993.

16 The designers of the reform learned the American method of Employment Shares Ownership Plan (ESOP). Yet this type of firm represents an important mechanism by which the state tries to transform a large number of factories in the non-strategic sectors.

17 For instance, the Stock Company Rules promulgated by the SCRES in May 1992 require that the minimum registered capital of a stock company should be 10 million *yuan*. If it is a company with foreign investment, the minimum is raised to 30 million. And approval for creation of such a company has to be jointly processed by a number of state agencies, the SCRES, SPC and the People's Bank of China.

18 *The Opinion on the Standardisation of Limited Liability Companies*, promulgated on 15 May 1992. See the appendix in Jin Jian (1992).

19 The legal grounds for keeping collective shares are that contracted factories can allocate a proportion of profits to be delivered as social welfare funds to workers. But the state imposes the proportion for each year's allocation. At the same time it allows the part exceeding the proportion to be accumulated in a separate book to be distributed to workers in the future, for instance when a given year's profits are not enough to maintain the current level of grants. Therefore, the accumulated funds have already changed the nature of ownership and factories have a strong case to argue.

20 It is necessary to explain that in the Chinese literature on the share reform, there arises common confusion about the terminology of the first two categories. Some economists use the term 'corporate shares' (*farengu*) to describe the state shares controlled by an enterprise. This is especially true for large state-owned enterprises where the proportion of factory ownership is small. Under the assumption that the state is only the theoretical ultimate owner, they simply equate state shares and corporate shares. Again, in some cases, corporate shares include both the state and the company's collective shares, indicating a weak distinction between the two, as the economists see the diminishing significance of the role of state ownership in a joint stock company.

21 Information from a number of joint stock companies in Beijing in 1992.

22 SCRES (1993, p. 37). A policy proposal by the SETC suggested a more conservative date than the SCRES's for the conversion of the first category, the end of this century, and this looks more feasible.

23 During my field research in China in 1992 I collected a number of cases of transformation along the lines of the fourteen types mentioned below. Yet because of the limits of this book, I can only present case studies of two of them, and it is important to note that the process of transformation may bring more questions than answers subject to comparison with western norms. So my concern is mainly focused on the changing relations between these factories and the state through the reform, rather than on how well the conversion goes.

24 To be qualified as a second-grade state factory, it has to have annual sales exceeding 10 million *yuan*.

25 This case was published in *Jingji ribao*, 3 January 1993, but key points were missing in the coverage, e.g. who approved the conversion, where the shares were sold, who were the corporate buyers, and so on. My own investigation

through personal correspondence obtained some additional information. The state agency that approved the transformation was the Provincial Commission for Restructuring the Economic System, the stocks were sold at the local banks (there is no stock market in Shandong to this date) and a fairly large number of factories, schools, government agencies and even the police department bought the corporate shares. Because of high demand and short supply, a lot of *guanxi* had to be employed to obtain shares.

26 What must be pointed out is that flawed implementation is actually a logical rejection of the government policy that allows people to possess stocks but restricts their trading.

27 The report submitted to the State Council by the SCRES and the State Council Production Office of the State Council, *Qiye gaige tungxun*, no. 3, 1992, p. 4.

28 According to an estimate by the SCRES, China can absorb only 4 per cent unemployment at any time. Social unrest will erupt when this percentage is exceeded. See SCRES (1993, p. 44). But the current official rate of unemployment of 2.5 to 3 per cent (excluding non-city dwellers) has already flashed a signal of unrest. Thus the room for sustainable unemployment is actually very small.

29 Sun Xiaoliang, speech on the shares system to a national conference on 26 September 1992.

9 THE CONSTRUCTION OF A NEW ECONOMIC MODEL

1 According to Lieberthal and Lampton (1992), there are six clusters of bureaucracy in China. This chapter concentrates on only one of them: economic bureaucracy.

2 It is interesting to note that for the first time the CCP used the phrase *xingzheng tizhi*, or administrative system, to characterise the reform, a departure from the term *xingzheng jigou*, or administrative structure, used previously. The difference is that while the former describes the aggregate of political relations and functions embodied in the system, the latter touches upon the operational mechanisms only. See Xing Zheng, 'Xia juexin zhuahao guanli tizhi he jigou gaige' (Resolutely pushing ahead with the reform of the administrative system and structure), *Zhongguo jigou yu bianzhi* (China's organisation and establishment), no. 12, 1992, pp. 4–7.

3 Jiang Zemin's political report to the party's Fourteenth National Congress, October 1992.

4 This is stated in the regulations on the Management of State Assets. Xie Cichang, head of the Policy Bureau of the National ABSP, revealed in a press conference in July 1993 that after five drafts the regulations would be submitted to the State Council in late 1993 (*China Central Television*, 21 July 1993).

5 In 1995 a national investment company and a state investment bank were created along these lines. The Construction Bank remains (some of its investment functions were taken over by the new investment bank) but it has become a commercial bank. The national investment company has registered capital of 6 billion *yuan* and is involved in 210 national investment projects as either the principal shareholder or the joint shareholder (*China Business Times*, 6 May 1995).

6 This was explained to me by a researcher in the Research and Policy Office of the State Council in late 1992. Zhu Rongji made a speech along similar lines to the Shanghai delegation to the Fourteenth Party Congress in October

1992. Later he published a theoretical discussion on the changing state/state-owned enterprises relations in *Zhongguo faxue*, no. 4, 1993, pp. 3–5.

7 Speech by Li Yining at a public seminar at Beijing University in November 1992.

8 Ironically it is these 'fixed spot' factories that have registered most debts. This is partly because the price of their products is kept under tighter scrutiny. More importantly, because of these paternalistic ties, they have not developed good market mechanisms, and cannot compete well in the changed situation.

9 Interviews with cadres in the Beijing municipal government in late 1992.

10 Ironically, however, these 'donations' have actually bought more business autonomy for these factories (information obtained from interviews with a number of factory managers in this category in 1992). They claimed that the local government could be 'handled very skilfully'.

11 These institutions include bureaux of culture, science and technology, public health and education and so on.

12 These first-grade legal entities exist on a temporary basis only, according to the country's reform programme. Their fate depends on whether they can fit into the market economy. Some of them have done well, as they assist their factories in marketing and purchasing. Others have actually become hindrances to their factories, as they interfere too much. The current policy is gradually to turn various blocs of corporations into independent economic concerns.

13 The case study is based on the detailed report of the country submitted to the Shanxi government and the SCRES, which I read while doing fieldwork in China in late 1992. Parts of the report were published in *Zhongguo jigou yu bianzhi*, no. 11, 1992, pp. 10–11.

14 By the first half of 1992, the number of state-owned enterprises which had entered into similar reform arrangements had reached 20,000 across the country, covering a significant percentage of China's large and medium-scale firms (*China Central Television*, 9 July 1992.)

15 It is not easy to define the nature of these corporations. On the one hand, they are not supposed to be administrative companies but they are still entrusted with a range of administrative missions. They are supposed to become economic entities, but without many key elements for conducting business they are largely empty shells. So the ambiguity of their status represents the characteristics of a command economy in transition.

16 There is no equivalent term in English to translate *fanpai gongsi*. Literally, the term means that a state agency has changed its nameplate and become a corporation overnight. In practice, things are more complicated. When the name is changed, it is likely that its functions will also have to change, and its status and position as regards the government will have to change. But these changes come much more slowly than the change in name.

10 CONCLUDING REMARKS

1 Interview with the cadre in 1992. It is interesting to note that when I compared the CCP reform with the late Qing reform and quoted a Qing high official as saying that 'the reform may save China but can't save the dynasty', he answered that if the people believed that the CCP could save China, they would vote for it when the time for open elections comes.

2 According to Deputy Labour Minister Zhu Jiazhen, the long-term reform goal for the industrial social welfare system is to change it from being enterprise-based to society-based with the assistance of the state (Zhu Jiazhen, 'Speech

to Liaoning Labour Conference', *Labour Science of China*, no. 6, 1992, pp. 6–8).

Bibliography

ENGLISH SOURCES

Amodio, Nicoletta (1993) 'From Ministries to Corporations', *The Journal of Communist Studies*, special issue: *From Gorbachev to Yeltsin*.

Barnett, A. Doak (1967) *Cadre, Bureaucracy, and Political Power in Communist China*, New York: Columbia University Press.

—— (1986) *Modernizing China: Post-Mao Reform and Development*, Boulder, Colo: Westview Press.

Bowles, Paul and White, Gordon (1992) 'The Dilemmas of Market Socialism: Capitalism Market Reform in China – Part II: Shares', *The Journal of Development Studies*, vol. 28, no. 4, July 1992, pp. 575–94.

Brugger, Bill (1976) *Democracy and Organization in the Chinese Industrial Enterprises, 1948–1953*, Cambridge: Cambridge University Press.

Burns, John P. (ed.) (1988) *Chinese Communist Party's Nomenklatura System*, Armonk, NY: M. E. Sharpe.

Byrd, William (1991) *The Market Mechanism and Economic Reform in China*, Armonk, NY: M. E. Sharpe.

Chan, Anita (1992) 'Dispelling Misconceptions about the Red Guards Movement', *The Journal of Contemporary China*, vol. 1, no. 1.

—— (1993) 'Revolution or Corporatism?', *The Australian Journal of Chinese Affairs*, no. 29, January 1993, pp. 31–62.

—— (1995) 'Setting up New Trade Unions and Collective Bargaining in South China', paper presented at workshop on 'The Development of Labour Resources and Economic Development in China's Coastal Regions', Shantou University, 8–11 December 1995.

Chan, Anita and Unger, Jonathan (1991) 'Voice from the Protest Movement in Chongqing: Class Accents and Class Tensions', in Jonathan Unger (ed.) *The Pro-Democracy Protests in China*, Armonk: M. E. Sharpe.

Chan, Anita, Madsen, Richard and Unger, Jonathan (1992), *Chen Village under Mao and Deng*, Berkeley: University of California Press.

Chang Pao-ming (1986) 'China: Problems and Pitfalls of Economic Reform', *Asia Pacific Community*, Winter 1986.

Chao, Howard and Xiaoping, Yang (1987) 'The Reform of the Chinese System of Enterprise Ownership', *International Law*, Summer 1987.

Chevrier, Yves (1991) 'Micro-politics and the Factory Director Responsibility System', in Deborah Davis and Ezra Vogel (eds) *Chinese Society on the Eve of Tiananmen*, Cambridge, Mass.: Harvard University Press.

Chi Hsi-Sheng (1991) *Political Disillusionment: The Chinese Communist under Deng Xiaoping, 1978–1989*, Armonk, NY: M. E. Sharpe.

Child, John (1994) *Management in China during the Age of Reform*, Cambridge: Cambridge University Press.

Clarke, Christopher M. (1986) 'Rejuvenation, Reorganization and the Dilemmas of Modernization in Post-Deng China', *Journal of International Affairs*, Winter 1986.

Dernberger, Robert (1986) 'China's Economic System: A New Model or Variations on an Old Theme', in Yu-ming Shaw (ed.) *Mainland China: Politics, Economics and Reform*, Boulder, Colo: Westview Press.

Des Forges, Roger (ed.) (1993) *Chinese Democracy and Crisis of 1989*, New York: State University of New York Press.

Dittmer, Lowell and Lu Xiaobo (1996) 'Personal Politics in the Chinese Danwei under Reform', *Asian Survey*, vol. 36, no. 3, March.

Domes, Jurgen (1985) *The Government and Politics of the PRC: A Time of Transition*, Boulder, Colo.: Westview Press.

Falkenheim, Victor C. (1989) 'Citizen and Group Politics in China', in Victor Falkenheim and Ilpyong Kim (eds) *Chinese Politics from Mao to Deng*, New York: Paragon House.

Feher, Ferenc, Heller, Agnes and Markus, Gyorgy (1983) *Dictatorship over Needs: An Analysis of Soviet Societies*, New York: Basil Blackwell.

Fewsmith, Joseph (1987) 'The PRC's Internal Political Dynamics', *Journal of Northeast Asian Studies*, Spring.

Friedman, Edward (1991) 'Technological Revolution and China's Tortuous Path to Democratizing Leninism', in Richard Baum (ed.) *Reform and Reaction in Post-Mao China*, New York: Routledge.

Gaddis, John Lewis (1992/3) 'International Relations Theory and the End of the Cold War', *International Security*, vol. 17, no. 3, Winter.

Glassman, Ronald (1991) *China in Transition: Communism, Capitalism, and Democracy*, New York: Praeger.

Gold, Thomas (1984) ' "Just in Time!" China Battles Spiritual Pollution on the Eve of 1984', *Asian Survey*, vol. 24, no. 9.

Goldman, Merle (1996) 'Politically-Engaged Intellectuals in the Deng–Jiang Era: Changing Relations with the Party-State', *China Quarterly*, no. 145.

Goodman, David (1992) 'The State and Capitalist Revolution', *Pacific Review*, vol. 5, no. 4.

Goodman, David and Segal, Gerard (1991) 'Introduction', in David Goodman and Gerald Segal (eds) *China in the Nineties: Crisis Management and Beyond*, Oxford: Clarendon Press.

—— (eds) (1994) *China Deconstructs: Politics, Trade and Regionalism*, London: Routledge.

Granick, David (1992) *Chinese State Enterprises: A Regional Property Rights Analysis*, Chicago: University of Chicago Press.

Guldin, Gregory Eliyu (ed.) (1992) *Urbanizing China*, New York: Greenwood Press.

Halpern, Nina P. (1985) 'China's Industrial Economic Reforms: The Question of Strategy', *Asian Survey*, December.

Han Jianwei and Motohiro, Morishima (1992) 'Labour System Reform in China and Its Unexpected Consequences', *Economic and Industrial Democracy*, vol. 13.

Hanami, Tadashi (1979) *Labour Relations in Japan Today*, London: John Martin.

Hanami, Yamamoto (1993) 'The Lifetime Employment System Unravels', *Japan Quarterly*, vol. 40, no. 4.

Harding, Harry (1981) *Organizing China*, Stanford, Calif.: Stanford University Press.

—— (1987) *China's Second Revolution: Reform after Mao 1978–1985*, Washington, DC: Brookings Institution.

—— (1989) 'China's Political Reforms', in Charles Morrison and Robert Dernberger (eds) *Asia-Pacific Report: China in the Reform Era*, Honolulu: East–West Center.

—— (1992) 'China at the Crossroads: Conservatism, Reform and Decay', Adelphi Paper 275.

Hartford, Kathleen (1991/2) 'Reform or Retrofitting? The Chinese Economy since Tiananmen', *World Policy Journal*, vol. IX, no. 1, Winter 1991–2.

Hasegawa, Tsuyoshi (1992) 'The Connection between Political and Economic Reform in Communist Regimes', in Gilbert Rozman (ed.) *Dismantling Communism: Common Causes and Regional Variations*, Washington, DC: The Woodrow Wilson Center Press.

Hemming, Richard and Mansoor, Ali (1988) 'Privatisation and Public Enterprises', Occasional Paper 56, Washington DC: International Monetary Fund.

Houn, Franklin (1961) *To Change a Nation: Propaganda and Indoctrination in Communist China*, Ann Arbor: Michigan State University Press.

Howard, Pat (1991) 'Rice Bowls and Job Security: The Urban Contract Labour System', *Australian Journal of Chinese Affairs*, no. 25, January 1991.

Huang Yasheng (1990) 'Web of Interests and Patterns of Behaviour of Chinese Local Economic Bureaucracies and Enterprises during Reform', *China Quarterly*, no. 123, September.

Huo Tai-chun and Myers, Ramon (1986) *Understanding Communist China: Communist China Studies in the United States and the Republic of China, 1949–1978*, Stanford, Calif.: Hoover Institution Press, Stanford University.

Jackson, Sukhan (1990) 'Post-Mao Wage Policy and Trends in the People's Republic of China', Discussion Paper in Economics, no. 32, The University of Queensland.

—— (1992) *Chinese Enterprise Management: Reforms in Economic Perspective*, Berlin: Walter de Gruyter.

Jia Hong and Wang Mingxia (1994) 'Market and the State: The Changing Central–Local Relations in China', in Jia Hong and Lin Zhimin (eds) *Changing Central Local Relations in China*, Boulder, Colo.: Westview Press.

Johnson, Simon, Kroll, Heidi and Eder, Santiago (1993) 'Strategy, Structure, and Spontaneous Privatisation in Russia and Ukraine', in Vedat Milor (ed.) *Changing Political Economies*, Boulder, Colo. Lynne Rienner.

Jowitt, Kenneth (1974) 'An Organisational Approach to the Study of Political Culture in Marxist-Leninist Systems', *American Political Science Review*, vol. 68, September 1974.

Kaser, Michael (1988) 'Comparing Soviet and Chinese Reforms', *The Pacific Review*, no. 1.

Katz, Daniel and Kahn, Robert (1966) *The Social Psychology of Organization*, New York: John Wiley.

Kelliher, Daniel (1991) 'Privatisation and Politics in Rural China', in Gordon White (ed.) *The Chinese State in the Era of Economic Reform*, London: Macmillan.

Kim, Samuel (1995) 'China in the Post-Cold War', in Stuart Harris and Gary Klintworth (eds) *China as a Great Power: Myths, Realities and Challenges in the Asia-Pacific Region*, New York and Melbourne: St Martin's Press and Longman.

Koo, Anthony Y. C. (1990) 'The Contract Responsibility System: Transition from a Planned to a Market Economy', *Economic Development and Cultural Change*, vol. 38, no. 4, July.

Kornai, Janos (1985) 'The Double Dependence of State Enterprises: The Hungary Experience', *Jingjin yanjiu*, no. 10.
—— (1986) *Contradictions and Dilemmas*, Cambridge, Mass.: MIT Press.
Kramer, Mark (1995) 'Introduction', *Communist and Post-Communist Studies*, vol. 28, no. 1.
Laaksonen, Oiva (1987) *Management in China during and after Mao in Enterprises, Government, and Party*, Berlin: Walter de Gryter.
Lampton, David (ed.) (1987) *Policy Implementation in China*, Berkeley: University of California Press.
Lampton, David and Keyers, Catherine (eds) (1988) *China's Global Presence*, Washington, DC: American Enterprise Institute.
Lee, Caro Hamrin (1986) *China's Establishment Intellectuals*, New York: M. E. Sharpe.
Lee, Hong Yung (1991) *From Revolutionary Cadres to Party Technocrats in Socialist China*, Berkeley: University of California Press.
Lee, Peter Nan-shong (1987) *Industrial Management and Economic Reform in China*, Oxford: Oxford University Press.
—— (1991a) 'Corporatism and the Chinese Economic Reform', *Ershiyi Shiji* (Hong Kong), vol. 7.
—— (1991b) 'The Chinese Industrial State in Historical Perspective: From Totalitarianism to Corporatism', in Womack Brantly (ed.) *Contemporary Chinese Politics in Historical Perspective*, Cambridge: Cambridge University Press.
Lewis, John Wilson (1963) *Leadership in Communist China*, Ithaca, NY: Cornell University Press.
Li Cheng and White, Lynn (1988) 'The Thirteenth Central Committee of the Chinese Communist Party', *Asian Survey*, April.
Lieberthal, Kenneth (1995) *Governing China: From Revolution through Reform*, New York and London: W. W. Norton.
Lieberthal, Kenneth and Lampton, David (eds) (1992) *Bureaucracy, Politics and Decision-Making in Post-Mao China*, Berkeley: University of California Press.
Lieberthal, Kenneth and Oksenberg, Michel (1998) *Policy Making in China: Leaders, Structures and Processes*, Princeton, NJ: Princeton University Press.
Link, Perry (1992) *Evening Chats in Beijing*, New York: W. W. Norton.
Lu Feng (1993) 'The Origins and Formation of the Unit (*danwei*) System', *Chinese Sociology and Anthropology*, vol. 25, no. 3, Spring.
McCormick, Barrett (1990) *Political Reform in Post-Mao China: Democracy and Bureaucracy in a Leninist State*, Berkeley: University of California Press.
Manion, Melanie (1985) 'The Post-Mao Cadre Management System: The Appointment, Promotion, Transfer and Removal of Party and State Leaders', *China Quarterly*, June.
Maxwell, Neville and McFarlane, Bruce (eds) (1984) *China's Changed Road to Development*, Sydney: Pergamon Press.
Meaney, Connie Squires (1991) 'Market Reform and Disintegrative Corruption in Urban China', in Richard Baum (ed.) *Reform and Reaction in Post-Mao China*, New York: Routledge.
Milanovic, Branko (1991) 'Privatisation in Post-Communist Societies', *Communist Economies and Economic Transformation*, vol. 3, no. 1.
Miller, Robert (1989) 'Theoretical and Ideological Issues of Reform in Socialist Systems: Some Yugoslav and Soviet Examples', *Soviet Studies*, vol. 41, no. 3.
—— (ed.) (1992) *The Development of Civil Society in Communist Systems*, Sydney: Allen & Unwin.
Montinola, Gabriella, Yingyi Qian and Weingast, Barry (1995) 'Federalism, Chinese Style', *World Politics*, vol. 48, no. 3.

Nathan, Andrew (1985) *Chinese Democracy: An Introduction into the Nature and Meaning of 'Democracy' in China Today*, New York: Alfred A. Knopf.
—— (1990) 'Is China Ready for Democracy?', *Journal of Democracy*, vol. 2, no. 1.
—— (1992) 'China's Path from Communism', *Journal of Democracy*, vol. 4, no. 2.
Naughton, Barry (1992) 'Hierarchy and the Bargaining Economy: Government and Enterprise in the Reform Process', in Kenneth Lieberthal and David Lampton (eds) *Bureaucracy, Politics and Decision-Making in Post-Mao China*, Berkeley: University of California Press.
—— (1996) 'The Dangers of Economic Complacency', *Current History*, September.
Nee, Victor (1992) 'Organization Dynamics of Market Transition: Hybrid Forms, Property Rights, and Mixed Economy in China', *Administrative Science Quarterly*, no. 37.
Nee, Victor and Stark, David (eds) (1989) *Remaking the Economic Institutions of Socialism: China and East Europe*, Stanford, Calif.: Stanford University Press.
Ng, Chee Yuen and Woon, Toh Kin (1992) 'Privatisation in the Asian-Pacific Region', *Asian-Pacific Economic Literature*, vol. 6, no. 2.
Nye, Joseph (1967) 'Corruption and Political Development: A Cost–Benefit Analysis', *American Political Science Review*, vol. 61.
Oi, Jean (1989) *State and Peasant in Contemporary China*, Berkeley: University of California Press.
—— (1992) 'Fiscal Reform and the Economic Foundations of Local State Corporatism in China', *World Politics*, vol. 45, October.
Pang Song and Han Gang (1987) 'The Party and State Leadership Structure: Historical Investigating and Prospects for Reform', *Social Sciences in China*, Winter 1987.
Pearson, Margaret (1993) 'Breaking the Bonds of "Organised Dependence": Managers in China's Foreign Sector', *Studies in Comparative Communism*, vol. 25, no. 1, March.
Pei Minxin (1996) 'Microfoundations of State-socialism and Patterns of Economic Transformation', *Communism and Post-Communism Studies*, vol. 29, no. 2.
Peng Yusheng (1992) 'Wage Determination in Rural and Urban China: A Comparison of Public and Private Industrial Sectors', *American Sociological Review*, vol. 57, April.
Perry, Elizabeth (1989) 'State and Society in Contemporary China', *World Politics*, vol. 61, no. 4.
Perry, Elizabeth and Wasserstrom, Jeffrey (eds) (1991) *Popular Protest and Political Culture in Modern China*, Boulder, Colo.: Westview Press.
Prybyla, Jan S. (1985) 'The Chinese Economy: Adjustment of the System or Systemic Reform?', *Asian Survey*, no. 5.
—— (1989) 'China's Economic Experiment: Back from the Market?', *Problems of Communism*, vol. 37, no. 1.
Putterman, Louis (1995) 'The Role of Ownership and Property Rights in China's Economic Transition', *China Quarterly*, no. 144.
Rawski, Thomas (1991) 'How to Study China's Economy Today', in Xu Dianqing *et al.* (eds) *China's Economic Reform: Analysis, Reflections and Prospects*, Hong Kong: The Chinese University of Hong Kong Press.
Redding, Gordon (1990) *The Spirit of Chinese Capitalism*, Berlin: Walter de Gruyter.
Scalapino, Robert (1989) *The Politics of Development: Perspective on 20th Century Asia*, Cambridge, Mass.: Harvard University Press.
—— (1992) 'Northeast Asia – Prospects for Cooperation', *Pacific Review*, vol. 5, no. 2.
Schurmann, Franz (1968) *Ideology and Organization in Communist China*, Berkeley: University of California Press.

Shambaugh, David (1984) *The Making of a Premier: Zhao Ziyang's Provincial Career*, Boulder, Colo.: Westview Press.

Shirk, Susan (1981) 'Recent Chinese Labour Policies and the Transformation of Industrial Organisation in China', *The China Quarterly*, no. 88, December.

—— (1984) 'The Decline of Virtuocracy in China', in James Watson (ed.) *Class and Social Stratification in Post-Revolutionary China*, Cambridge: Cambridge University Press.

—— (1993) *The Political Logic of Economic Reform in China*, Berkeley: University of California Press.

Shue, Vivienne (1988) *The Reach of the State: Sketches of the Chinese Body Politic*, Stanford, Calif.: Stanford University Press.

Solinger, Dorothy (1989) 'China's Transition from Socialism', *Problems of Communism*, vol. 38, no. 1.

—— (ed.) (1993) *China's Transition from Socialism: Statist Legacies and Market Reform 1980–1990*, Armonk, NY: M. E. Sharpe.

Solnick, Steven (1996) 'The Breakdown of Hierarchies in the Soviet Union and China', *World Politics*, vol. 48, no. 1.

Stavis, Benedict (1986) *China's Political Reforms: An Interim Report*, New York: Praeger.

Szelenyi, Ivan (1988) *Socialist Entrepreneurs: Embourgeoisement in Rural Hungary*, Madison: University of Wisconsin Press.

Tadashi, Hanami (1979) *Labour Relations in Japan Today*, London: John Martin.

Takahara, Akio (1992) *The Politics of Wage Policy in Post-Revolutionary China*, London: Macmillan.

Teiwes, Frederick (1979) *Politics and Purges in China: Rectification and the Decline of Party Norms 1950–1965*, New York: M. E. Sharpe.

Totten, George and Zhou Shuliang (eds) (1992) *China's Economic Reform: Administering the Introduction of Market Mechanism*, Boulder, Colo.: Westview Press.

Tsou Tang (1984) 'Political Change and Reform: The Middle Course', in Norton Ginsburg and Bernard Laror (eds) *China: The 80s Era*, Boulder, Colo.: Westview Press.

—— (1986) *The Cultural Revolution and Post-Mao Reforms: A Historical Perspective*, Chicago: University of Chicago Press.

Tung, Rosalie (1982) *Chinese Industrial Society after Mao*, New York: Lexington Books.

Unger, Jonathan (1987) 'The Struggle to Dictate China's Administration: The Conflict of Branches vs Areas vs Reform', *Australian Journal of Chinese Affairs*, no. 18, July.

—— (1991) (ed.) *The Pro-Democracy Protests in China*, Armonk, NY: M. E. Sharpe.

Unger, Jonathan and Chan, Anita (1995) 'China, Corporatism and the Eastern Asian Model', *Australian Journal of Chinese Affairs*, no. 33, January.

Van Ness, Peter (ed.) (1989) *Market Reforms in Socialist Societies*, Boulder, Colo.: Lynne Rienner.

Vogel, Ezra (1991) *The Four Little Dragons: The Spread of Industrialization in East Asia*, Cambridge, Mass.: Harvard University Press.

Walder, Andrew (1986) *Communist Neo-Traditionalism: Work and Authority in Chinese Industry*, Berkeley: University of California Press.

—— (1987) 'Wage Reform and the Web of Factory Interests', *China Quarterly*, no. 109, March.

—— (1989a) 'Factory and Manager in an Era of Reform', *China Quarterly*, no. 118, June.

—— (1989b) 'The Political Sociology of the Beijing Upheaval of 1989', *Problems of Communism*, September–October 1989.

Walder, Andrew and Gong Xiaoxia (1993) 'Workers in the Tiananmen Protests: The Politics of the Beijing Workers' Autonomous Union', *Australian Journal of Chinese Affairs*, no. 29, January.

Wank, David (1995) 'Private Business, Bureaucracy and Political Alliance', *Australian Journal of Chinese Affairs*, no. 33, January.

Watson, James (ed.) (1984) *Class and Social Stratification in Post-Revolution China*, Cambridge: Cambridge University Press.

White, Gordon (1991) *The Chinese State in the Era of Economic Reform*, London: Macmillan.

—— (1993) *Riding the Tiger: The Politics of Economic Reform in Post-Mao China*, London: Macmillan.

Whyte, Martin (1991) 'State and Society in the Mao Era', Kenneth Lieberthal, Joyce Kallgren, Roderic MacFarquhar and Frederic Wakeman (eds) *Perspective on Modern China*, Armonk, NY: M. E. Sharpe.

Wilson, Ian and You Ji (1990) 'Leadership by "Lines": China's Unresolved Succession', *Problems of Communism*, vol. 39, January.

Wilson, Jeanne L. (1990) 'Labour Policy in China: Reform and Retrogression', *Problems of Communism*, September–October.

Winckler, Edwin (1992) 'Taiwan in Transition?', in Tun-jen Cheng and Stephan Haggard (eds) *Political Change in Taiwan*, Boulder, Colo.: Lynne Rienner.

Womack, Brantly (1990) 'Party/State Democracy: A Theoretical Exploration', in King-yuh Chang (ed.) *Mainland China after the 13th Party Congress*, Boulder, Colo.: Westview Press.

—— (ed.) (1991a) *Contemporary Chinese Politics in Historical Perspective*, Cambridge: Cambridge University Press.

—— (1991b) 'Transfigured Community: Neo-Traditionalism and Work Unit Socialism', *China Quarterly*, no. 126.

Wong, Linda (1994) 'Privatisation of Social Welfare in post-Mao China', *Asian Survey*, vol. 34, no. 4.

Wu Jiaxiang (1989) 'Shareholding Enterprises: An Approval to Future Reform', *Chinese Economic Studies*, vol. 23, no. 1.

Wu Yu-Shan (1990) 'Reforming the Revolution: Industrial Policy in China', *Pacific Review*, vol. 3, no. 3.

Yang, Mayfair Mei-hui (1989) 'Between State and Society: The Construction of Corporateness in a Chinese Socialist Factory', *Australian Journal of Chinese Affairs*, no. 22.

You Ji (1991) 'Zhao Ziyang and the Politics of Inflation', *Australian Journal of Chinese Affairs*, no. 25, January.

—— (1995) 'Corporatisation, Privatisation and the New Trends in China's Economic Reform', *Issues and Studies*, vol. 31, no. 4, March.

—— (1996) 'Jiang Zemin: in Struggle for the post-Deng Supremacy', in Maurice Brosseau, Suzanne Pepper and Tsang Shu-ki (eds) *China Review 1996*, Hong Kong: The Chinese University of Hong Kong Press.

Young, Graham (ed.) (1985) *China: Dilemmas of Modernization*, London: Croom Helm.

Yuen, Ng Chee and Woon, Toh Kin (1992) 'Privatisation in the Asian-Pacific Region', *Asian-Pacific Economic Literature*, vol. 6, no. 2.

Zhao Minhua and Nichols, Theo (1996) 'Management Control of Labour in State-Owned Enterprises: Cases from Textile Industry', *China Journal*, no. 36.

Zhou, H. (1994) 'Behaviour of State Enterprises in Hybrid Economy with Imperfect Market', *Economic System*, vol. 18, no. 1.

Zhou Shuliang (1992) 'Reform of the Planned Economy and Planning System', in George Totten and Zhou Shuliang (eds) *China's Economic Reform*, Boulder, Colo.: Westview Press.

CHINESE SOURCES

Beijing Party Organisation Department (POD) and Beijing Party School (PS) (1990) 'Jianguo yilai gongye qiye lingdao zhidu de yange' (The evolution of the leadership structure in state-owned enterprises), in COD (ed.) *Dangjian guangyi* (The discussion on party-building), Beijing: Zhongyang dangxiao chubanshe, 1990.

Bianji xiaozu (1990) *Liyi gongtongti chutan* (The research of the community of common interests), Beijing: Zhongguo gongren chubanshe.

Bo Yibo (1990) 'Zhaijinian Li Fuchun danchen jiushi zhounian dahuishang de jianghua' (Speech at the memorial meeting of Li Fuchun's 90th birthday), in Li Guangan *et al.*, *Jinian Li Fuchun* (In memory of Li Fuchun), Beijing: Zhongguo jihua chubanshe.

—— (1991) *Ruogan zhongda juece yu shijian de huigu* (Review of several major events and decisions), Beijing: Zhonggong zhongyang dangxiao chubanshe.

CASS (1992) 'A Feasible Approach to State Enterprise Reform', *Jingji yanjiu*, no. 7.

—— (1996) 'Zhongguo jingji fengxi yu yuce' (Analysis and forecast on the economic trend in China), *Jingji yanjiu*, no. 6.

Central Party School (CPS) (1991) *Tansuo tizhi gaige zhilu* (Exploring the road for the systemic reforms), Beijing: Qushi chubanshe.

Chang Kai (1995) *Laodong guanxi, laodongze, laoqun* (Labourer, labour relations and labour rights), Beijing: Zhongguo laodong chubanshe.

Chen Wentong (1995) 'Zhengqi nanfan de genyuan' (The reasons why it is difficult to achieve separation of government and business), *Jingjigaige neican*, no. 22.

Chen Xiaohong (1996) 'Guoyou qiye de xianzhuang he zhuyao wenti' (The current situation of state-owned enterprises and their major problems), *Guanli shijie*, no. 2.

Chen Yongjie (1995) 'Zujian guojie konggu gongsi: buyao xinping zhuang juju' (In creating shareholding companies, do not put old wine in the new bottle), *Jingjigaige neican*, no. 16.

Chen Yuan (1991) 'Woguo jingji de shenceng wenti he xuanze' (The problems in the deeper economic structure and our reform choices), *Jingjin yanjiu*, no. 4.

Cheng Xinsheng *et al.* (eds) (1987) *Zhongguo 2000 nian de xiaofei* (China's consumption in the year 2000), Beijing: Zhongguo shehui kexue chubanshe.

Chi Fulin and Huang Hai (1988) *Deng Xiaoping zhengzhi tizhi gaige sixiang yanjiu* (Research of Deng Xiaoping's thought on political reform), Beijing: the Central Party School Press.

China Enterprise Reform and Development Research Centre (1992) '1992 Zhongguo qiye gaige mianlin de zhuyao renwu' (The major tasks of the enterprise reform in 1992), *Qiye gaige tongxun*, no. 1.

China Social Survey Institute (1990) *Zhongguo guoqing baogao* (The report on China's basic situation), Liaoning: Renmin chubanshe.

COD (1990) *Dangjian guangyi* (The discussion on party-building), Beijing: Zhongyang dangxiao chubanshe.

COD and the Personnel Ministry (1991) 'Quanmin suoyouzhi qiye pinyongzhi ganbu guanli zhanxing guiding' (The provisional regulation of contract cadres in state-owned enterprises), *Renfafa*, no. 5.

Dangdai chanqun jizhi ketizu (1992) 'Guoyou qiye xiandai chanquan zhidu yanjiu' (Study on contemporary state property mechanisms), *Xinhua wenzhai*, no. 2.

Deng Liqun (1985) *Dangdai Zhongguo jingji tizhi gaige* (Reform of the economic system in contemporary China), Beijing: Renmin chubanshe.

Deng Xiaoping (1983) *Deng Xiaoping wenxuan* (Selected works of Deng Xiaoping), vol. I, Beijing: Renmin chubanshe.

—— (1987) *Jianshe you Zhongguo tese de shehui zhuyi* (On building socialism with Chinese characteristics), Beijing: Renmin chubanshe.

—— (1988) *Deng Xiaoping wenxuan* (Selected works of Deng Xiaoping), vol. II, Beijing: Renmin chubanshe.

Di Linyu (1995) 'Congdaili lilun kanguoyou qiye gaige fangxiang' (Agency theory and orientation of reform in China's state enterprises), *Jingji yanjiu*, no. 2.

Ding Xianjiu and Yong Weiguo (1992) 'Guoying qiye gongxiao guagou qianyi' (A brief analysis of the linkage reform in state-owned enterprises), *Zhongguo laodong kexue*, no. 7.

Dong Ping (1994) 'Zhubu duixing jiti tanpan qianding jiti hetong' (Implementing collective bargaining and collective contract step by step), *Labour Science of China*, no. 11.

Du Mingkun (1994) 'Shixin liangdiyu shi zouxiang shichang jiuding gongzhi de gudu banfa' (The two-below principle is a transitional measure to realise the goal of letting the market decide on wage distribution), *Zhongguo laodong kexue*, no. 4.

Du Yaohua (1987) 'XinZhongguo jianli yihou geshiqi qiye lingdao zhidu de bijiao' (The comparison of leadership systems at the different eras since the founding of the PRC), in Sha Ye (ed.) *Zemyang shixing changzhang fuzezhi* (How to implement the director responsibility system), Zhejiang renmin chubanshe.

Fan Zhu (1991) *Oiye wenhua daolun* (The general theory of the enterprise culture), Beijing: Shijia zhishi chubanshe.

Feng Tongqing (1993) *Zhongguo zhigong zhuangkuang* (The current situation of Chinese workers), Beijing: The Chinese Social Science Publishing House.

—— (1996) '1995–1996 Zhongguo zhigong zhuangkuan fenxi he yuce' (Analysis of Chinese workers in 1995–1996 and forecast), in Jiang Liu, Lu Xueyi and Shang Tienlun (eds) *Shehui lanpishu 1995–1996* (Social Blue Book 1995–6), Beijing: Zhongguo shehui kexue chubanshe.

Gao Qixiang (1990) 'Cong shige fangmian tan Zhao Ziyang tongzhi gangjian guandian de cuowu' (Talk from ten directions on Zhao Ziyang's mistakes on party building), *Zhibu shenghuo* (Beijing), no. 8.

Gao Shangqun (1990) 'Shenhua gaige de zhongdian shi qiye gaige' (The priority in reform is enterprise reform), *Jingyi yanjiu*, no. 8.

—— (1992) 'Guanyu shichang jingji de jige wenti' (On some issues of the market economy), *Qiye gaige tongxun*, no. 6.

—— (1993a) 'Shi qiye zhenzheng chengwei shichang jingzhen de zhuti' (To transform state-owned enterprises into true competitive entities in the market), *Qiye gaige tongxun*, no. 11.

—— (1993b) 'Shi qiye zhenzheng chengwei shichang jingzhen de zhuti' (To make enterprises the true entities of market competition), *Qiye gaige tongxun*, no. 14.

—— (1994) 'Shiqiye zhenzheng chengwei shichang de zhuti' (Make enterprises true entities of competition in the market), *Qiye gaige tongxun*, no. 14, May 1994.

Gao Zimin (1993) 'Lun zhuanbian zhenfu zhineng' (On changing government functions), *Qiye gaige tongxun*, no. 7.

Gong Hua (ed.) (1988) *Zenyang gaohuo qiye* (How to enliven state-owned enterprises), Beijing: Xinghua chubanshe.

Gu Jiaqi (1995) 'Shehui zhuyi tiaojian xiade hangye guanli' (Sectoral management under the socialist market economy), *Zhongguo jigou yubianzhi*, no. 7.

Guan Xiaofeng (1992) 'Dui qiye dangjian gongzuo de sikao' (On building factory party cells), *Xinchangzheng*, no. 11.

Guan Yonghui *et al.* (1994) 'Cong gaige de shijian tangtao hongguan diaokong gongzhi de banfa' (Seeking new ways to improve macro wage controls), *Zhongguo laodong kexue*, no. 4.

Guo Yanxi (1995) 'Lun jingying zhe nianxinzhi' (On the idea of annual salary for managers), *Jingji yanjiu*, no. 11.

Guo Zhenyi (1992) 'Guanyu wuguo suoyouzhi jieguo de jige wenti' (Several problems about China's ownership structure), *Jingji yanjiu*, no. 2.

Guojia jingwei (ed.) (1987) *Gaohuo qiye neibu fenpei wanshan jingji zerenzhi* (Do a good job in the inner factory distribution and improve the economic responsibility system), Beijing: Energy Publishing House.

Shixing Changzhang fuzezhihuo qiye dangwei ruhe gongzuo (How to conduct party work in factories practising the director responsibility system), Beijing: The PLA Political College Press, 1985.

Han Hai (1995) 'Huachu hangye guanli de jingwei' (Drawing a blueprint for sectoral guidance), *Zhongguojiguo*, no. 11–12.

Hauagan, W. and Zhang Jun (1996) 'Gaige qidian yu gaige lujing: yige hexing de moni' (On the starting point and path of economic reform), *Jingji yanjiu*, no. 1, pp. 3–10.

Hu Chengfu (1991) 'Shilun dangqian woguo renji guanxi bianhua de erxiangxing' (On current dual changes in human relations in China), *Shehuixue yu shehui diaocha*, no. 4.

Hu Keming (1994) 'Laodongfa qicao guocheng zhong de ruogan nandian wenti' (Some difficult questions regarding the draft of the Labour Law), *Labour Science of China*, no. 11.

Hua Gong (1988) *Zenyang gaohuo qiye* (How to enliven state-owned enterprises), Beijing: Xinghua chubanshe.

Huang Chuhua (1987) *Changzhang fuzezhi: chenggong yu cuozhe bashili* (The director responsibility system: eighty cases of success and failures), Shanghai jiaotong University Press.

Huang Weituan (1992) *Zhongguo de yingxing jingji* (China's hidden economy), Beijing: Zhongguo shangye chubanshe.

Huang Yuan (1990) *Choushade qishi* (Revelation of murderers: killings of Chinese entrepreneurs in the 1980s), Beijing: Zhongguo wenlian chubanshe.

Jiang Liu, Lu Xueyi and Shang Tienlun (eds) (1996) *Shehui lanpishu 1995–1996* (Social Blue Book 1995–6), Beijing: Zhongguo shehui kexue chubanshe.

Jiang Yiwei (1990) 'Guanyu shenhua qiye gaige wenti de tantao' (Thoughts on the deepening of enterprise reform), *Gaige*, no. 5.

Jin Guangtao and Liu Qingfeng (1990) *Xingsheng yu weiji* (Prosperity, crisis and opportunities), Taipei: Fengyun shidai Publishing House.

Jin Jian (1992) *Zhongguo gufen jingji gailun* (On the stock economy of China), Guangzhou: South China University of Science and Technology Press.

Jingji yanjiu (ed.) (1990) *Zhongguo shehui zhuyi jingji wenti zhengming* (The debate on the socialist economic theory), Beijing: Zhongguo caijing chubanshe.

Ke Meicheng (1995) 'Zhengqi fengkai: congbumen guanli zhuanxiang hongye guanli' (From department control to sectoral guidance), *Jingji gaige neican*, no. 23.

Li Beilin (1996) *Zhongguo xinshiqi jieceng baogao* (Social stratification in the market transition in China), Liaoning: Renmin chubanshe.

Li Chunting (1996) 'Zhuada faxiao shigaohao guoyou qiye de zhengque zhanlie' (The centre's strategy of revitalising large state firms and letting go small ones is a sound strategy), *Xinhua wenzhai*, no. 1.

Li Ming (1992) 'Jiceng danzuzhi zai shehui zhuanxingqi de zuoyong' (The functions of the grassroots party cells in the era of social change', *Dangjian luntan*, no. 6.

Li Mu (1989) 'Sulian dongou guojia qiye dangzuzhi de jiegou he huodong xingshi' (The industrial party cells in the USSR and East Europe), *Zuzhi shenghuo*, no. 4.

Li Peilin (1992) *Zhuanxing zhongde Zhongguo qiye* (The Chinese enterprise in transition), Jinan: Shandong renmin chubanshe.

Li Yining (1992) *Zhongguo jingji gaige yu gufenzhi* (China's economic reform and the stock system), Beijing: Beijing University Press.

Liaowang (1996) 'Tanjiaqiang guoyou qiye dangde gongzuo' (On strengthening party work in state-owned enterprises), no. 28.

Lin Yunhui, Wang Hongmo and Cong Jin (eds) (1991) *1949–1989 de Zhongguo: Kege xinjing de shiqi* (China: 1949–89, a period of march with victory songs), Henan: Renmin chubanshe.

Liu Guoguang (1988) *Zhongguo jinji tizhi gaige moshide yanjiu* (The study on the reform model of China's economic system), Beijing: Zhongguo shehui dexue chubanshe.

Liu Hongru (1993) 'Woguo de gufenzhi he zhengjuan shichang' (The stock system and securities market in China), *Oiye gaige tongxun*, no. 10, January.

Liu Kegu (1988) 'Dangzheng jiguo gaige yanjiu' (Study of the reform of party and government institutions), Beijing: *Renmin ribao* chubanshe.

Liu Qingtang, Zhao Yan and Peng Jinyun (eds) (1989) *Oiye gongzi gaige fangan de sheji yu fanli* (The good wage reform designs), Beijing: Beijing Institute of Economics Press.

Liu Wei (1991) 'Suoyouqun de jingjixingzhi, singshi ji qunneng jiegao' (The economic nature, form and structure of property rights), *Jingji yanjiu*, no. 4.

Long Xianying and Guo Hanxian (1990) 'Some Thoughts on the Linkage between Wages and Efficiency', *Zhongguo laodong kexue*, no. 7.

Lu Feng (1989) 'Danwei: yizhong teshu de shehui zhuzhi xingshi' (*Danwei*: a special type of social organisation), *Social Sciences in China*, no. 1, pp. 71–88.

Lu Guotai (1996) 'Chongxin goujian zhengfu jingji zhinong yiji yunxing fangshi' (Reshaping government economic functions and operational mechanisms), *Zhongguojigou*, no. 6.

Lu Jianhua (1990) 'Danghai qingnian de zhengzhi jiazhiguan' (The value system of contemporary youth), *Qingnian yanjiu*, no. 2.

Lu Ren (1992) *Sheilai dan gudong* (Who will become the shareholders), Beijing: The Chinese People's University Press.

Lu Wanxin (1992) 'Qiye gongsihua, gongsigufenhua' (State-owned enterprises should be corporatised in the form of stock companies), *Qiye gaige tongxun*, no. 7.

Lun Yuan (1991) 'Buke hushi qiye zhigong qinshuhua qinxiang' (Tendency towards a workforce of relatives should not be ignored), *Zhongguo laodong kexue*, no. 1.

Ma Bin (1986) *Jianchi gaige, jianchitangsuo, jianchi yuanzhe* (Upholding reform, creation and principles), Beijing: Zhongguo zhanwan chubanshe.

Ma Hong (1980) *Beijing Diyi jichuangchang diaocha* (The survey of the Beijing Number One Machine Tools Factory), Beijing: Zhongguo shehui kexue chubanshe.

—— (1988) 'Guangyu guoying qiye chengbao jingying de jida wenti' (Major issues in the contract system in state-owned enterprises), in Zhuo Shulian (ed.) *Qiye chengbao jingying gongzuo shuoce* (The handbook for the contract system), Beijing: Zhongguo caijing bubanshe.

Mao Zedong (1990) *Jianguo yilai Mao Zedong wengao no. 1: 1949 jiuyue – 1950 shieryue* (The selected works of Mao Zedong: September 1949 – December 1950), Beijing: Zhongyang wenxian chubanshe.

Maomao (1986) 'Zaijiangxi de rizhili' (The Jiangxi days), in Zhou Ming (ed.) *Lishizai zheli chensi: 1966–1976 jishi* (History is pondering here: record of 1966–76), Beijing: Huaxia chubanshe.

Ni Di (1992) 'Zhongyang zhengfu jigou gaige qianzhan' (A preview of the structural reform of the central government), *Zhongguo jigou yu bianzhi*, no. 7.

OD of the Zibo Party Committee (1988) 'Ziboshi jiji tuijin shudi lingdao gongzuo' (Zibo City is pushing hard the work to localise party industrial leadership), *Zhibu shenghuo* (Shandong), no. 6.

Pan Zhenmin and Lu Shouchu (1988) *Shehui zhuyi weiguan jingji junhenglun* (Equilibrium in a socialist micro economy), Shanghai: Sanlian chubanshe.

Peng Maoan (1991) 'Laodong gongzi jihua tizhi gaige de jiben silu' (The basic guidance for the reform of the wage and labour system), *Zhongguo laodong kexue*, no. 6.

Peng Xianzhi (1989) *Mao Zedong heta de mishu Tien Jiaying* (Mao Zedong and his secretary Tien Jiaying), Beijing: Zhongyang dangxiao chubanshe.

Pu Guangzhong (1986) 'Shixian jihua zhidaoxia de pinrenzhi shirencai guanli zhidu gaige de yixiang zhongda gaige' (The contract system: a major breakthrough in the management of talents), in Shanghai POD (ed.) *Zuzhi renshi zhidu gaige tantao lunwenxuan* (Selected essays on the organisation and personnel reform), Shanghai: Renmin chubanshe.

Qiu Jinji (1992) 'Tantan qiye jituan de jige wenti' (On some issues of enterprise groups), *Qiye gaige tongxun*, no. 9, December 1992

Ruan Chongwu (1992) 'Tuidong laodong yonggong, gongzhi fengpei he shehui baoxian zhidu de gaige' (Boost reforms in the area of labour, wage and welfare), *Zhongguo laodong kexue*, no. 2.

SCRES (1988) *Qiye jizhi gaige chutan* (An initial study of the enterprise reform), Beijing: Zhongguo shangye chubanshe.

—— (1993) 'Guanyu guoyou dazhongxing qiye zhuanhuan jingying jizhi de yanjiu baogao' (Report on the changing operational mechanisms of the large and medium-sized state-owned enterprises), *Gaige*, no. 2.

SETC (1994) 'Jianli yu sheshui zhuyi shichang jingji xianshiying de xiandai qiye zhidu' (Creating a modern enterprise mechanism that suits the market), *Xinhua wenzai*, no. 2.

Sha Ye (ed.) (1987) *Zenyang shixing changzhang fuzezhi* (How to implement the director responsibility system), Zhejiang renmin chubanshe.

Shandong Shengwei (1990a) 'Zai changye gongren zhong fazhan dangyuan de diaocha' (Survey on recruiting party members among workers), *Zhibu shenghuo* (Shandong), no. 1.

—— (1990b) 'Dangqian dangqun guanxi zhuangkuang de diaocha yu sikao' (Survey and analysis on the current party/mass relations), *Zhibu shenghuo*, no. 6.

Shi Jian (1990) 'Wei bushenqing dengji de dangyuan chuangzao hexie de huanjing' (To create an easy atmosphere for party members who do not want to register), *Zhibu shenhuo* (Beijing), no. 4.

Shi Wei (1990) 'Fushipin jiage butie xianzhuang yu tiaozhen cuoshi' (Situation of price subsidies for non-staple food and adjustment measures), *Jingji lilun yu jingji guanli*, no. 9.

Shi Xin (1993) 'Bushe zhuanye sijiu de shexiang shi zenyang shixiande' (How the plan to remove the specialised bureaux was realised), *Zhongguo jigou yu bianzhi*, no. 5.

Sicular, T. (1995) 'Zhongguo guoyou qiye weishenmo kuison' (The reasons why China's state-owned enterprises make a loss), *Jingji yanjiu*, no. 4.

Song Guohuang (1988) *Qiyefa zhinan* (The guide to the Enterprise Law), Beijing: Jingji guanli chubanshe.

SPC (1991) 'Qiye gongzi zonger tong jingji xiaoyi guagoude yanjiu' (On the mechanism to link the wage bill to economic efficiency), *Zhongguo gongye jingji yanjiu*, no. 3.

Special writing group of Heilongjiang (1984) *Jianguo yilai qiye lingdao zhidu yanbian shilie* (The history of the enterprise leadership system), Heilongjiang: Renmin chubanshe.

Su Hainan (1990) *Qiye gongzhi gaige fangan sheji shouce* (The handbook for the design of the plans for the industrial wage reform), Beijing: Zhongguo laodong chubanshe.

Sun Zhen (1990) 'On the Problems and Counter Measures in the Deepening of Wage Reform', *Zhongguo laodong kexue*, no. 5.

—— (1992) 'Shuli da gongzi guannian' (Observe wage matters from the macro perspective), *Zhongguo laodong kexue*, no. 10.

Tang Daiwang *et al.* (1990) *Xiandai renshi guanlixue jiaocheng* (The textbook for modern personnel management), Beijing: Zhongguo renshi chubanshe.

Tang Fengyi (1995) 'Zhengfu gaige bu daowei qiye gaige nanshenhua' (If the administrative reform is not in place, enterprise cannot progress), *Jingjigaige neican*, no. 22.

Tang Ji (1992) 'Gaige tupokou de liangdong xiaoying' (The domino effects at the breaking points in the reform), *Zhongguo jigou yu bianzhi*, no. 11.

Tang Jin (1993) 'Weirao zhuanbian zhineng zhongxin huangjie sannian wancheng jigou gaige renwu' (Focusing on changing functions, completing the administrative reform in three years), *Zhongguo jigou yu bianzhi*, no. 4.

Tigaisuo (1986) *Gaige: Women mianling de wenti yu silu* (Reform: our questions and thinking), Beijing: Jingji guanli chubanshe.

Tigaisuo and SCRES (1988) *Gaige zhong de shichang jiegou he qiye zhidu* (The changing market structure and enterprise organisation), Sichuan: Renmin chubanshe.

Tong Zongkun (1993) 'Guo you chanqun zhidu jianshe de dangwu zhiji' (The urgent task in reconstructing the state property system), *Gaige*, no. 2.

United Survey Team (1992) 'Shanghai dier fangzhi jijiechang zhengqang huoli de diaochia' (Survey on the Shanghai Second Textile Machine Plant), *Qiye gaige tongxun*, no. 1.

Wang Haili (1991) 'Dang xiaozu shenghuohui weishenma kai buhao' (Why could not the party group studies be conducted well?), *Zhibu shenghuo* (Beijing), no. 6.

Wang Hongming (1996) 'Gonghui, zhigong de baohusang' (The trade unions, workers' protection shield?), *Sangyuefeng*, no. 6.

Wang Jian *et al.* (1992) *Zhongguo gupao shichan wenti zhengming* (The debate on the Chinese stock reform), Tianjing: Nankai University Press.

Wang Jianxin (1986) *Ganbu guanli gailun* (The outline of cadre management), Liaoning University Press.

Wang Kezhong (1991) 'Ba chengbao jingying zerenzhi jianlizhai jiazhi guiliu jichushang' (The contract system of managerial responsibility should be established according to the law of value), *Fudan xuebao*, no. 5.

Wang Shuanxi (1992) 'Santiao huiliu, gengjia tongchang' (Three ways out and a smooth transition), *Zhongguo jigou yu bianzhi*, no. 12.

Wang Xiaoguang (1995) 'Guoyou qiye gaige qunmian zhankai jiuwu jiangqude tupo' (Reform of state-owned enterprises will go a long way and achieve a major breakthrough in the Ninth Five-Year Plan period), *Liaowang Weekly*, no. 44.

Wang Xiaolu (1996) 'Chanpin guanli tizhi: qiye mianlin de wenti' (A study on the management system of products in large and medium enterprises), *Jingji yanjiu*, no. 9.

Wang Yiqing (1987) 'Guanyu dazhongxing guoying qiye shixing dangdaibiao zhi de guoxiang' (A proposal on establishing the party representative system on state-owned enterprises), in Nie Gaomin *et al.* (eds) *Dangzheng fenkai lilun tantao* (Study on the theory of separating the party and government), Beijing: Chunqiu chubanshe.

Wen Wen (1990) 'Ganbu pinrenzhi de shijian yu tansuo' (The practice and study of the cadre contract system), *Xingzheng yu renshi*, no. 10.

Wu Wenying (1993) 'Zhuanbian zhineng, jiaqiang huaxue gongye hangye guanli (Changing functions to enhance sectoral management in the chemical industry), *Zhongguo jigou yu bianzhi*, no. 5.

Wu Zhiqing (1991) *Xinshiqi qiye dang de jianshe* (Party building in enterprises in the new era), Nanchang: Jiangxi renmin chubanshe.

Xia Zhiqiang (1992) *Quanmin suoyouzhi gongye qiye zhuanhuan jingying jizhi tiaoli* (The Regulation on Changing Enterprise Managerial Mechanisms), Beijing: Zhongguo dabaike qunshu chubanshe.

Xiao Liang (1989) 'Qianyan: *Zhongguo de siying jingji*' (The preface to the book: *Chinese private economy*), Beijing: Zhongguo shehui kexue chubanshe.

Xiao Mei (1993) 'Kangzhun fangxiang, xiangang qilai zaishuo' (See the direction, let's do it first), *Zhongguo jigou yubianzhi*, no. 3.

Xiao Wei (1992) 'Xia de xuewen' (The way of stepping down), *Zhibu shenghuo* (Beijing), no. 5.

Xiao Yu (1990) 'Xunqiu guanshu de yuanwang shizenyang changsheng de' (How the will of indoctrination was maintained), *Zhibu shenghuo* (Beijing), no. 12.

Xie Ping (1992) 'An Analysis of the Structure of Chinese Financial Capital', *Jingji yanjiu*, no. 11.

Xie Qiuhan (1992) *Guoyu zichan jingying yuanli yu shijian* (The theory and practice of managing state property), Beijing: Jingji kexue chubanshe.

Xu Songtao, Liu Jialin and Zhang Xianyang (eds) (1988) *Zhongguo gongzi zhidu gaige* (The reform of the Chinese wage system), Beijing: Zhongguo caizheng jingji chubanshe.

Xu Yanjun (1995) 'Dui zhiding qiye gongzi zhenzhang zhidaoxian de sikao' (Some ideas on industrial guidance line for wage rises), *Zhongguo laodong kexue*, no. 2.

Xu Yue (1996) 'Shengji zhengfu jiguo gaige conglan' (The summary of provincial administrative reform), *Chongguojigou*, no. 2.

Xue Muqiao (1988) 'Tonghuo pengzhang yu wujia shangzhang zhi guanxi' (The relations between inflation and price rises), *Gaige*, no. 4.

Yan Pengyuan (1990) *Jiceng dangwei gongzuo shouce* (Handbook for grassroots party committees), Liaoning: Changbai chubanshe.

Yan Shiqu (1987) 'Shilun hongguan huanjing dui qiye dang zuzhi gongneng jiegou de yingxiang' (The influence of macro-environment on the functional structure of party cells in state-owned enterprises), *Zhengzhixue yanjiu*, no. 4.

Yan Zhi (1988) 'Qishiye danwei dangzuzhi shixing shudihua guanli wenda' (Questions and answers on localising party management in the industrial units), *Zhibu shenghuo* (Shandong), no. 5.

Yang Rueilong (1995) 'Guoyou qiye gufengzhi gaizao de lilun sikao' (Theoretical thinking on share-system reform of state-owned enterprises), *Jingji yanjiu*, no. 2.

Yang Songtang (1993) 'Fan guojia tigaiwei fuzhuren Hong Hu' (Interview with Hong Hu), *Zhongguo jingji tizhi gaige*, no. 7.

Yao Lantang (1989) 'Buyao ba dangyao guandan yangbianwei dangzhi guandang' (Not to change 'the Party should manage its affairs' to 'the Party should only manage its internal affairs'), *Zhibu shenghuo* (Shandong), no. 8.

Ye Guangzhao (1989) *Gaige zhi lu* (The road of reform), Beijing: Jingji guanli chubanshe.

Ye Wen (1996) '2010 nianqian zhengfu gaige de liangda jingcheng' (The two major phases in government reform before the year 2010), *Zhongguojiguo*, no. 4.

Yin Guohua (1993) 'Zheci jigou gaige de jiben tedian' (The basic features of this administrative reform), *Zhongguo jigou yu bianzhi*, no. 5.

—— (1995) 'Gongye jingji bumen jiguo gaige de xin tansou' (The new creations in the reform of the industrial management system), *Chongguo xingzheng yubianzhi*, no. 4.

Ying Hao (1987) 'Weirao shengchan jingying zhongxin tansuo dangde gongzuo' (Explore the party work around production as the centre), in Huang Chuhua (ed.) *Changzhang fuzezhi: chenggong yu cuozhe bashilia* (The director responsibility system: eighty cases of success and failures), Shanghai Jiaotong University Press.

Yu Hongji (1991) 'Qiye shengchan yixian dangyuan shao de yuanyin ji duice' (The reason why there are fewer party members in the first line work posts), *Zhibu shenghuo* (Shandong), no. 5.

Yu Jingfu (1996) 'Shenhua guoyou qiye gaige bujing jianchi guojia zhudao' (Deepening enterprise reform should not be state-dominated), *Jingji yanjiu*, no. 5.

Yu Shaoxuan (1988) 'Penglaixian qiye dangde gongzuo chuxian sige bianhua' (The four changes in party work in Penglai County), *Zhibu shenghuo* (Shandong), no. 12.

Yu Zhenbo (1987) 'Ganbu xuanba gongzuo de chuantong yu biange' (The tradition and change of the cadre's selection and promotion system), in the Zhejiang Shengwei zuzhibu (ed.) *Zuzhi renshi gongzuo xintan* (The new exploration of organisational and personnel work), Zhejiang University Press.

Yuan Baohua (1985) *Renzhen gaohao qiyi lingdao tizhi gaige* (Do a good job in reforming the leadership structure in state-owned enterprises), Beijing: Gongren chubanshe.

Yuan Yong (1991) 'Yige lanyong chengbaoqun de dianxing' (A typical example of abuse of power through the contract responsibility system), *Zhibu shenghuo* (Beijing), no. 12.

Yue Guangzhao (1989) *Zhongguode laodong zhengce he zhidu* (The Chinese labour policies and system), Beijing: Jingji guanli chubanshe.

Yue Qifeng (1992) 'Guanyu jianli qiye jishu gezao jizhi de sikao' (On establishing technological renovation mechanisms in state-owned enterprises), *Qiushi*, no. 9.

Yue Xiuwu (1990) *Zuzhi gongzuo lilun yanjiu* (Research on the theory of organisation), Beijing University Press.

Zhang Chenglian (1991) *Xin tizhi, dasilu* (The new system and general line of thinking), Beijing: Gaige chubanshe.

Zhang Guoxiang (1994) 'Xiandai qiye bixu tuixin jiti hetong zhidu' (The collective contract must be practised in modern corporations), *Zhongguo laiodong kexue*, no. 8.

Zhang Jun (1990) 'On the Present Financial Plight of Our Country', *Jingji yanjiu*, no. 12, December 1990.

Zhang Rongde (1994) 'Liangdi liangbao gongzhi zuoliang hongguan tiaokong fuhe shichang jingji de yaoqiu' (The 'two below' macro regulation method suits the market economy), *Zhongguo laodong kexue*, no. 11.

Zhang Shenhui (1991) *Guoyou qiye lingdao zhidu de yange* (The evolution of the leadership structure), Beijing: Zhongyang danxiao chubanshe.

Zhang Shuguang (1996) '90 niandai zhongguo gaige yu hongguan jingji' (China's economic reform and macro-economic situation in the 1990s), *Jingji yanjiu*, no. 6.

Zhang Wenmin (1990) 'Shehui zhuyi de shouru fenpai' (The socialist income distribution), in *Jingjin yanjiu* (ed.) *Zhongguo shehui zhuyi jingji lilun wenti zhengming* (The debate on the socialist economic theory), Beijing: Zhongguo caijing chubanshe.

Zhang Zhailun (1985) *Changzhang fuzezhi* (The director responsibility system), Beijing: Jingji kexue chubanshe.

Zhang Zhanbin (1988) *Xin Zhongguo qiyelingdao zhidu* (The enterprise leadership structure in new China), Beijing: Chuanqiu chubanshe.

Zhang Zhijian (1992) 'Qunli xiafang: shenhua gaige de zhongyao neirong' (Devolution: the key to the deepening of reform), *Zhongguo jigou yu bianzhi*, no. 11.

Zhao Dongwan (1991) 'Yao jianchi he wanshan ganbu pinyong zhidu' (To improve the cadre contract system), *Renshi zhengce fagui zhuankan*, no. 11.

Zhao Qizheng (1986) *Ganbu renshi gongzuo shouce* (The handbook for cadre and personnel work), Shanghai: Renmin chubanshe.

Zhao Renwei (1992) 'Woguo zhuanxingqi zhong shouru fenpai de teshu yixie xianxiang' (Some special phenomena in income distribution in social transition), *Jingji yanjiu*, no. 1.

Zhao Shenghui (1987) *Zhongguo gongchandang zuzhishi gangyao* (The outline of the CCP's organisation history), Anhui: Renmin chubanshe.

Zheng Honglang (1992) 'Gaige guozheng zhong de guoyou qiye xingwei' (The behaviour of state-owned enterprises in the process of the reform), *Jingji yanjiu*, no. 5.

Zhongguo qiqe yanjiu zhongxin (1992) '1992 Zhongguo qiye gaige mianlin de zhuyao renwu' (The major tasks of enterprise reform in 1992), *Qiye gaige tungxun*, no. 1.

Zhongyang bianwei (1995) *Zhongyang zhengfu zhuzhi jiguo* (The organisation and structure of the Central Government), Beijing: Zhongguo fazhan chubanshe.

Zhou Shulian and He Cung (1988) *Qiye jingying chengbao zerenzhi shouce* (The handbook for the contract responsibility system), Beijing: Zhongguo caijing chubanshe.

Zhou Zhibin (1990) 'Qiye sixiang zhengzhi gongzuo baoruo de shehuixue sikao' (A sociological analysis of political and ideological work in enterprises), *Shehuixue yanjiu*, no. 2.

Zhu Jiazhen (1992) 'Zai liaoning laodong gongzuo huiyi shang de jianghua' (Speech to Liaoning Labour Conference), *Zhongguo laodong kexue*, no. 6.

—— (1994) 'Laodongfa shishi zhongde jige wenti' (Several questions concerning implementing the Labour Law), *Zhongguo laodong kexue*, no. 10.

—— (1995) 'Zhai quunguo laodong gongzuo huiyi shangde zhongjie baogao' (The summary speech at the 1994 national conference on labour affairs), *Zhongguo laodong kexue*, no. 2.

Zuo Chunwen (1995) 'Fahui shoutu zhengce de hongguan tiaokong zuoyong' (Use effectively the macro levers to regulate people's income), *Xinhua wenzhai*, no. 6.

Index

Note: page numbers in italics refer to figures or tables where these are separated from their textual reference.